OXFORD STUDIES IN EUROPEAN LAW

*Series Editors*

PAUL CRAIG
*Professor of English Law at St John's College, Oxford*

GRÁINNE DE BÚRCA
*Professor of Law at New York University School of Law*

# Subnational Authorities in EU Law

# OXFORD STUDIES IN EUROPEAN LAW

*Series Editors*:
Paul Craig, Professor of English Law at St John's College, Oxford and
Gráinne de Búrca, Professor of Law at New York University School of Law

The aim of this series is to publish important and original research on EU law. The focus is on scholarly monographs, with a particular emphasis on those which are interdisciplinary in nature. Edited collections of essays will also be included where they are appropriate. The series is wide in scope and aims to cover studies of particular areas of substantive and of institutional law, historical works, theoretical studies, and analyses of current debates, as well as questions of perennial interest such as the relationship between national and EU law and the novel forms of governance emerging in and beyond Europe. The fact that many of the works are interdisciplinary will make the series of interest to all those concerned with the governance and operation of the EU.

OTHER TITLES IN THIS SERIES

**Accessing Asylum in Europe**
**Extraterritorial Border Controls and Refugee Rights under EU Law**
Violeta Moreno-Lax

**National Parliaments after the Lisbon Treaty and the Euro Crisis**
**Resilience or Resignation?**
Davor Jančić

**Environmental Integration in Competition and Free-Movement Laws**
**Julian Nowag**
EU Agencies

**Legal and Political Limits to the Transformation of the EU Administration**
Merijn Chamon

**Coherence in EU Competition law**
Wolf Sauter

**Foreign Policy Objectives in European Constitutional Law**
Joris Larik

**Economic Governance in Europe**
**Comparative Paradoxes and Constitutional Challenges**
Federico Fabbrini

**Private Regulation and the Internal Market**
**Sports, Legal Services, and Standard Setting in EU Economic Law**
Mislav Mataija

**The EU Deep Trade Agenda**
**Law and Policy**
Billy A. Melo Araujo

**The Human Rights of Migrants and Refugees in European Law**
Cathryn Costello

# Subnational Authorities in EU Law

MICHÈLE FINCK

*Fellow in Law at the London School of Economics and Lecturer at Keble College, University of Oxford*

OXFORD
UNIVERSITY PRESS

OXFORD
UNIVERSITY PRESS

Great Clarendon Street, Oxford, OX2 6DP,
United Kingdom

Oxford University Press is a department of the University of Oxford.
It furthers the University's objective of excellence in research, scholarship,
and education by publishing worldwide. Oxford is a registered trade mark of
Oxford University Press in the UK and in certain other countries



First Edition published in 2017



Published in the United States of America by Oxford University Press
198 Madison Avenue, New York, NY 10016, United States of America

British Library Cataloguing in Publication Data
Data available

Library of Congress Control Number: 2017947329

ISBN 978–0–19–881089–6

# *Foreword*

As Michèle Finck herself states, this book is an argument about the legal imagination, and in particular the legal imagination in relation to the 'constitutional' structure of the European Union. Imagination may, at first sight, not appear a lawyerly word. But as Ursula Le Guin once wrote, imagination 'is not detached from reality: imagination acknowledges reality, starts from it, and returns to enrich it'[1]. This book does exactly that. Michèle builds on the existing literature which addresses the place of local and regional authorities (or 'subnational authorities') in European Union law and policy, and adds her own rich and thoughtful examination of the trends and tensions. Michèle's examination, in the best tradition, is marked by a profoundly interesting blend of detailed appreciation of the law - the Treaty, the secondary legislation, the case law – and the wider implications which are revealed. Most of all, she uses the narratives of the 'outsider' – which treats the EU legal order as the property of the EU itself and its Member States, thereby excluding subnational actors – and the 'insider' – which admits and embraces subnational authorities as direct contributors to the development of EU law and policy. Her claim, amply substantiated in this work, is that both narratives have their truths. This leads to her a compelling depiction of the European legal order as a site of polycentricity.

That depiction is particularly important in these times of contestation about the nature of the EU. Le Guin distinguishes imagination from wishful thinking. Wishful thinking, she states, is 'thinking cut loose from reality, a self-indulgence that is often merely childish, but may be dangerous' (108). Michèle Finck's analysis, grounded as it is in a painstaking analysis of primary materials and offering a nuanced account of two different narratives, provides a robust foundation on which to have a more intelligent debate about the structural nature of the EU.

This book, while very much an evolution beyond its initial form, originated as a doctoral thesis that we supervised between 2012 to 2015 while Michèle was a graduate research student in Oxford. The life of the supervisor of graduate research students is varied. Some students need support, others need coaxing; some students are in want of firm guidance, others respond

[1] Ursula K. Le Guin, *Words Are My Matter: Writings About Life and Books 2000-2016* (Small Beer Press 2016) 109.

better to nudging; some need to be pushed to focus on the detail, others need to be helped to see the big picture. Michèle needed none of this and, in truth, she scarcely needed supervision. For those three years it was simply an immense pleasure for both of us to meet with her and hear of her latest insights. She was, from the very start, in command of her material, able to engage fully with all relevant literature, and consistently perceptive and subtle in her analysis. In particular, she was committed to ensuring that her analysis lay in a robust and rigorous appreciation of the material she was working with. She was also someone always committed to ensuring that legal imagination both acknowledges reality and enriches it.

Liz Fisher and Stephen Weatherill

# *Series Editors' Preface*

The relationship between the state and subnational entities therein is shaped by a plethora of factors, including those of a political, constitutional, cultural, and sociological nature. This is true irrespective of whether the subnational entities take the form of local authorities, cities and regions, although the relative importance of the preceding factors may well differ depending on the nature of the particular type of subnational entity. It is the relationship between the EU and subnational entities that is the focus of this book by Michèle Finck. The topic is interesting and timely, and the analysis instructive. The book is structured around two competing narratives concerning the role of subnational authorities in EU law, which the author terms the outsider and insider narrative respectively.

The outsider narrative is predicated on a formal conception of the relationship between states and the EU. It assumes a bi-centric relation between the Member State and the Union. Thus, unlike Member States, subnational authorities have no formal legal status as a matter of EU law. It is the state that accedes to the EU; it is the state that formally accords the EU competence in the areas specified in the Treaty; it is the state that engages in law-making through the Council; and it is the state that exercises high-level executive authority through the European Council. The formal account draws on conventional theories of public international law, and is reflected in the terms of the constituent Treaties. From the formal perspective, the relationship between EU law and subnational authorities is indirect, interstitial and marginal, with the consequence that such authorities are conceived to be primarily domestic phenomena, of little relevance for supranational law. Finck identifies three features that characterize the outsider narrative. The first is that Member States are conceived as sovereign equals, subject to the principle of national institutional autonomy, and as monolithic entities. The second characteristic is that the division of public authority in the EU is bipolar and bi-centric, with the division, whatsoever it might be in substantive terms, being between the EU and the Member State. The third feature is that it is the Member States, as masters of the Treaties, which have the exclusive rights and obligations flowing from the Treaty; local and regional authorities benefit from no analogous status.

The insider narrative, as developed by Finck, is functional in nature. The argument is that, notwithstanding the lack of any formal legal status, local and regional authorities have assumed a pivotal role in the administration of EU law and the development of the supranational legal order. The author deploys the concepts of polycentricity and porosity to frame the ensuing analysis. Polycentricity connotes the idea that the EU is constituted and shaped by a plurality of nodes of public authority rather than just two, while porosity captures the idea that the borders delimitating these spheres are porous, thereby permitting mutual cross- fertilization and intertwining to occur. There are, Finck argues, four different ways in which subnational authorities can be seen to contribute to European integration: they can influence the substantive development of EU law; they have become important EU allies in achieving supranational objectives; a relation of loyalty between the EU and subnational authorities has developed as a result of these interactions; and subnational authorities have become important insiders of EU law in their capacity as market participants.

The author draws on federalism theory to consider the implications of these co- existing narratives, arguing that the changing role of subnational authorities is indicative of, and reflects, changes relating to the structure of the European legal order itself, and the polycentric nature of contemporary governance challenges.

The book will be interest to all lawyers and political scientists concerned with the governance of the EU, and the way in which it interacts with Member States and the subnational entities therein.

Paul Craig and Gráinne de Búrca

# *Acknowledgements*

This monograph is based on my doctoral thesis, completed at the University of Oxford between 2012 and 2015. I started working on this project during my LLM at the European University Institute. My path then took me to Oxford, where I had the immense fortune to be supervised by Liz Fisher and Steve Weatherill. Liz and Steve continuously encouraged me to write about what I was really interested in and to believe in my intellectual capacities. Maybe most importantly, Liz and Steve set a strong example as to what kind of academic I continue to aspire to be. During my doctorate I also had the opportunity to spend a year at New York University (NYU), which I benefitted enormously from.

The thesis was accordingly written in many different places: Florence, Oxford, New York City and Luxembourg, whereas the monograph was completed between London and Berlin. In these various places I have met many inspiring and supportive people, many of them now friends. I have also had the chance to meet a number of great legal minds that have generously taken time to discuss my work. I should single out Giorgio Monti (the supervisor of my LLM thesis) and Loïc Azoulai at the European University Institute. At NYU I benefitted from generous discussions with Gráinne de Búrca as well as Peter Zimroth, Kenji Yoshino, Barry Friedman, Arie Rosen, Wojciech Sadurski, Antoine Vauchez, Chris McCrudden, Anne Dienelt, Azin Tadjdini along with all the participants of the JSD Forum. In Oxford I received invaluable input from Stefan Enchelmaier and Nicolas Bamforth. Angus Johnston in particular has been a constant guide and examiner of my thesis. I am grateful to him, as well as to Joanne Scott, the second examiner, whose insightful advice guided me in adding the final touches to the project. I also gratefully acknowledge funding for my doctorate from the Luxembourg National Research Fund and the Faculty of Law of the University of Oxford.

Gratitude also goes to the Law Department of the London School of Economics, which I joined as a fellow just after finishing the doctorate. In the Law Department I have found a welcoming and intellectually inspiring home to finish this book and start new projects. I will forever cherish that time not only for the intellectual inspiration received, but also for meeting many wonderful colleagues and friends. I must mention in particular the entire GOLEM crew and special thanks go to Floris de Witte, who read parts of this book during the final stages of completion.

This book is dedicated to those without which none of this would have been possible: my family—in particular my parents, who patiently and lovingly raised me and stood by in difficult times—and to Moritz, my partner in life.

# *Table of Contents*


*Table of Cases* xv
*Table of Legislation* xix
*List of Abbreviations* xxi

**1. The Status of Subnational Authorities in EU Law** 1
Introduction 1
A. The Outsider Narrative and the Insider Narrative 4
1. The outsider narrative 4
a. The monolithic nature of statehood 6
b. The bi-centric interaction between the EU and the Member States 10
c. Member States have a special status in EU law by virtue of being masters of the Treaties 13
2. The insider narrative: a polycentric conception of the European legal order 15
a. Polycentricity 17
b. Porosity 21
c. Member States and SNAs can be assimilated 25
B. The Evolving Structure of the European Legal Order 27
1. The nature of European integration 28
2. The nature of contemporary governance challenges 32

**2. SNAs in the Contemporary European Union** 37
Introduction 37
A. A Wide Diversity of Subnational Authorities 38
B. SNAs' Norm-Generating Capacity 40
C. Subnational Authorities and European Integration 45
D. The Committee of the Regions 48
E. Associations of Regions and Localities 50
F. SNAs and International Relations 53
G. The Constant Evolution of Subnational Autonomies 56

**3. Subnational Authorities as Outsiders of EU Law** 61
Introduction 61
A. Manifestations of the Outsider Narrative in EU Law 62
1. The Member States as masters of the Treaties 62

2. Member States have special rights by virtue of being masters of the Treaties 67
   a. Standing under Article 263 TFEU 67
   b. Only Member States can engage in closer cooperation 72
   c. Member States have special obligations by virtue of being masters of the Treaties 74
   d. Direct responsibility 74
   e. Indirect responsibility 82
3. Member States are monolithic entities 84
   a. The doctrine of purely internal situations 85
   b. The bi-centric nature of the ordinary legislative procedure 88
   c. The Court adheres to the monolithic nature of statehood under EU law 91
   d. The outsider narrative is characterized by the paradigms of division and separate spheres of public authority 92
4. Explicit references to SNAs in the EU Treaties 95
   a. Article 4(2) TEU 96
   b. Article 5(3) TEU 100

**4. The Insider Narrative** 109

Introduction 109

A. SNAs as Contributors to EU Law's Substantive Development 110
1. The *Omega* case 110
   a. Omega and the protection of national identities under EU law 114
   b. The protection of human dignity as a general principle of EU law 116
   c. The public policy exemption 118
   d. The justification of the local measure 120

B. Polycentricity 122
1. *Horvath* 122
2. *Digibet* 125
3. The Covenant of Mayors 130
4. The Pact of Amsterdam and the Committee of the Regions' Charter on Multi-Level Governance 132
5. The European Citizens' Initiative 134

C. Porosity 136
1. *Casagrande* 136
2. *Regione Sardegna* 139
3. Cross-border cooperation in the polycentric union 141
4. The Regions of Knowledge Initiative 142
5. The European Grouping of Territorial Cooperation 144

D. Subnational Authorities as Allies in the Achievement of Supranational Objectives 146
1. *Carbonati Apuani* 147
2. *Josemans* 150
3. *Walloon Waste* 153
4. SNAs' duty of loyalty towards the EU 155
5. Tripartite contracts 160
E. The Assimilation of Member States and SNAs 162
1. *Flemish Care Insurance* 163
2. *Aragonesa* 167
3. *Anton Las* 169
4. The smart specialization agenda 171
F. Subnational Authorities as Internal Market Participants 172
1. Public procurement law 173
a. Rüffert 174
b. Coditel Brabant 177
2. State aid law 179
a. Azores and the 'sufficiently autonomous' test 183
b. Azores and SNAs as insiders 188

**5. Conclusion** 191

*Bibliography* 197
*Index* 211

# *Table of Cases*

## CASE LAW OF THE COURT OF JUSTICE OF THE EUROPEAN UNION


Case 26/62 *Van Gend en Loos* [1963] EU:C:1963:1 . . . . . . . . . . 82
Case 6/64 *Costa v ENEL* [1964] EU:C:1964:66. . . . . . . . . . 31
Case 13/68 *Salgoil* [1968] EU:C:1968:54 . . . . . . . . . . 9
Joined Cases 2/69 and 3/69 *Brachfeld and Chougol* [1969] EU:C:1969:30. . . . . . . . . .30&148
Joined Cases 51/71 to 54/71 *International Fruit Company and Others* [1971] EU:C:1971:128 . . . . . . . . . .9&123
Case 39/72 *Commission v Italy* [1973] EU:C:1973:13 . . . . . . . . . . 75
Case 9/74 *Donato Casagrande v Landeshauptstadt München* [1974] EU:C:1974:74. . . . . . . . . . 136
Case C-41/71 *Van Duyn v Home Office* [1974] EU:C:1997:300. . . . . . . . . .113&119
Case 43/75 *Defrenne* [1976] EU:C:1976:56. . . . . . . . . . 64
Case 175/78 *R v Saunders* [1979] EU:C:1979:88. . . . . . . . . . 85
Case 115/78 *Knoors* [1979] EU:C:1979:31 . . . . . . . . . . 166
Case C-69/81 *Commission v Belgium* [1982] EU:C:1982:26 . . . . . . . . . .77&79
Case 96/81 *Commission v Netherlands* [1982] EU:C:1982:192. . . . . . . . . .9&77–80
Case C-8/81 *Becker v Finanzamt Münster-Innenstadt* [1982] EU:C:1982:7 . . . . . . . . . . 155
Case 230/81 *Luxembourg v European Parliament* [1983] EU:C:1983:32. . . . . . . . . . 67
Joined Cases 205/82 to 215/82 *Deutsche Milchkontor* [1983] EU:C:1983:233. . . . . . . . . . 9
Case 222/83 *Commune de Differdange v Commission* [1984] EU:C:1984:266. . . . . . . . . . 68
Case 179/84 *Bozzetti* [1985] EU:C:1985:306 . . . . . . . . . . 9
Case C-152/84 *Marshall v Southampton and South-West Hampshire Area Health Authority* [1986] EU:C:1986:84. . . . . . . . . . 155
Case 248/84 *Germany v Commission* [1987] EU:C:1987:437. . . . . . . . . .181&182
Case 20/87 *Gauchard* [1987] EU:C:1987:532 . . . . . . . . . . 86
Case 131/86 *United Kingdom v Council* [1988] EU:C:1988:86 . . . . . . . . . . 67
Joined Cases 227-230/85 *Commission v Belgium* [1988] EU:C:1988:6. . . . . . . . . . 77–80
C-289/86 *Vereniging Happy Family Rustenburgerstraat* [1988] EU:C:1988:360. . . . . . . . . . 151
Case C-103/88 *Fratelli Costanzo* [1989] EU:C:1989:256. . . . . . . . . . 16, 146, 154–9
Case 3/88 *Commission v Italy* [1989] EU:C:1989:606 . . . . . . . . . . 121
Case C-8/88 *Germany v Commission* (Suckler Cow Premium) [1990] EU:C:1990:241 . . . . . . . 80
Case 1/90 *Aragonesa* [1991] EU:C:1991:327 . . . . . . . . . . 23, 167–9, 192–3
Case C-33/90 *Commission v Italy* [1991] EU:C:1991:476 . . . . . . . . . . 80
Joined Cases C-6/90 and 9/90 *Francovich & Bonifaci v Italy* [1991] EU:C:1991:428. . . . . . . . . 82
Case 2/90 *Walloon Waste* [1992] EU:C:1992:310. . . . . . . . . . 23, 146, 153–4, 193
Case C-156/91 *Hansa Fleisch v Landrat des Kreises Schleswig-Flensburg* [1992] EU:C:1992:423 . . . . . . . . . . 76–7, 123
Case C-163/90 *Legros and Others* [1992] EU:C:1992:326 . . . . . . . . . . 149
Case C-19/92 *Kraus* [1993] EU:C:1993:125 . . . . . . . . . . 166
Case C-419/92 *Scholz* [1994] EU:C:1994:62. . . . . . . . . . 166
Joined Cases C-363/93, C-407/93 to C-411/93 *Lancry and Others* [1994] EU:C:1994:315 . . . . . . . . . . 30, 86, 148–9
Case C-486/93 *Simitzi* [1995] EU:C:1995:281 . . . . . . . . . . 149
Joined Cases C-46/93 and 48/93, *Brasserie du Pêcheur/Factortame III* [1996] EU:C:1996:79 . . . . . . . . . . 82

Case C-5/94 *Hedley Lomas* [1996] EU:C:1996:205 . . . 83
Case C-194/94 *CIA Security International v Signalson & Securitel* [1996] EU:C:1996:172 . . . 173
Case C-95/97 *Région Wallonne v Commission* [1997] EU:C:1997:184 . . . 69
Case C-180/97 *Regione Toscana v Commission* [1997] EU:C:1997:451 . . . 69
Case T-238/97 *Comunidad Autonoma de Cantabria* [1998] EU:T:1998:126 . . . 70
Case T-214/95 *Het Vlaamse Gewest* [1998] EU:T:1998:77 . . . 70
Case C-323/96 *Commission v Belgium* [1998] EU:C:1998:411 . . . 77
Case T-288/97 *Friuli Venezia Giulia* [1999] EU:T:2001:115 . . . 70
Case C-302/97 *Konle* [1999] EU:C:1999:271 . . . 74&83
Case C-18/95 *Terhoeve* [1999] EU:C:2006:703 . . . 86
Case C-158/98 *Coffeeshop 'Siberië'* [1999] EU:C:1999:334 . . . 151
Case C-224/97 *fA* [1999] EU:C:1999:212 . . . 156–7
Case C-424/97 *Haim* [2000] EU:C:2000:357 . . . 74, 83–4
Case C-236/99 *Commission v Belgium* [2000] EU:C:2000:374 . . . 77
Case C-387/97 *Commission v Greece* [2000] EU:C:2000:356 . . . 79
Case C-247/98 *Commission v Spain* [2000] EU:C:2001:4 . . . 77
Case C-54/99 *Église de Scientologie* [2000] EU:C:2000:124 . . . 114&119
Joined Cases C-400/97, C-401/97 and C-402/97 *Juntas Generales de Guipúzcoa and Diputación Foral de Guipúzcoa* [2000] EU:C:2000:87 . . . 181–2
Case C-324/98 *Telaustria and Telefonadress* [2000] EU:C:2000:669 . . . 177–8
Case C-377/98 *Netherlands v Parliament and Council* [2001] EU:C:2001:523 . . . 117
Case C-143/99 *Adria-Wien Pipeline* [2001] EU:C:2001:598 . . . 180
Case 268/99 *Jany* [2001] EU:C:2001:616 . . . 119
Cases C-301/97 and C-452/98 *Nederlandse Antillen* [2001] EU:C:2001:623 . . . 69
Case C-383/00 *Commission v Germany* [2002] EU:C:2002:289 . . . 77, 79, 80
Case C-482/99 *France v Commission* ('*Stardust Marine*') [2002] EU:C:2002:294 . . . 180
Joined Cases T-127/99, T-129/99 and T-148/99 *Disputación Foral de Álava and Others v Commission* [2002] EU:T:2002:59 . . . 181
Case C-224/01 *Köbler* [2003] EU:C:2003:513 . . . 74&82
Case C-388/01 *Commission v Italy* [2003] EU:C:2003:30 . . . 77&81
Case C-198/01 *Consorzio Industrie Fiammiferi* [2003] EU:C:2003:430 . . . 156–7
Case C-112/00 *Eugen Schmidberger* [2003] EU:C:2003:333 . . . 112&120
Case C-243/01 *Gambelli* [2003] EU:C:2003:597 . . . 120
Case C-103/01 *Commission v Germany* [2003] EU:C:2003:301 . . . 80
Case C-358/03 *Commission v Austria* [2004] EU:C:2004:824 . . . 14, 77–80
Case C-357/03 *Commission v Austria* [2004] EU:C:2004:681 . . . 77
Case C-87/02 *Commission v Italy* [2004] EU:C:2004:363 . . . 14, 77–8
Joined Cases C-397/01 to C-403/01 *Pfeiffer* [2004] EU:C:2004:584 . . . 156
Case C-36/02 *Omega* [2004] EU:C:2004:614 . . . 1, 22–3, 110–21, 125, 128, 136, 152, 193
Case C-72/03 *Carbonati Apuani* [2004] EU:C:2004:506 . . . 30–1, 140, 146–9
Case T-308/00 *Salzgitter v Commission* [2004] EU:T:2013:30 . . . 181
Case C-148/04 *Unicredito Italiano* [2005] EU:C:2005:774 . . . 180
Case C-88/03 *Portugal v Commission* [2006] EU:C:2006:511 . . . 30, 180
Case C-406/06 *Landtag Schleswig-Holstein v Commission*, EU:C:2007:90 [2007] . . . 67
Case C-341/05 *Laval un Partneri Svenska byggnadsarbetareförbundet* [2007] EU:C:2007:809 . . . 112, 174, 176
Case C-438/05 *International Transport Workers' Federation v Viking* [2007] EU:C:2007:772 . . . 112, 174, 176
Case C-346/06 *Rüffert* [2008] EU:C:2008:189 . . . 23, 174–6
Case C-324/07 *Coditel Brabant* [2008] EU:C:2008:621 . . . 177–9

Joined Cases C-428/06 to C-434/06 *Union General de Trabajadores de La Rioja* [2008] EU:C:2008:488 . . . . . 183–7
Case T-211/04 *Government of Gibraltar v Commission* [2008] EU:T:2008:595. . . . . 87–88, 185
Case C-212/06 *Government of the French Community and Walloon Government v Flemish Government* [2008] EU:C:2007:398 . . . . . 85, 163
Case C-428/07 *Horvath* [2009] EU:C:2009:47 . . . . . 26, 122–8
Case C-169/08 *Presidente del Consiglio dei Minsitri v Regione Sardegna* [2009] EU:C:2009:709 . . . . . 139
Case C-46/08 *Carmen Media Group* [2010] EU:C:2010:505. . . . . 127, 158–60
Case C-444/09 *Rosa María Gavieiro* [2010] EU:C:2010:819. . . . . 157
Case C-137/09 *Josemans* [2010] EU:C:2010:774. . . . . 20, 128, 146–53
Case C-341/08 *Petersen* [2010] EU:C:2010:4 . . . . . 157
Case C-429/09 *Günter Fuß* [2010] EU:C:2010:717. . . . . 83
Case T-262/10 *Microban v Commission* [2011] EU:T:2011:623. . . . . 70
Joined Cases C-403/08 & C-429/08 *FA Premier League v Media Protection Services Ltd* [2011] EU:C:2011:631 . . . . . 173
C-391/09 *Runevic-Vardyn and Wardyn* [2011] EU:C:2011:291 . . . . . 170
Joined Cases C-106/09 P and C-107/09 P, *European Commission, Kingdom of Spain v Government of Gibraltar and United Kingdom* [2011] EU:C:2011:732 . . . . . 185
Case T-18/10 *Inuit Tapiriit Kanatami* [2011] EU:T:2011:419 . . . . . 70
Case C-288/11 P *Mitteldeutsche Flughafen* [2012] EU:C:2012:821 . . . . . 187
Case C-97/11 *Amia* [2012] EU:C:2012:306 . . . . . 157
Joined Cases C-274/11 and C-295/11 *Spain and Italy v Council* [2012] EU:C:2013:240. . . . . 73
Case C-202 /11 *Anton Las v PSA Antwerp NV* [2013] EU:C:2013:239 . . . . . 23
Opinion 2/13 on the Accession of the EU to the ECHR [2014] EU:C:2014:2454 . . . . . 22
Joined Cases C-473/13 and C-514/13 *Bero and Bouzalmate* [2014] EU:C:2014:2095 . . . . . 91, 159–60
Case C-156/13 *Digibet* [2014] EU:C:2014:1756. . . . . 99, 117–29
Case C-333/14 *Scotch Whisky* [2015] EU:C:2015:845 . . . . . 91–2

## ADVOCATE GENERAL OPINIONS

Advocate General Tesauro had previously done in his opinion in Joined Cases C-363, 407-411/93 *Lancry & Others v Direction Générale des Douanes & Others* [1994] EU:C:1998:179 . . . . . 86
Opinion of Advocate General Capotorti in Case 68-73/81 *Belgium v Commission* [1982] EU:C:1982:30 . . . . . 76
Opinion of Advocate General Mischo in Case C-424/97 *Haim* [2000] EU:C:1999:253 . . . . . 84
Opinion of Advocate General Jacobs in Case C-156/91 *Hansa Fleisch v Landrat des Kreises Schleswig-Flensburg* [1992] EU:C:1992:423 . . . . . 77
Opinion of Advocate General Jacobs in Case C-256/97 *DMT* [1999] EU:C:1999:332 . . . . . 180
Opinion Advocate General Jacobs of 10 January 1991 in *Walloon Waste* [1991] EU:C:1991:344 . . . . . 153
Opinion of Advocate General Léger in Cases C-301/97 and C-452/98 *Nederlandse Antillen* [2001] EU:C:2001:623 . . . . . 69
Opinion of Advocate General Sharpston in Case C-212/06 *Government of the French Community and Walloon Government v Flemish Government* [2008] EU:C:2007:398 . . . . . 86
Opinion of Advocate General Szpunar in Case C-591/15 *Gibraltar Betting and Gaming Association* [2017] EU:C:2017:32. . . . . 87
Opinion of Advocate General Trstenjak in Case C-428/07 *Horvath* [2009] EU:C:2009:47 . . . . . 26

## GERMAN CONSTITUTIONAL COURT

BVerfGE 6, 32 *Elfes* (1957) (1BvR 253/56) . . . . . . . . . . 115
BVerfGE 7 198, *Lüth* (1958) (1BvR 400/51) . . . . . . . . . . 115
BVerfGE 89, 155 (Maastricht Decision) [1994] CMLR 57 . . . . . . . . . . 6
BVerfGE 45, 187, *Lebenslange Freiheitsstrafe* (1977) (1 BvL 14/76) . . . . . . . . . . 115

## CZECH CONSTITUTIONAL COURT

Nález Ústavního Soudu čj. 19/08 / 2008 / Sbírka nálezu a usnesení Ústavního soudu (Cz.); http://angl.concourt.cz/angl_verze/doc/pl-19-08.php (in English, paragraphs 101, 102, 108) . . . . . . . . . . 7

# Table of Legislation

## EUROPEAN UNION SECONDARY LEGISLATION


Act concerning the Conditions of Accession and the Adjustments to the Treaties of the Kingdom of Denmark, Ireland, and the United Kingdom of Great Britain and Northern Ireland [1972] OJ L73/14 . . . . . . . . 87
Council Directive 85/73/EEC of 29 January 1985 on the financing of health inspections and controls of fresh meat and poultry meat [1985] OJ L 32 . . . . . . . . 76
Convention implementing the Schengen Agreement of 14 June 1985 between the Governments of the States of the Benelux Economic Union, the Federal Republic of Germany and the French Republic on the gradual abolition of checks at their common borders [1985] OJ L239/19. . . . . . . . 151
Council Decision 88/408/EEC of 15 June 1988 on the levels of the fees to be charged for health inspections and controls of fresh meat pursuant to Directive 85/73/EEC [1988] OJ 1988 L 194 . . . . . . . . 76
Council Directive 91/676/EEC of 12 December 1991 concerning the protection of waters against pollution caused by nitrates from agricultural sources [1991] OJ L 375/1 . . . . . . . . 79
Council Directive 96/82/EC of 9 December 1996 on the control of major-accident hazards involving dangerous substances [1997] OJ L 10/13 . . . . . . . . 80
Council Directive 98/83/EC of 3 November 1998 on the quality of water intended for human consumption [1998] OJ L 330/32 . . . . . . . . 26
Directive 2000/60/EC of the European Parliament and of the Council of 23 October 2000 establishing a framework for Community action in the field of water policy [2000] OJ L 327/1. . . . . . . . 26
Council Regulation (EC) No. 1782/2003 establishing common rules for direct support schemes under the common agricultural policy and establishing certain support schemes for farmers and amending Regulations (EEC) No 2019/93, (EC) No 1452/2001, (EC) No 1453/2001, (EC) No 1454/2001, (EC) No 1868/94, (EC) No 1251/1999, (EC) No 1254/1999, (EC) No 1673/2000, (EEC) No 2358/71 and (EC) No 2529/ 2001 [2003] OJ L270/269. . . . . . . . 123
Regulation (EC) No 1082/2006 of the European Parliament and of the Council of 5 July 2006 on a European grouping of territorial cooperation (EGTC) [2006] OJ L 210/19. . . . . . . . 53, 144
Council Decision 2009/937/ EU adopting the Council's Rules of Procedure [2009] OJ L325/35 . . . . . . . . 89
Regulation (EU) No 211/2011 of the European Parliament and of the Council of 16 February 2011 on the Citizens' Initiative [2011] OJ L65/1. . . . . . . . 44, 134


## INTERNATIONAL TREATIES


Council of Europe. 'European Charter of Local Self-Government.' *Council of Europe Treaty Series 122* 1985. . . . . . . . 179
Vienna Convention on the Law of the Treaties (1969) 1155 UNTS 331, 8 ILM 679. . . . . . . . 7, 66, 87

## LEGISLATION OF THE UNITED KINGDOM

Scotland Act 1998 . . . . . 57
Government of Wales Act 1998 . . . . . 57
Greater London Authority Act 1999 . . . . . 38
Constitutional Reform Act 2005 . . . . . 57
Government of Wales Act 2006 . . . . . 57
Greater London Authority Act 2007 . . . . . 38
Scotland Act 2012 . . . . . 57

## UNITED KINGDOM CASE LAW

*The Scotch Whisky Association and Others v The Lord Advocate and the Advocate General* (2016) [2016] CSIH 77 P762/12 . . . . . 92

## UNITED STATES SUPREME COURT

*New State Ice Co v Liebmann* 285 U.S. 262 (1932) . . . . . 24

# *List of Abbreviations*

| | |
|---|---|
| AER | Assembly of European Regions |
| CALRE | Conference of European Regional Legislative Assemblies |
| CAP | Common Agricultural Policy |
| CoR | Committee of the Regions |
| ECI | European Citizens' Initiative |
| ECJ | European Court of Justice |
| EGTC | European Groupings of Territorial Cooperation |
| EU | European Union |
| EWS | Early Warning System |
| GDP | Gross Domestic Product |
| INTERREG | a series of programmes funded by the European Regional Development Fund |
| OECD | Organisation for Economic Co-operation and Development |
| OJ | Official Journal of the EU |
| OMC | Open Method of Co-Ordination |
| PWD | Posted Workers Directive |
| REGLEG | Conference of European Regions with Legislative Powers |
| SNA | Subnational Authority |
| TACIS | Technical Aid to the Commonwealth of Independent States |
| TEU | Treaty on European Union |
| TFEU | Treaty on the Functioning of the European Union |

# 1

# The Status of Subnational Authorities in EU Law

## Introduction

Every student of EU law is familiar with the *Omega* case.[1] In particular, the case's implications for the interaction between fundamental freedoms and fundamental rights, the role of general principles of Union law, and the respect for national identities in the supranational legal order are often studied on the basis of this seminal decision. Enquiring into these various domains of EU law, *Omega*, as are most cases, is studied as raising the question of the interaction between the Member State and the European Union. Yet the domestic regulation that conflicted with the freedom to provide services in this instance was not that of a Member State, but rather that of a city, Bonn. This highlights our bias in studying various domains of EU law, as our perspective is habitually that of the bi-centric relation between the Member State and the Union. The present book's aim consists in surveying the implications of such subnational dimensions both for our understanding of the status of regional and local authorities in EU law, but also the nature of the European legal order itself. Indeed, despite their increasingly important role in addressing contemporary governance challenges, relatively little has been written about local and regional authorities (referred to generically as 'subnational authorities' or SNAs[2]) from the perspective of European Union law. This book introduces two distinct narratives of subnational authorities in EU law that reveal competing narratives of the nature of the supranational legal order itself.

[1] Case C-36/02 *Omega Spielhallen-und Automatenaufstellungs-GmbH v Oberbürgermeisterin der Bundesstadt Bonn* [2004] EU:C:2004:614 (hereafter *Omega*).

[2] The definition of what constitutes an SNA and their respective competences varies considerably depending on the respective domestic context. For the sake of simplicity I refer to them generically as 'SNAs'. The pronounced differences between SNAs within and between different Member States are addressed more fully in Chapter 2.

A formal analysis of EU law reveals the bi-centric interaction between Member States and the Union. Unlike Member States SNAs have no formal legal status as a matter of supranational law.[3] Primary law maps the Union and the States' respective relationship and spheres of competence.[4] Member States enjoy a set of special rights and obligations by virtue of their capacity as masters of the Treaties, a status SNAs cannot aspire to.[5] This reflects the fact that the EU is 'constitutionally a Union between Member States, and arguably between their peoples'.[6] Chapter 3 highlights that the references to SNAs in Articles 4(2) TEU and 5(3) TEU are unable to alter that conclusion, for they consider the subnational implications of EU integration to be for the Member States, rather than the EU, to process. The EU's bi-centric make-up has a profound impact on our constitutional imagination, that is to say the assumptions we take for granted when evaluating a certain legal phenomenon.[7] As Max Weber had alerted us, ideas generate 'world images' that 'like switchmen, determine[d] the tracks along which action has been pushed by the dynamic of interest'.[8] This book's mission is two-fold. I will first map the tension between the formal and the functional in developing two narratives of the European legal order, the 'outsider narrative' and the 'insider narrative', which respectively underline that while SNAs are outsiders of EU law from a formal point of view, a functional account reveals them to be insiders. I will then, secondly, ponder the implications of these co-existing narratives. Relying on federalism theory I will illustrate that SNAs' status in EU law unveils changes pertaining to the structure of the European legal order itself. Indeed, as the process of integration has progressed, SNAs' status necessarily became subject to modification. A second reason for the changing role of SNAs in EU law, and with it the changing structure of EU law itself, is identified, namely the polycentric nature of contemporary governance challenges.

Whereas we typically think of the States and EU institutions (and arguably citizens) as insiders of the European legal order, SNAs are outsiders. This notion refers to the fact that unlike the Member States SNAs entertain no

[3] It will be seen that the references to local and regional self-government in Articles 4(2) and 5(3) TEU do not alter that conclusion.

[4] See for instance Articles 1 and 48 TEU.

[5] See Article 263(1) TFEU and Articles 4(1) and 5(2) TEU.

[6] Niilo Jääskinen, 'The Case of the Åland Islands—Regional Autonomy versus the European Union of States' in Stephen Weatherill and Ulf Bernitz (eds), *The Role of Regions and Sub-National Actors in Europe* (Hart 2005) 89.

[7] See also Lorraine Weinrib, 'Postwar Paradigm and American Exceptionalism' in Sujit Choudhry (ed), *The Migration of Constitutional Ideas* (Cambridge University Press 2007) 110 ('[c]onstitutional conceptions organize our understanding of our particular domestic arrangements').

[8] Hans Gerth and Charles Wright (eds), *From Max Weber: Essays in Sociology* (Oxford University Press 1946) 280.

direct relation to the Union.[9] Ideas of local authority are made to conform to pre-existing ideas about public power.[10] The perception of SNAs is moreover rooted in the fact that we conceive of SNAs as actors whose influence doesn't exceed the borders of their own States. This is in particular the case with respect to local governments. When it comes to the legal understanding of cities, paradigms of the world as it used to be shape our understanding of the world as it is.[11] The image of an SNA as a powerless and subordinate administrative entity, addressing purely 'local' issues, and the influence of which is confined to local territory remains prevalent.[12] As a consequence these levels of public authority are, if at all, studied from the perspective of domestic public law, assuming that the relevance of these actors is confined to domestic borders.

Yet, in addition to this conservative formal account of local and regional authorities a functional account indicates that SNAs can be insiders of EU law. This notion flags the direct relations that have emerged between the Union and subnational authorities. The functional perspective captures the reality that supranational law is polycentric, for SNAs relate to this legal order in manifold ways. In recent years it has become increasingly plain that the EU is unable to govern in relating merely to the Member States to the exclusion of their subnational components. This book maps manifold instances underlining that the success of supranational objectives oftentimes hinges on SNAs. This insider narrative of SNAs in EU law illustrates that, as our unit of analysis changes, our perception of EU law does as well. If, as customary in legal scholarship, we take the Member States as our looking glass, EU law appears as a bi-centric structure. This book, however, underscores that if SNAs are the relevant units of analysis, the polycentric nature of supranational law becomes apparent. These developments hint at the tension that spans throughout the material examined in this book: the formal appraisal of subnational authorities and their functional status in European Union law. SNAs are devoid of any legal status under EU law, yet they have become crucial actors from a functional point of view. We will indeed trace the shift from isolation to interconnection throughout this book.

[9] Looking towards EU *law* to determine the relation between various levels of public authority is appropriate as '[l]aw determines the conditions in which political actors in the EU cooperate'. See Gráinne de Búrca, 'Rethinking Law in Neofunctionalist Terms' (2006) 12 Journal of European Public Policy 310, 320.

[10] Gerald Frug, 'The City as a Legal Concept' (1980) 93 Harvard Law Review 1059, 1079.

[11] Politically, economically, and legally powerful local governments are, however, in no way historically unprecedented, as the example of the German Hanse underlines.

[12] For a powerful critique, see Frug (n 10).

## A. The Outsider Narrative and the Insider Narrative

This section introduces two narratives of subnational authorities in EU law that will be further explored throughout the book. While these narratives operate on a spectrum, having stronger expressions in some domains than in others, they illustrate two distinct constitutional imaginations of SNAs in EU law as well as of the supranational legal order itself. Pursuant to the outsider narrative subnational authorities are outsiders of EU law and its substantive development, leaving intact the formal abstraction of the bi-centric nature of the supranational legal order. The insider narrative in contrast indicates that from a functional perspective SNAs constitute an integral part of the polycentric European legal order and entertain direct relations to the European Union and its law. It will be seen that these distinct narratives also portray different aspects of the European legal order itself. The outsider narrative reconstructs norms and institutional behaviours to identify the formal state of the supranational legal order. The insider narrative on the other hand focuses on the operation of formal rules in action, adopting a functional analysis, to highlight the actual interaction between SNAs and the EU. The book's concluding section will reflect on wider implications of the coexistence of the outsider and insider accounts of SNAs' status in EU law and the observed disconnect between the law on the books and the law in action.

### 1. The outsider narrative

The outsider narrative depicts EU law as a bi-centric structure in which the Member States and the Union have a central function, but SNAs do not: they are mere outsiders. SNAs' status as 'outsiders' highlights that local and regional authorities have no formal status under EU law and are not entertaining direct relations with the EU institutions. As a consequence SNAs are unable to contribute to EU law's substantive development. This account, reminiscent of conventional theories of public international law, is at its clearest when looking at the formal letter of the Treaties that map the respective spheres of competence and mutual relations between the Union and the States. In this imagination of supranational law the relation between subnational authorities and the EU is at best of an indirect nature, reflecting the States' pivotal role in the process of European integration and the construction of the European legal order.[13] SNAs are a purely domestic phenomenon of little relevance for supranational law. The notion of the 'outsider' equally

[13] As I will explain below, the fact that Articles 4(2) and 5(3) TEU now refer to local and regional authorities is unable to alter that conclusion.

reflects the fact that SNAs are bound to comply with EU law's inherent rights and obligations but that they are unable to contribute to their making. The outsider narrative is characterized by three main features: first, that Member States are sovereign equals subject to the principle of national institutional autonomy; secondly, that the division of public authority in the EU is bipolar; and thirdly, that SNAs cannot be assimilated to Member States.

As a preliminary step, it should be noted that the outsider narrative is not analogous to the narrative of blindness that some have identified. In 1966 the German scholar Ipsen indeed wrote that the EU and its legal order are *landesblind*, that is to say blind towards the presence of SNAs in the Member States.[14] While this assertion dates back to the early stages of European integration, it was also affirmed more recently that EU law manifests 'blindness towards the internal distribution of competences within the Member States'.[15] For some, European integration initially 'neglected anything other than State-national governments'.[16] This blindness was said to constitute 'just one element of the democratic deficit of the EU'.[17] The absence of a 'strong legal status for the regions', Martinico elaborated further, is one of the EU's most important 'constitutional wounds'.[18] The notion of blindness thus continues to loom in the background of studies of SNAs in EU law. None of these authors suggests that blindness is absolute and all-encompassing. There certainly are varying degrees of agreement as to how far the notion reflects reality. The blindness narrative nonetheless frequently functions as a starting point for the study of SNAs in EU law.

The outsider narrative is distinct from the blindness account. SNAs' existence is indeed recognized under both narratives but the capacity in which they are acknowledged varies.[19] Under the outsider narrative SNAs are considered to be purely domestic phenomena of little relevance to the EU, whereas the insider narrative captures them as key subjects of EU law. Now that it has been established that EU law's eyes are open, rather than closed, towards

[14] Vienna Convention on the Law of the Treaties (1969) 1155 UNTS 331, 8 ILM 679. See, further, Hans Ipsen, 'Als Bundesstaat in der Gemeinschaft' in Walter Hallstein, Ernst von Caemmerer, Hans Jürgen Schlochauer, and Ernst Steindorff (eds), *Probleme des europäischen Rechts. Festschrift für Walter Hallstein zu seinem 65. Geburtstag* (Klostermann 1966) 203, 248, 256.

[15] Jan Kottmann, 'Europe and the Regions: Subnational Entity Representation at Community Level' (2001) 26 European Law Review 159, 161.

[16] Joxerramon Bengoetxea, 'Autonomous Constitutional Regions in a Federal Europe' in Geert De Baere, Elke Cloots, and Stefan Sottiaux (eds), *Federalism in the European Union* (Hart 2012) 235 (stating further that '[t]he initial scenario was one of regional blindness').

[17] Ibid. [18] Ibid.

[19] The Treaty of Rome could already not be characterized as completely *landesblind* as its preamble stipulated that: 'to ensure [a] harmonious development by reducing the differences existing between the various regions and the backwardness of the less favoured regions'.

SNAs' existence, we will enquire about the capacity in which the latter are seen.[20] What follows is an observation of SNAs' actual status in EU law rather than what it ought to be. Indeed, in the words of Van Zeben, '[u]nderlining the importance of understanding the EU's effects on local government, and vice versa, does not necessitate the adoption of a normative position as to the "correct" spheres of influence of the EU and its Member States'.[21] The analysis below introduces the three central characteristics of the outsider narrative, starting with an analysis of the monolithic nature of statehood.

### *a. The monolithic nature of statehood*

EU law perceives Member States as monolithic entities, a status that derives from the concept of sovereign equality. The monolithic nature of statehood prevents the recognition of any formal legal status for SNAs. The EU has indeed long grappled with 'the difficulties of reconciling its nature as a Union of Member *States* with the particularities of these Member States' constitutional settlements that challenge traditional notions of sovereignty'.[22] The EU's authority is derived entirely from the Member States' delegation of competence.[23] Each State is considered to have preserved 'the quality as a sovereign State in its own right and the status of sovereign equality with other States within the meaning of Article 2(1) of the United Nations Charter'.[24] The principle of sovereign equality has been incorporated into the body of primary law under Article 4(2) TEU, which provides that '[t]he Union shall respect the equality of Member States before the Treaties'. Formally speaking, all Member States are equal, abstracting from obvious differences between, say, Germany and Luxembourg. Such abstraction may be considered unavoidable given that equality and partnership appear as preconditions for the continued avoidance of hegemonic conflict in Europe. This state of

[20] Jo Shaw, 'European Union Legal Studies in Crisis? Towards a New Dynamic' (1996) 16 Oxford Journal of Legal Studies 231, 242 ('[t]he task for the lawyers is to develop a conception of the legal order which can adequately reflect the sophistication of new models and go beyond the old simplicities of the unified legal order').

[21] Josephine van Zeben, 'Local Governments as Subjects and Objects of EU Law' in Samo Bardutzky and Elaine Fahey (eds), *Framing the Subjects and Objects of EU Law* (forthcoming, Edward Elgar 2017) 2 (hereafter van Zeben, 'Local Governments').

[22] Suzanne Kingston, 'The European Court of Justice and the Devolution of Taxation Powers' in Elke Cloots, Geert de Baere, and Stefan Sottiaux (eds), *Federalism in the European Union* (Hart Publishing 2012) 250.

[23] See BVerfGE 89, 155 (Maastricht Decision) [1994] CMLR 57 (hereafter '*Maastricht decision*') (judgment in English). For an analysis in English, see Ulrich Everling, 'The Maastricht Judgment of the German Federal Constitutional Court and the Significance for the Development of the European Union' (1994) 14 Yearbook of European Law 1.

[24] *Maastricht decision* (n 23) 91.

affairs entails, however, that the EU has to be formally indifferent to SNAs' existence and this even in respect of a Member State such as Belgium where SNAs are in many respects more important than the State itself.[25] It follows that even those SNAs with pronounced economic, demographic, and territorial magnitude enjoy no formal recognition under EU law.[26] Indeed, even 'constitutional regions' that is to say regions with pronounced legislative or constitutional competences, such as Scotland, Flanders, or Catalonia, are 'purely internal phenomena'.[27]

Member States' privileged status is the direct result of their quality as masters of the Treaties and echoes principles of public international law, such as Article 27 of the 1969 Vienna Convention on the Law of the Treaties.[28] Public international law and many aspects of EU law indeed 'choose to treat the State as a single entity, fully responsible for securing conformity with the law on its own territory'.[29] It follows that making sense of SNAs is burdened by two principles intimately connected to sovereign equality: the institutional autonomy of the State on the one hand, and, the principle of international legal personality of the State on the other.[30] In spite of the progress of European integration State sovereignty remains formally unaltered. The Czech Constitutional Court for instance considers that the transfer of state competences 'arises from the free will of the sovereign and ... is not a conceptual weakening of the sovereignty of a state, but, on the contrary, can lead to strengthening it within the joint actions of an integrated whole'.[31]

Given that supranational law awards equal treatment to each Member State notwithstanding their respective territorial, demographic, or socio-economic divergences they are, legally speaking, monolithic entities. This legal status prevents EU law from differentiating between Member States on the basis of domestic decentralization arrangements. This state of affairs is widely

[25] Laurence Sharpe, 'The European Meso: An Appraisal' in *The Rise of Meso-Government in Europe* (Sage Publications 1993).

[26] Examples would include Bavaria, Scotland, and Lombardy.

[27] Joxerramon Bengoetxea, 'Autonomous Constitional Regions in a Federal Europe' in Elke Cloots, Geert de Baere, and Stefan Sottiaux (eds), *Federalism in the European Union* (Hart Publishing 2012) 230 (hereafter Bengoetxea, 'Autonomous Constitutional Regions').

[28] This provision reads as follows: '[a] party may not invoke the provisions of its internal law as justification for its failure to perform a treaty'. See Robert Jennings and Arthur Watts (eds), *Oppenheim's International Law* (Longman 1992) 84–5 and Anthony Aust, *Modern Treaty Law and Practice* (Cambridge University Press 2000) Chapter 10.

[29] Stephen Weatherill, 'The Challenge of the Regional Dimension in the European Union' in Stephen Weatherill and Ulf Bernitz (eds), *The Role of Regions and Sub-National Actors in Europe* (Hart Publishing 2005) 2.

[30] Bengoetxea, 'Autonomous Constitutional Regions' (n 27) 235.

[31] Czech Constitutional Court, Treaty of Lisbon I case, Pl ÚS 19/08, para 106 (hereafter 'Czech Constitutional Court').

recognized and seldom questioned by the Member States or indeed SNAs themselves. In addition, '[t]he idea that arrangements pertaining to local government are, and should, be outside the scope of EU law has gone largely unquestioned by EU legal scholars'.[32] Monolithic statehood is of course also firmly grounded in the concept of indivisible sovereignty, the flipside of sovereign equality.[33] European constitutionalism as a matter of fact 'still insists on the indivisibility of (State) sovereignty'[34] and 'the European Court of Justice, and Union practice generally tend to attach [importance] to state sovereignty'.[35] Formally speaking, all sovereign powers sit with the State. Indivisibility is apparent both in respect of sovereignty's internal and external dimensions. The State's supreme authority within its own territory, internal sovereignty, implies that EU law cannot recognize that oftentimes significant competences are devolved to subnational actors in accordance with domestic power-sharing arrangements. Similarly, SNAs also exercise considerable influence on a given State's foreign relations, the external dimension of its sovereignty, but EU law is unable to recognize this. When the Walloon Parliament threatened to block the EU–Canada Comprehensive Economic and Trade Agreement in 2016, the EU treated this as a Belgian failure to agree even though it was more than apparent that the Belgian federal government was starkly opposed to Wallonia's stance.[36]

Given that the Member States have founded the Union and empowered it through the transfer of domestic competences, the rules on competence division clearly underline the centrality of the States, and the irrelevance of domestic arrangements, including the question whether the transferred competences belonged to the national or subnational level.[37] In accordance with the principle of conferral, the Treaties map regulatory competence as belonging either to the European Union or the Member States.[38] This pictures public authority as being divided alongside two centres, not acknowledging that,

[32] Van Zeben, 'Local Governments' (n 21) 1.

[33] Julian Franklin, *Bodin on Sovereignty: Four Chapters from The Six Books of the Commonwealth* (Cambridge University Press 1992) ('sovereignty is the absolute and perpetual power of a commonwealth ... , that is, the highest power of command'). See also Jean-Jacques Rousseau, *Du Contrat Social* (Flammarion 2001) Chapter 2 (my own translation). This was echoed by Article 1-III of the French Constitution of 1791 that stated that 'la souveraineté est une, indivisible, inaliénable et imprescriptible'.

[34] Robert Schütze, *From Dual to Cooperative Federalism: The Changing Structure of European Law* (Oxford University Press 2009) 345.

[35] Andrew Evans, 'Regional Dimensions to European Governance' (2003) 52 International and Comparative Quarterly 21, 21.

[36] On this, see further Chapter 3.

[37] See Article 4(1) TEU as well as Articles 5(1) and 5(2) TEU.

[38] See for example Article 2 TFEU.

on a domestic scale, SNAs can themselves have significant regulatory competence, and see this diminished where a competence is allocated to the EU or influenced by supranational acts.

An additional implication of the monolithic nature of statehood is that all rights and obligations arising under EU law fall on Member States alone. It is well established that 'the EU cannot look into the internal organisation of its Member States'.[39] This has been widely documented by the Court, which systematically refuses to peek below the veil of statehood into domestic power-sharing arrangements when assessing the compatibility of a given measure with supranational law.[40] The flipside of monolithic statehood is that Member States are free to internally organize themselves as they see fit, and allocate obligations flowing from EU membership accordingly. They are, for example, at liberty to determine which domestic institution should transpose directives. EU law is indifferent to the level in charge of transposition; all it is concerned with is whether transposition occurs in compliance of supranational standards.[41] The Court has held time and time again that Member States' ability to organize themselves internally as they see fit must be reconciled with the need for the uniform application of EU law.[42] All regulatory authority is supposed to belong to the State. While EU law recognizes that the State can delegate such competence upwards to the Union it recognizes only timidly that regulatory authority can also be delegated downwards to SNAs.[43]

The above overview has illustrated that the sovereignty paradigm continues to exercise a strong hold on the nature and perception of statehood in the EU. Under the outsider narrative the supranational legal order is based on clear hierarchies and the separation of regulatory spheres. This underscores that only Member States are formal insiders with a distinct legal status and a direct relation to the EU. SNAs are devoid of these characteristics and accordingly outsiders to the privileged relationship between the Union and the States. This inevitably entails that interactions between levels of public authority under the formal outsider narrative are bi-centric as only the States and the Union engage in direct communication.

[39] Bengoetxea, 'Autonomous Constitutional Regions' (n 27) 231.

[40] Maite Zelaia Garagarza, 'The Spanish State Structure and EU Law: The View of the Spanish Constitutional Court' in Elke Cloots, Geert de Baere, and Stefan Sottiaux (eds), *Federalism in the European Union* (Hart Publishing 2012) 385.

[41] Joined Cases 51–54/71 *International Fruit Company II* [1971] EU:C:1971:128, para 4 and Case 96/81 *Commission* v *Netherlands* [1982] EU:C:1982:192; Case 13/68 *Salgoil* [1968] EU:C:1968:54; Case 179/84 *Bozzetti* [1985] EU:C:1985:306.

[42] Joined Cases 205/82 to 215/82 *Deutsche Milchkontor* [1983] EU:C:1983:233.

[43] Article 5(1) TEU.

### b. *The bi-centric interaction between the EU and the Member States*

It logically follows from the monolithic nature of statehood that EU law solely accounts for the bi-centric interactions between the Member States and the EU. Bi-centricity labels the structure of supranational law under the outsider narrative. As only the Member States and the EU belong to this structure, local and regional authorities are left with an outsider position. It is indeed apparent that the EU Treaty system 'contemplates only two levels of government—the European [Union] and the Member States'.[44] Article 1 TEU reflects this state of affairs in providing that the Member States have established the Union and conferred competences on it 'to attain objectives they have in common'. Bi-centricity also lies at the heart of Article 5(1) TEU according to which competence is delegated by the Member States to the Union.[45] It follows that while a given competence may be that of an SNA according to domestic arrangements it is that of the State from the perspective of EU law.[46]

This bipolar structure stands in the way of recognizing a formal legal status for local and regional authorities. Articles 4(2) and 5(3) TEU, the most significant references to SNAs in primary law, are unable to alter that conclusion. Article 4(2) TEU provides that '[t]he Union shall respect the equality of Member States before the Treaties as well as their national identities, inherent in their fundamental structures, political and constitutional, inclusive of *regional and local self-government*'.[47] Some have argued that this provision, introduced by the most recent Treaty amendment, amounts to a direct recognition and status for SNAs in EU law.[48] This argument has to be rejected. Looking at its very wording it is clear that Article 4(2) TEU merely recognizes that subnational self-government may be a feature of a States' constitutional identity but no direct recognition is granted to SNAs. The same conclusion arises from the examination of Article 5(3) TEU. The subsidiarity principle, redrafted in 2009 to include this reference to local and regional self-government, formulates a two-part, and not a three-part test. It does not enquire whether regulation is more adequately passed at (i) supranational, (ii) national, or (iii) subnational, level but rather whether (i) the EU, or (ii) the

[44] Andrea Ross and Mayte Salvador Crespo, 'The Effect of Devolution on the Implementation of European Community Law in Spain and the United Kingdom' (2003) 28 European Law Review 210, 216–17.

[45] See also Article 4(1) TEU.

[46] This is echoed by Article 5(3) TEU.

[47] Emphasis added.

[48] Claudio Mandrino, 'The Lisbon Treaty and the New Powers of Regions' 10 European Journal of Law Reform (2008) 515.

Member States should act.[49] This echoes the Westphalian ideal that regulatory competence exclusively lies with the State as the sole bearer of sovereignty.[50] EU law is only interested in whether the supranational or national level regulates but does not enquire which level within the Member State should do so. It follows that neither Article 4(2) TEU nor Article 5(3) TEU can be read as allocating a legal status to SNAs and hence altering the bi-centric structure of EU law. Formally speaking, SNAs are outsiders of the bi-centric supranational legal order.

The exclusive and exclusionary relationship between the Member States and the Union can also be observed in the structure of the EU's checks-and-balances model. The Union's institutional structure foresees the interaction of institutions representing different interests. Under the ordinary legislative procedure, the Commission, the Council, and Parliament must reach agreement on draft legislation.[51] Whereas the European Parliament represents European citizens, the Commission represents supranational interests, and the Council those of the Member States. SNAs are not represented in this institutional structure. The Committee of the Regions was designed to represent SNAs at Union level but its involvement in law-making is of a purely consultative nature.[52] The centrality of the States and the Union can be explained by the fact that the Member States have collectively created the EU and are bound by the obligations they have agreed to assume on this occasion. Member States have the ability to ensure that the EU does not exceed its conferred competence when legislating whereas the Commission can take action against non-complying Member States that disregard obligations falling on them as masters of the Treaties.[53] Local and regional authorities are not formally involved in this checks-and-balances model.[54]

Member States' influence on supranational law extends beyond the ordinary legislative procedure. As masters of the Treaties they are also makers of primary legislation.[55] This is crucial as the main instrument of constitutional

[49] On this, see further Michèle Finck, 'Challenging the Subnational Dimension of Subsidiarity in EU Law' (2015) 8 European Journal of Legal Studies 5.

[50] The Westphalian paradigm is used in reference to the Peace of Westphalia of 1648, which ended the Thirty Years' War. It refers to an international legal reality constituted solely by sovereign Nation-States. See Kanishka Jarasuriya, 'Globalization, Law, and the Transformation of Sovereignty: The Emergence of Global Regulatory Governance' (1999) 6 Indiana Journal of Global Legal Studies 425.

[51] Article 289 TFEU.

[52] Article 13(4) TEU and Article 300 TFEU. On the Committee of the Regions, see further Chapter 2.

[53] Article 258 TFEU.

[54] I develop this idea further in Michèle Finck, 'Fragmentation as an Agent of Integration' International Journal of Constitutional Law (forthcoming 2018).

[55] Article 48 TEU.

change in the EU remains the 'revision treaty', that is, an international agreement between the Member States of the European Union making amendments to the so-called 'founding treaties'.[56] Member States moreover have a pivotal function in relation to the construction of the European legal space beyond primary and secondary law. In addition to their explicit legislative capacity, they influence EU law through their norms. The interaction between national and supranational norms, and the generative effect thereof on the European legal order is made explicit by Article 6(3) TEU, which recognizes that '[f]undamental rights ... as they result from the constitutional traditions common to the Member States, shall constitute general principles of the Union's law'. The ordinary legislative procedure as well as the States' influence on secondary legislation and general principles of law confirms that Member States contribute to EU law's substantive development but SNAs do not.

The exclusive nature of the reciprocal relationship between the States and the Union should not be understood as blindness towards SNAs. Bi-centricity rather confirms that SNAs are devoid of any formal legal status under EU law. This is confirmed by Article 16(2) TEU, which provides that '[t]he Council shall consist of a representative of each Member State at ministerial level, who may commit the government of the Member State in question and cast its vote'. The formulation 'at ministerial level' was fashioned to allow Member States to send regional ministers to the Council.[57] Panara has operated a detailed examination of the implementation of this provision, showing that regional ministers have for instance represented Austria, Belgium, Spain, and Germany.[58] EU law hence recognizes the existence of SNAs and even allows them to participate in the supranational legislative procedure. Crucially, however, from the perspective of EU law these ministers do not represent their SNAs, but the Member State. Their participation is the result of domestic arrangements and EU law considers them to be delegates of the States, upholding bi-centricity.[59]

The bi-centric nature of EU law is moreover echoed by the mutual obligations between the EU and its Member States in which SNAs take no part. Article 4(3) TEU for instance obliges the States and the Union to entertain a

[56] Bruno de Witte, 'Treaty Revision in the European Union: Constitutional Change Through International Law' (2004) 35 Netherlands Yearbook of International Law 51, 51–2.

[57] The Council's rules of procedure also foresee that ministers may be accompanied by 'officials who assist them' which allows sub-national representatives to travel with them. In this scenario, what is visible at EU level is the representative of the Member State. Annex to Council Decision 2009/937/EU adopting the Council's Rules of Procedure [2009] OJ L325/34, art 5(3).

[58] Carlo Panara, *The Sub-National Dimension of the EU* (Springer 2015) 20–1 (hereafter Panara, *The Sub-National Dimension*). With respect to Germany, see Article 23(6) of the German Basic Law.

[59] On this, see further Chapter 3.

relation of loyalty and in the context of their common relations; both scales have undertaken a number of mutually enforceable rights and obligations. Member States must for instance comply with EU law and are held responsible where they fail to do so.[60] The above elements indicate that the interaction between the Member States and the Union is of a direct nature and characterized by bi-centricity and exclusivity. In accordance with this perception the EU is a polity in which 'the only relevant actors for its governance are the states and the federal government'.[61] As masters of the Treaties, Member States have a special and privileged role in the Union. This clearly demarcates Member States and SNAs and explains why SNAs are devoid of any formal legal status and unable to directly interact with the EU. Devoid of statehood, SNAs cannot be formal members of the Union.[62] While EU law doesn't deny the existence of SNAs, countering any theory of pure blindness, their status diverges considerably from that of the Member States. SNAs must comply with EU law's inherent obligations but have no formal involvement in its substantive development.[63] The outsider narrative captures the dissimilarities between the States' and SNAs' status and the related implications for EU law. This confirms SNAs as being domestic phenomena deprived of any formal legal status in Union law, and leads to the conclusion that Member States and SNAs constitute two different categories of public actors that cannot be assimilated.

### c. *Member States have a special status in EU law by virtue of being masters of the Treaties*

The outsider narrative is firmly rooted in the assumption that a Member State has a fundamentally different status from that of an SNA. Under the outsider narrative, actors are defined in accordance with their formal status, or lack thereof. SNAs, being wanting of a formal legal status under EU law and not entertaining any direct relations with the EU, are framed as outsiders of EU law. Member States' capacity as masters of the Treaties grounds their privileged status by virtue of which they hold exclusive rights and obligations and sovereign equality is at the root of their formal monolithic nature. Devoid of sovereign equality, local and regional authorities benefit from no analogous status.

60 This is examined further in Chapter 3.

61 Fernanda Nicola, 'Invisible Cities in Europe' (2012) 35 Fordham International Law Journal 1282, 1285.

62 Article 49 TEU only allows States to join the European Union.

63 See Article 49 TEU.

Chapter 3 studies manifold areas of supranational law that confirm the divergence between Member States' formal status and SNAs' lack thereof. This can, for example, be observed in the context of the implementation of EU secondary legislation. In many Member States the 'implementation of EU law by the regions is common practice'.[64] SNAs indeed often have an implementing capacity, especially where secondary legislation relates to their competences.[65] The Pact of Amsterdam further acknowledges that EU law is 'to a large extent implemented in Urban Areas and has direct and indirect implications for Urban Authorities'.[66] EU law, however, considers that any action carried out at domestic level is that of the State. Time and time again, the Court has affirmed that where an SNA fails to implement correctly, the Member State is responsible.[67] Thus even where the SNAs is causally responsible for the breach it cannot, unlike Member States, be legally responsible as a matter of supranational law. The impossibility of assimilation between Member States and SNAs is for instance also highlighted in respect of standing under Article 263 TFEU in Chapter 3.

The monolithic nature of statehood and the bi-centric structure of EU law indicate that from a formal standpoint it proves impossible to assimilate the Member States and the Union. Subnational authorities enjoy no direct recognition in supranational law, as this would negate Member States' monolithic nature. Local and regional authorities are accordingly unable to enjoy any direct recognition as a matter of EU law. It follows that only Member States have the capacity to contribute to EU law's substantive development. Local and regional authorities are outsiders of the European legal order given that, unlike the insider States, they do not benefit from a formal legal status or the ability to entertain direct relations with the Union. In light of the obvious formal divergences between SNAs and Member States they are actors of a fundamentally different nature that cannot be assimilated. The outsider narrative is thus characterized by three different features defining the relationship between subnational authorities and EU law: Member States'

[64] Maite Zelaia Garagarza, 'The Spanish State Structure and EU Law: The View of the Spanish Constitutional Court' in Elke Cloots, Geert de Baere, and Stefan Sottiaux (eds), *Federalism in the European Union* (Hart Publishing 2012) 386.

[65] Article 23(6) of the German Basic Law for instance attributes responsibility for the implementation of European directives to the Länder wherever they concern an area of their competence.

[66] European Union, Establishing an Urban Agenda for the EU, 'Pact of Amsterdam' (2016) Agreed at the Informal Meeting of EU Ministers Responsible for Urban Matters on 30 May 2016 in Amsterdam, The Netherlands, available online: http://ec.europa.eu/regional_policy/sources/policy/themes/urban-development/agenda/pact-of-amsterdam.pdf (hereafter referred to as 'Pact of Amsterdam').

[67] See by way of example Case C-358/03 *Commission* v *Austria* [2004] EU:C:2004:824, para 13; Case C-87/02 *Commission* v *Italy* [2004] EU:C:2004:363, para 38.

sovereign equality and the principle of national institutional autonomy, bi-centricity, and the impossibility of assimilating SNAs and the Member States. The insider narrative highlights, however, that a parallel imagination of EU law can be detected.

## 2. The insider narrative: a polycentric conception of the European legal order

Beyond the formal letter of EU law a parallel yet distinct narrative can be identified according to which SNAs are insiders of supranational law and its substantive development. If we approach Union law from a functional perspective it hardly appears to be the formalistic, bi-centric structure in which only States and the Union play a significant role. The insider narrative pinpoints that in the contemporary EU, not merely formal competence and authority matter but also, and increasingly, informal relations between various levels of public authority, including SNAs. In spite of being devoid of any formal legal status, local and regional authorities have, via the relations they entertain, taken on a pivotal role in the administration of EU law and the development of the supranational legal order. Through their active role in the construction of the European legal order they have acquired an insider status that is in many manners analogous to that of the Member States. The insider narrative highlights that SNAs are in many respects active insiders of supranational law and its substantive development. This becomes obvious when we focus on SNAs' functional role in the EU context, which is addressed in further detail in Chapter 4.

As a result of SNAs' de facto status in supranational law, sovereign equality and bi-centricity are unable to reflect the multidimensional interactions between public authorities that are occurring. The section below introduces two notions that can better frame these dynamics: polycentricity and porosity. Polycentricity indicates that the Union is made up and shaped by a plurality of nodes of public authority rather than just two, whereas porosity denotes that the borders delimitating these spheres are porous, permitting mutual cross-fertilization and intertwining to occur. Four distinct dynamics that frame SNAs' contributing role to the development of European integration can be distilled. *First*, that SNAs are capable of influencing EU law's substantive development. Chapter 4 singles out numerous occasions where the interaction between a subnational norm and a norm of EU law modified EU law's substantive core, for instance through the development of the derogations regime under free movement law.[68] *Second*, SNAs have become important

[68] On this see further Chapter 4.

EU allies in achieving supranational objectives. While the Union continues to rely on States to ensure the success of its policies, recruiting SNAs to do the same has multiplied the enforcing agents of supranational objectives.[69] *Third*, it will be seen that these interactions have given rise to a relation of loyalty between the EU and SNAs. Loyal cooperation is imperative for the implementation and enforcement of supranational law, but it has also triggered a relation of trust and co-dependency of the EU towards SNAs.[70] *Fourth*, it will be highlighted that subnational authorities have become important insiders of EU law in their capacity as market participants.

Key to the insider narrative is the assumption that looking at actors' relations tells us more about their role and status than formal principles. Indeed, as Azoulai has argued in another context, 'we need to understand, and attend to, the complex set of *relations* that constitute integration'.[71] In the United States, an influential school of federalism studies has developed in recent years, which highlights that fragmentation can serve integration.[72] My study reveals that in the European context, SNAs' functional importance becomes particularly lucid when we consider their relations with other actors. This is reminiscent of the Czech Constitutional Court's position mentioned earlier, according to which States strengthen their sovereignty through EU membership, indicating how public actors can augment their respective powers through interconnection rather than isolation.[73] This has definitely proven to be accurate in relation to SNAs, which, while certainly having witnessed a diminishment of some of their formal domestic competences as a consequence of European integration, have also been able to magnify their influence, both externally and internally, through the intermediary of the European Union.[74]

Taking SNAs' relations to the EU rather than their lack of formal status as our looking glass, their impetus to European integration, as well as that process itself, emerge in a different light. Expanding our constitutional imagination beyond formal labels enables us to evaluate SNAs, but also the European legal order from a different perspective. Traditional paradigms anchored in narratives of separate spheres and hierarchical relations cannot explain the role SNAs have assumed over the past decades. In the contemporary Union

[69] Pact of Amsterdam (n 66).

[70] In *Fratelli Costanzo*, the Court established that SNAs are subject to a duty of loyalty towards the European Union. Case C-103/88 *Fratelli Costanzo* [1989] EU:C:1989:256.

[71] Loic Azoulai, '"Integration Through Law" and Us' (2016) 14 International Journal of Constitutional Law 449, 460 (emphasis in original).

[72] Judith Resnik, 'Law's Migration: American Exceptionalism, Silent Dialogues, and Federalism's Multiple Ports of Entry' (2006) 115 Yale Law Journal 1564; Heather Gerken, 'Federalism All the Way Down' (2010) 124 Harvard Law Review 4.

[73] Czech Constitutional Court (n 31).

[74] On this, see further Chapter 4.

authority and law-making are as a matter of fact divided between multiple actors, including SNAs. Control has slipped upwards and downwards from the States to the extent that public authority is more accurately understood as a network rather than in the hands of a single sovereign. The result is the fragmentation of decision- and law-making capacity and pronounced interconnection between the various actors involved. The central dynamics of the insider narrative have also been highlighted by authors that have examined different aspects of the European legal order. Writing about new governance, Scott and Trubeck have for instance found that '[w]hereas a traditional conception of law looks for a unitary source of ultimate authority, new governance is predicated upon a dispersal and fragmentation of authority, and rests upon fluid systems of power sharing'.[75] In order to best capture the imagination of supranational law inherent to the insider narrative its three key characteristics are now outlined: (i) polycentricity, (ii) porosity, and (iii) the assimilation between SNAs and Member States.

### a. *Polycentricity*

The following chapters document a range of different instances of interaction between SNAs and the EU. Such interactions cannot be explained on the basis of the outsider narrative as they skew bi-centricity and the monolithic conception of statehood. A more suitable functional conceptualization is that of polycentricity. The notion draws attention to the existence of a legal space that encompasses not only Member States and the EU but also SNAs. Polycentricity stresses the existence of a plurality of centres of public authority and norm-generation within the Union. Regulation is being crafted in a polycentric fashion at the international, supranational, national, regional, and local levels. The notion first emerged in Polanyi's *Logic of Liberty* in 1951, polycentricity being referred to as an organizational system where 'participants enjoy the freedom to make individual and personal contributions'.[76] It was then developed more comprehensively by the Ostroms and their collaborators. Vincent Ostrom, Tiebout, and Warren first introduced polycentricity, as applied here, in 1962.[77] They framed the notion as connoting:

[75] Joanne Scott and David Trubek, 'Mind the Gap: Law and New Approaches to Governance in the European Union' (2002) 8 European Law Journal 1, 8.

[76] Ibid. For an overview of the notion's evolution, see Paul Aligica and Vlad Tarko, 'Polycentricity: From Polanyi to Ostrom, and Beyond' (2012) 25 Governance: An International Journal of Policy, Administration, and Institutions 237, 238 (hereafter Aligia and Tarko, 'Polycentricity').

[77] Charles Tiebout, Robert Warren, and Vincent Ostrom, 'The Organization of Government in Metropolitan Areas: A Theoretical Inquiry' (1961) 55 The American Political Science Review 831 (hereafter Tiebout, Warren, and Ostrom, 'The Organization of Government'). The notion also

many centres of decision' making, which are formally independent of each other.... To the extent that they take each other into account in competitive relationships, enter into contractual and cooperative undertakings or have recourse to central mechanisms to resolve conflicts, the various political jurisdictions in a metropolitan area may function in a coherent manner with consistent and predictable patterns of interacting behaviour.[78]

Elinor Ostrom subsequently developed her own definition according to which:

Polycentric systems are characterized by multiple governing authorities at differing scales rather than a monocentric unit (see Ostrom, 1999). Each unit within a polycentric system exercises considerable independence to make norms and rules within a specific domain (such as a family, a firm, a local government, a network of local governments, a state or province, a region, a national government, or an international regime). Participants in a polycentric system have the advantage of using local knowledge and learning from others who are also engaged in trial-and-error learning processes.[79]

The merit of these definitions consists in stressing the dispersal of regulatory authority and the related interconnection of norms originating at various scales.[80] Importantly, the concept captures that not only the Union and Member States but also the Union and SNAs relate directly to another. Polycentricity can encompass many systems in which public authority is divided including multilevel governance and federalism. Polycentricity serves as an umbrella notion capable of encompassing these concepts. Aligica and Tarko for instance consider with respect to the United States that 'designing the American constitution could be viewed as an experiment in polycentricity while federalism could be seen as one way to capture the meaning and to operationalize one aspect of this type of order'.[81] Polycentricity moreover has the advantage that contrary to federalism it contains no normative preconception as to the desirability of centralization or decentralization.[82] Vincent

appeared in Michael Polanyi, *The Logic of Liberty* (University of Chicago Press 1951) (hereafter Polanyi, *The Logic of Liberty*) and Lon Fuller, 'The Forms and Limits of Adjudication' (1978) 92 Harvard Law Review 353.

[78] Tiebout, Warren, and Ostrom, 'The Organization of Government' (n 77) 831.

[79] Elinor Ostrom, 'Polycentric Systems for Coping with Collective Action and Global Environmental Change' (2010) 20 Global Environmental Change 550, 552.

[80] I concentrate on public authority, not private or hybrid initiatives, without however denying their importance in many regulatory fields.

[81] Aligica and Tarko, 'Polycentricity' (n 76) 245.

[82] Interestingly, these connotations vary depending on the system at stake. While federalism is most often associated with decentralization in the US, it generally denotes a normative preference for centralization in the European context.

Ostrom noted himself that '[n]o a priori judgment can be made about the adequacy of a polycentric system of government as against a single jurisdiction'.[83] In light of the above, polycentricity emerges as a suitable description of the structure of EU law as seen through a functional lens.[84] It is at this stage interesting to note that while polycentricity was long an exotic notion in EU discourse, it has now made its appearance as an official description of the supranational legal order, as the 2016 Urban Agenda proclaims that '[t]he Urban Agenda for the EU acknowledges the *polycentric structure* of Europe'.[85]

Polycentricity captures the reality that from a functional perspective we must account for more than just the Member States and the EU to understand the contemporary structure of Union law. This book's study of SNAs reveals that many aspects of the construction and execution of supranational law cannot be comprehensively mapped if we solely focus on actors with a formal legal status. Below the surface of such formality the supranational, national, and subnational overlap and interact in complex and variegated manners. Whereas my study relates to polycentricity specifically in EU law it can be qualified as a broader phenomenon. As de Búrca observed, 'the relevant centres and dimensions of political and legal decision-making' have grown 'in number and complexity' as not only 'local and regional entities, along with nation states and supranational players' play a role in governance but also the international and transnational spheres.[86] This phenomenon occurs more widely and expressions thereof have been identified by various authors in various contexts, for instance in public international law.[87]

In the EU as elsewhere, the emergence of polycentricity in governance networks and law emerges alongside the polycentric nature of numerous contemporary governance challenges, such as climate change.[88] Indeed '[i]n

[83] Tiebout, Warren, and Ostrom, 'The Organization of Government' (n 77) 838.

[84] It could also merely be stated that this aspect of EU law is of a 'sui generis' nature but that would arguably have little explanatory value at all considering that all legal orders can be qualified as 'sui generis' in their own way.

[85] Pact of Amsterdam (n 66) 4 (emphasis added).

[86] Gráinne de Búrca, 'Reappraising Subsidiarity's Significance After Amsterdam' (1999) Jean Monnet Working Paper 7/99 http://www.jeanmonnetprogram.org/archive/papers/99/990701.html, 5.

[87] On this, see by way of example Yishai Blank, 'Localism in the New Global Legal Order' (2006) 47 Harvard Journal of International Law 263 (hereafter Blank, 'Localism in the New Global Order'); Helmut Aust, 'Auf dem Weg zu einem Recht der globalen Stadt? "C40" und der "Konvent der Bürgermeister" im globalen Klimaschutzregime' (2013) 73 Zeitschrift für ausländisches öffentliches Recht und Völkerrecht 673.

[88] On this, see by way of example Joanne Scott, 'The Multi-Level Governance of Climate Change' in Paul Craig and Gráinne de Búrca (eds), *The Evolution of EU law* (Oxford University Press 2001); Joyeeta Gupta, Michele Betsill, and Harriet Bulkeley, 'Cities and the Multilevel Governance of Global Climate Change' (2006) 12 Global Governance 141.

controversies over topics as diverse as the use of the Internet, immigration policy, terrorism, and the current financial crisis, policy-makers struggle with the appropriate role of multiple levels of government'.[89] The emergence of polycentricity mirrors our interconnected contemporary world where many problems necessitate regulation at scales that are at times smaller and at times larger than the State.[90] Such transfers of competence to the subnational 'should not be seen as a simple transfer of powers from central to city and region level, but rather as a process that requires multi-level partnership and networking'.[91] Local and regional authorities are indeed not gaining prominence because they are increasing their sphere of autonomy vis-à-vis Member States or the Union but rather because their interconnection with these actors increases, enabling them to exert more influence on them. The multiplication of levels of public authority and their inherent intertwining undoubtedly challenge Westphalian paradigms.

While the formal structure of the European legal order remains bi-centric, we can observe the emergence of polycentricity in numerous domains of EU law that are covered more comprehensively in Chapter 4. Examples include the polycentric realization of the EU's objectives. The Riga Declaration emphasizes that '[c]ities and towns play a significant role in ... achieving the EU 2020 objectives, due to the concentration of people, services, dwellings, economic activity and transport nodes'.[92] The Urban Agenda for the EU, on the other hand, 'strives to involve Urban Authorities in the design of policies, to mobilise Urban Authorities for the implementation of EU policies, and to strengthen the urban dimension in these policies'.[93] In *Josemans* the CJEU considered the city of Maastricht to be an ally in the fight against drug addiction and crime and, even more noticeably, the upholding of European public order.[94] The EU's Smart Specialization regime on the other hand stresses the primordial function of regions in achieving supranational internal market objectives.[95] All of these expressions of the insider narrative are subject to more detailed coverage in Chapter 4 but it should already be stressed that

[89] Hari Osofsky, 'Is Climate Change "International?" Litigation's Diagonal Regulatory Role' (2009) 49 Virginia Journal of International Law 585, 589.

[90] See Parag Khanna, *Connectography: Mapping the Future of Global Civilization* (Random House 2016) (hereafter Khanna, *Connectography*).

[91] OECD, *Devolution and Globalisation. Implications for Local Decision-Makers* (2001): https://www.oecd.org/cfe/leed/devolutionandglobalisationimplicationsforlocaldecision-makers.htm,10.

[92] Declaration of Ministers Towards the EU Urban Agenda (2015): http://www.ectp-ceu.eu/images/stories/PDF-docs/Riga_Declaration_agreed_10062015.pdf, 1.

[93] Pact of Amsterdam (n 66) 5.

[94] Case C-137/09 *Josemans* [2010] EU:C:2010:774.

[95] See further Chapter 4.

they highlight the functional interrelation between the subnational and the supranational.

The interactions highlighted above underline the polycentric nature of the contemporary European legal order. Such intertwining is not, however, limited to the various levels of public authority themselves but equally extends to their norms. Indeed, in contrast with the outsider narrative, the insider narrative contains no presumption that normative interaction occurs only between EU and Member State norms.[96] The second characterizing feature of the insider narrative, porosity, underscores that the dividing borders between the different levels of public authority are permeable, allowing for symbiosis to take place not solely between EU and Member State norms but also those of SNAs. Through such porosity local and regional authorities have been able to contribute to EU law's substantive development.

### *b. Porosity*

Porosity alludes to the interconnection and intertwining of the norms of different levels of public authority. The denomination flags that the various scales of public authority that polycentricity captures are permeable rather than self-contained. Porosity enables policies to leak from one level to another, leading to a dynamic and creative process of cross-fertilization. In this process, experimentation and mutual learning take place. Porosity thus describes the dynamics that arise as a consequence of the interaction of international, EU, national, and subnational norms. The creation of norms at different scales leads to their mutual interaction and SNAs' ability to influence the development of EU law. It is of course hardly a novel statement that the domestic and European legal orders are interconnected.[97] Porosity is also recognized under the outsider narrative in relation to Member State and EU norms. Such bipolar porosity has indeed been widely documented

[96] The recognition that there is a multiplicity of scales of public authority also leads to a multiplication of borders between them, somewhat countering the presumption that we are navigating towards a world without borders. See further Saskia Sassen, 'The City: Today's Frontier Zone' (2014) 1 Glocalism: Journal of Culture, Politics and Innovation 1, 4.

[97] See by way of example Jacques Ziller (ed), *L'européanisation des droits constitutionnels à la lumière de la Constitution pour l'Europe* (L'Harmattan 2003); Monica Claes, 'The Europeanization of National Constitutions in the Constitutionalization of Europe: Some Observations against the Background of the Constitutional Experience of the EU-15' (2007) 3 Croatian Yearbook of European Law and Policy 1; Matej Avbelj and Jan Komárek (eds), *Constitutional Pluralism in the European Union and Beyond* (Hart 2012); and Jörg Gerkrath, 'The Figure of Constitutional Law of the "Integrated State": The Case of the Grand Duchy of Luxembourg' (2014) 10 European Constitutional Law Review 109.

in legal scholarship.[98] According to Pernice, 'national constitutions and the European constitutional level are closely interwoven and interconnected in both their institutions and their substantive law'.[99] Besselink determined that 'the European constitution is more than the constitution of the organization entitled the EU; it also includes the constitutions of the Member States'.[100] Bi-centric porosity is, for instance, evident in the EU's fundamental rights regime as general principles are inspired by the constitutional traditions of the Member States and the ECHR.[101] Domestic constitutional concepts' influence on the development of the body of general principles of EU law is widely accepted.[102] Transnational judicial dialogues are moreover one of the more explicit expressions of porosity as they allow norms from one level to influence the interpretation or content of those at a different level.[103] Porosity is also expressed through primary law's engagement with the influence national policies have on the supranational legal order.[104] The fusion of national and supranational norms is thus well established. While the outsider narrative recognizes such interactions occurring between the States and the EU, the insider narrative frames that subnational norms are not excluded from that phenomenon.

Chapter 4 confirms that porosity plays out between subnational and supranational norms in many contexts. Cases that arise out of such conflicts abound. Some of them are well-known judgments that have significantly shaped free movement law, such as *Omega*, where the Court endorsed Bonn's particular, and isolated, interpretation of the federal constitutional

[98] See for instance Ingolf Pernice, 'The Treaty of Lisbon: Multilevel Constitutionalism in Action' (2009) 15 Columbia Journal of European Law 349, 374.

[99] Ibid 379.

[100] Leonard Besselink, *A Composite European Constitution* (Europa Law Publishing 2007) 4.

[101] Article 6(3) TEU. See also Paul Gragl, 'A Giant Leap for European Human Rights? The Final Agreement on the European Union's Accession to the European Convention on Human Rights' (2014) 51 Common Market Law Review 13, 13–14 (arguing that the Accession Agreement 'constitutes the last step of a growing interlocked system of fundamental rights'). Note, however, Opinion 2/13 on the Accession of the EU to the ECHR [2014] EU:C:2014:2454.

[102] There is an abundant literature engaging with these dynamics. For an example, see Jacques Ziller, 'National Constitutional Concepts in the New Constitution for Europe' (2005) 1 European Constitutional Law Review 247, 452. On the interconnection between domestic and EU law, see further Lord Reed, 'EU Law and the Supreme Court' Sir Thomas Moore Lecture 2014: https://www.supremecourt.uk/docs/speech-141114.pdf.

[103] On judicial dialogues in the EU context, see Anne-Marie Slaughter, 'Judicial Globalization' (2000) 40 Virginia Journal of International Law 1103; Anne-Marie Slaughter, 'A Global Community of Courts' (2003) 44 Harvard International Law Journal 191; Monica Claes and Maartje de Visser, 'Are You Networked Yet? On Dialogues in European Judicial Networks' (2012) 8 Utrecht Law Review 100; and Michal Bobek, *Comparative Reasoning in European Supreme Courts* (Oxford University Press 2013).

[104] See by way of example Article 120 TFEU.

principle of human dignity and incorporated it into the body of supranational law.[105] In *Aragonesa* the Court was faced with an incompatibility between a Catalan ban on alcohol advertising and the free movement of goods.[106] *Walloon Waste* was the consequence of a conflict between a Walloon ban on waste imports and Article 34 TFEU.[107] In the more recent *Scotch Whisky* case the Court clarified the scope of public health derogations in relation to the free movement of alcoholic goods when examining planned Scottish legislation.[108] In *Anton Las* the Court shed light on the legal treatment of national linguistic identity on the basis of a conflict between Article 35 TFEU and Flemish employment contract legislation.[109] Labour law protections from Lower Saxony conflicting with the Posted Workers' Directive[110] set the background of the *Rüffert* case.[111] In each of these cases, porosity is unintended as it occurs as a result of a conflict between a subnational and a supranational norm. Porosity can, however, also be intentional and the intention to bring it about is shared not only by subnational actors but indeed also the European Union. An expression of intentional porosity can be readily observed in the EU's 'Smart Specialisation Platform', an online interface enabling the exchange of information between all scales on matters of smart specialization.[112] In this context the EU encourages the cross-influence of policies initiated at various scales, including the subnational. Other examples include the innumerable networks that have formed between groupings of local and regional actors around shared thematic or geographical interests.[113]

The Ostroms but also Polanyi have emphasized the significance of processes of experimentation and learning in polycentric systems.[114] The various trial-and-error processes in place between subnational authorities, Member States, and the EU will indeed be highlighted throughout the book. Experimentalism allows local and national regulators to gather more

[105] *Omega* (n 1). [106] Case 1/90 *Aragonesa* [1991] EU:C:1991:327.

[107] Case 2/90 *Walloon Waste* [1992] EU:C:1992:310.

[108] Case C-333/14 *Scotch Whisky* [2015] EU:C:2015:845.

[109] Case C-202/11 *Anton Las v PSA Antwerp NV* [2013] EU:C:2013:239. For a comment, see Elke Cloots, 'Case C-202/11, Anton Las v. Psa Antwerp NV, Judgment of the Court of Justice (Grand Chamber) of 16 April 2013' (2014) 51 Common Market Law Review 623.

[110] Directive 96/71/EC concerning the posting of workers in the framework of the provision of services [1996] OJ L 18/431.

[111] Case C-346/06 *Rüffert* [2008] EU:C:2008:189.

[112] The website of this platform is at http://s3platform.jrc.ec.europa.eu/home.

[113] David Smith and Michael Timberlake, 'Hierarchies of Dominance Among World Cities' in Saskia Sassen (ed), *Global Networks, Linked Cities* (Routledge 2002).

[114] Polanyi, *The Logic of Liberty* (n 77).

information on a phenomenon, but also its relation to existing legal frameworks.[115] While the technique goes back significantly in time it is particularly valuable in contexts that are subject to rapid transformation, and gains ground due to the 'social and technological acceleration of society'.[116] This acceleration also impacts on normative orders given that legal frameworks need to adapt to the pace surrounding them.[117] Porosity between the various scales in the polycentric European legal space facilitates the communication between the various actors involved, enabling regulatory solutions employed successfully in one context to influence regulation in a different context.

The constitutional imagination grounding the insider narrative captures subnational norms' impact on the European legal order. As polycentricity creates opportunities for engagement between regional, local, national, supranational, and international regulators, porosity allows their respective norms to interact. The communication between different levels—whether implicit or explicit—allows norms to influence each other, channelling agreement or disagreement. Porosity also extends to the international context as international and transnational law-making increases. SNAs elsewhere have been found to import international legal standards into the domestic regulatory bodies where the national level has been reluctant to do so. Resnik has observed that in the United States 'laws (like people) migrate, and seepage is everywhere'.[118] The examples provided above underline the existence of a similar phenomenon in the EU, confirming that norms 'do not respect lines that people draw across land'.[119] The dividing lines drawn by the formal letter of EU law could indeed not prevent porosity between the subnational and the supranational legal order from occurring.

Once we acknowledge that porosity takes place it is impossible to exclusively think of Member States as outsiders of the European legal order. Porosity rather underlines that SNAs and their norms exist in the same sphere of interaction as the Member States and the Union. While a formal analysis of supranational law has revealed that SNAs are not engaging in direct relations with the Union, a functional analysis reveals a different truth. Just as Member

[115] It is for this reason that subnational authorities are often referred to as 'laboratories'. For the origin of the states-as-laboratories idea in the United States, see *New State Ice Co v Liebmann* 285 U.S 262 (1932) Brandeis J, dissenting.

[116] William Scheuerman, *Liberal Democracy and the Social Acceleration of Time* (John Hopkins University Press 2004).

[117] Wolfgang Hoffman-Riem, 'Législation expérimentale en Allemagne' in Charles Morand (ed), *Evaluation législative des lois expérimentales* (Presses Universitaires d'Aix Marseille 1992) 177.

[118] Judith Resnik, 'Law's Migration: American Exceptionalism, Silent Dialogues, and Federalism's Multiple Ports of Entry' (2006) 115 Yale Law Journal, 1564, 1576.

[119] Ibid, 1576.

States' norms, those of local and regional authority directly interact with and have the potential to influence the supranational legal order. In light of the conclusion that subnational norms can, just as those of the Member States, influence the substantive development of supranational law we must conclude that, despite their formal differences, in some scenarios Member States and SNAs can be assimilated from a functional perspective.

### c. *Member States and SNAs can be assimilated*

The outsider narrative posits Member States and SNAs as actors of a fundamentally different nature. Member States are masters of the Treaties and correspondingly have a privileged formal status SNAs cannot aspire to. The insider narrative underscores, however, that in some domains of supranational law Member States and subnational authorities are functionally aligned. This is, for instance, the case in relation to their respective norms. The ECJ treats subnational norms in the same manner as those of the Member State, attributing them identical value and respect, even though the regulatory capacity of SNAs is, as such, not recognized by EU law. This means, for example, that a subnational regulation conflicting with a provision of EU law can be justified on the same grounds as those of a Member State. In allowing subnational norms to interact with EU norms under the same circumstances as Member State norms, subnational norms can influence the EU's law's substantive development. This can occur where a conflict between a subnational and a supranational provision leads to the development of the derogations regime under free movement law.[120]

This assimilation between Member States and SNAs reaches much wider. The Commission has for instance considered that SNAs can further supranational objectives more efficiently than Member States. In relation to the smart specialization agenda, a key component of the Europe 2020 growth strategy, and 'a crucial part of Europe's response to the economic crisis',[121] SNAs are encouraged to identify their respective comparative advantage and focus their efforts on its development.[122] The rationale is that 'by concentrating knowledge resources and linking them to a limited number of priority economic activities, countries can become—and remain—competitive in the

[120] For a detailed analysis, see Chapter 4.

[121] Research EU Focus, A Competitive Europe. Research Regionally Develop Globally (March 2009): https://ec.europa.eu/research/regions/pdf/publications/research_focus_02.pdf, 8.

[122] For an overview, see Assembly of European Regions, Smart Specialisation Website, online at http://aer-www.ameos.net/knowledge-centre/thematic-expertise-thematic-issues/economy-research-innovation/smart-specialisation.html.

global economy'.[123] In this context, the Commission has stressed that the 'national level is ineffective when it comes to stimulating new regional poles of activity'.[124] In the eyes of the Commission, SNAs are sometimes in a better position to achieve EU objectives than the Member States. This makes them insiders in the achievement of such objectives, but also of European law as such, given the direct relation that emerges between the EU and SNAs.

SNAs' key role in realizing supranational objectives is frequently made explicit by EU secondary legislation. Despite always being formally addressed to the States numerous directives and regulations consider SNAs to be important agents in achieving the objectives they formulate. The Water Directive, for instance, provides that its success 'relies on close cooperation and coherent action at [EU], Member State and local level'.[125] The Drinking Water Directive in turn stresses that 'the natural and socio-economic differences between the regions of the Union require that most decisions on monitoring, analysis, and the measures to be taken to redress failures be taken at a local, regional or national level'.[126] It has also been argued that the decentralized administration of EU law presents benefits that could not be achieved without subnational intervention. Advocate General Trstenjak has, for instance, emphasized the benefits of fragmentation in light of 'the demands of the Common Agricultural Policy for devolved and differentiated implementation'.[127] The devolved organization of agricultural law acknowledges that 'regional differentiation is entirely necessary' to account for the 'structural and natural disparities between the various agricultural regions'.[128]

This section has drawn attention to two parallel yet distinct narratives of SNAs in EU law, which are also contrasting narratives of European integration itself. The outsider narrative captures the reality that local and regional authorities are devoid of any formal legal status and recognition as a matter of supranational law. It moreover captures the fact that no direct relations exist between the EU and SNAs. As a consequence, the structure of the European

[123] EU Smart Specialisation Platform, Guide to Research and Innovation Strategies for Smart Specialisation: http://ec.europa.eu/regional_policy/sources/docgener/presenta/smart_specialisation/smart_ris3_2012.pdf, 12.

[124] European Commission FOREN Network, 'A Practical Guide to Regional Foresight' (2011) http://foresight.jrc.ec.europa.eu/documents/eur20128en.pdf, 11.

[125] Recital 14 of Directive 2000/60/EC of the European Parliament and of the Council of 23 October 2000 establishing a framework for Community action in the field of water policy (2000) OJ L 327/1.

[126] Recital 4 of Council Directive 98/83/EC of 3 November 1998 on the quality of water intended for human consumption (1998) OJ L 330/32.

[127] Opinion of Advocate General Trstenjak in Case C-428/07 *Horvath* [2009] EU:C:2009:47, para 89.

[128] Ibid, para 92.

legal order can only be understood to be formally bi-centric. The insider narrative, on the other hand, draws attention to the functional significance of SNAs in the supranational legal order as significant executers of EU obligations and shapers of EU law's substantive development. Seen from this perspective, supranational law is characterized by polycentricity and porosity. The remainder of the present chapter enquires into the reasons underlying the co-existence of both narratives. Two central arguments are put forward in this respect. It will firstly be maintained that the coexistence of both narratives relates to the evolution of the European legal order itself, and, secondly, that such coexistence can be explained in light of the nature of contemporary governance challenges.

## B. The Evolving Structure of the European Legal Order

The preceding analysis has highlighted that two narratives of SNAs coexist in the EU: the outsider narrative and the insider narrative. These parallel yet dissimilar narratives of European law highlight the divide between the formal (SNAs' lack of any formal status and direct relation to the EU) and the functional (SNAs' manifold interactions with the EU and their practical importance in the supranational legal order). Whereas law's very purpose consists in operating abstractions I contend that the present disconnect between the formal and the functional hints at a deeper phenomenon. It has been seen that the outsider narrative echoes the strong attachment the EU retains towards sovereign statehood, apparent through the States' singular rights and obligations as masters of the Treaties. The insider narrative, on the other hand, highlights the evolution of European integration and that relations between various actors are as revealing as their formal status. Over the past decades, the supranational legal order has matured as integration has progressed to encompass actors other than States. This is well documented and acknowledged in relation to European citizens and the development of the concept of European citizenship.[129] This book makes the point that the same is true in relation to local and regional authorities, arguing that while SNAs were initially considered irrelevant for supranational integration, time has revealed a different truth. The second dynamic identified to make sense of the coexistence of both narratives is the nature of contemporary governance challenges.

[129] For an overview of the evolution of the concept of European citizenship, see Francis Jacobs, 'Citizenship of the European Union—A Legal Analysis' (2007) 13 European Law Journal 591; Niamh Nic Shuibhne, 'Limits rising, duties ascending: The changing legal shape of Union citizenship' (2015) 52 Common Market Law Review 889.

I will illustrate that many of these challenges are themselves of a polycentric nature, mandating a correspondingly polycentric regulatory response.

## 1. The nature of European integration

SNAs' functional status as insiders of EU law can be framed as a natural consequence of the integration process, which has had, and continues to have, formative effects on the structure of supranational law. This section relies predominantly on federalism theory to frame that finding. That does not convey, however, that the author considers the EU to be of a federal structure. Rather, in the words of Walker, while the notion of federalism might be of 'limited or even negative value' in the EU, federalism 'when drawing on its deeper historical roots and considered instead as a basis for imaginative reflection on the nature and proper trajectory of an unprecedented political configuration, fares rather better'.[130] Federalism theory is accordingly a helpful tool assisting qualifications of supranational law, a conclusion which does not imply that we have to think of the EU in terms of a federal entity.

The transition from the dual to the cooperative nature of inter-level relations in the EU, pinpointed by Schütze, can be considered to have entered its next phase, as the levels affected by this dynamic are transitioning from two to many. As a consequence a functional account of EU law reveals a multi-directional polycentric interconnection that encompasses not only Member States but also local and regional authorities. SNAs have become functionally vital ingredients of European integration. This structural transformation, it is claimed, should be understood from the perspective of European integration itself. It is well established that EU law's structure has been subject to evolution over the past decades. Schütze famously documented that, due to the increased cooperation and interconnection between Member States and the Union, the European legal order transitioned from a structure of dual to one of cooperative federalism.[131] His study, as most in EU law, was however limited to the Union and the States only, not enquiring whether Member States' internal authorities were equally affected by the said transition. This book indicates that the interconnection provoked by cooperation has spread to also include local and regional authorities. The European legal order is accordingly evolving not merely towards more connection (from dualism to cooperation) but moreover towards including more and more actors (from

[130] Neil Walker, 'Federalism in 3D, The Reimagination of Political Community in the European Union' Edinburgh School of Law Research Paper No 2016/13, 1.

[131] Geert De Baere and Timothy Roes, 'EU Loyalty as Good Faith' (2015) 64 International and Comparative Law Quarterly 829.

bi-centricity to polycentricity). Integration emerges as a performative phenomenon, for it concerns not merely that which is explicitly planned, namely the increased cooperation between the Union and the States, but also aspects that were not explicitly envisaged initially, including SNAs' involvement.

The 1950 Schuman Declaration recognized that 'Europe will not be made all at once', recognizing the gradual evolution of European integration and anticipating the spillover effects that would take place.[132] The theory of neofunctionalism captures how spillover occurs within the EU. It was first employed to make sense of how cooperation on coal and steel in the context of the European Coal and Steel Community had given rise to the European Economic Community and Euratom.[133] Ernst Haas, the champion of neofunctionalism in the EU, considered that the 'expansive logic of sector integration' arises where integration in one sector entails pressure for States to also integrate other sectors.[134] Niemann and Schmitter have highlighted that the logic behind this phenomenon is that of interconnection, as 'some sectors are so interdependent that it is impossible to isolate them from the rest' which makes integration in one sector only practicable in combination with the integration of additional sectors.[135] The same can be readily observed in the case of territorial as opposed to sectoral dynamics. Haas acknowledged that spillover may also come to have a geographical dimension[136] and others have indeed attempted to shed light on the EU's enlargement process through the lens of neofunctionalism.[137] We can also apply the spillover logic to the relationship between the EU and subnational authorities. While it is clear that initially the objective was to merely integrate the Member States, time has revealed that SNAs' integration is equally necessary to achieve supranational objectives, especially as they expanded in scope and depth. We will indeed see that the achievement of many supranational policies was merely feasible thanks to SNAs' contribution and it is difficult to imagine how the objectives inherent to supranationalism could be upheld without the collaboration of local and regional authorities.

[132] The Schuman Declaration (1950) http://europa.eu/european-union/about-eu/symbols/europe-day/schuman-declaration_en.

[133] For an overview, see Arne Nieman and Philippe Schmitter, 'Neofunctionalism' in Antje Wiener and Thomas Diez (eds), *European Integration Theory* (Oxford University Press 2009) (hereafter Nieman and Schmitter, 'Neofunctionalism').

[134] Ernst Haas, *The Uniting of Europe: Political, Social and Economic Forces 1950–1957* (Stevens 1958) 383 (hereafter Haas, *The Uniting of Europe*). See also Ernst Haas, *Beyond the Nation State* (Stanford University Press 1964).

[135] Nieman and Schmitter, 'Neofunctionalism' (n 133) 49.

[136] Haas, *The Uniting of Europe* (n 134) 313–17.

[137] Nieman and Schmitter, 'Neofunctionalism' (n 133) 61–3.

The Court itself has recognized the functional impetus behind the transition from bi-centricity to polycentricity. In *Carbonati Apunani* it applied a bi-centric Treaty provision in a polycentric manner and provided an intriguing justification for doing so.[138] Article 30 TFEU refers solely to the States in providing that: '[c]ustoms duties on imports and exports and charges having equivalent effect shall be prohibited between Member States'. The Court held that its explicit wording doesn't prevent the prohibition from equally applying to SNAs as their measures have the same distortive effects on free movement.[139] If the Treaties only make express reference to States, the Court elaborated, that is 'because the framers of the Treaty took it for granted that there were no charges exhibiting the features of a customs duty in existence within the Member States'.[140] The framers' constitutional imagination was bi-centric in that they considered only the Member States and the Union as relevant levels of public authority for the purposes of EU law. Yet subsequent decades have revealed that the objectives inherent to European integration cannot be achieved if only Member States and not SNAs are bound by obligations such as that enshrined in Article 30 TFEU. The internal market would be doomed to fail if Member States were to tear down any borders but SNAs could keep theirs. The SNA is an insider in this respect, as its actions directly influence the supranational scale and its cooperation is imperative to secure the achievement of supranational objectives.

Fuller has explained the notion of polycentricity by reference to a spider's web in which a 'pull on one strand will distribute tensions after a complicated pattern throughout the web as a whole'.[141] Cases such as *Carbonati Apuani* reveal the Court's awareness that, despite the Treaties' silence, SNAs are pivotal partners in the project of European integration as their policies have, just as those of the Member States, the potential to pull on the strands of the polycentric Union and distribute tension or stimulus through the entire web. SNAs further supranational goals where they adhere to them, yet they can also endanger the ideal of the internal market without borders where they reinstate fiscal borders.[142] Similarly SNAs' endorsement of supranational objectives strengthens their success. This underlines that with the passing of time, the spiders' web has broadened to catch actors other than States, famously

[138] Case C-72/03 *Carbonati Apuani* [2004] EU:C:2004:506 (hereafter *Carbonati Apuani*).

[139] Para 22, citing Joined Cases 2/69 and 3/69 *Brachfeld and Chougol* [1969] EU:C:1969:30; para 14 and Joined Cases C-363/93, C-407/93 to C-411/93 *Lancry and Others* [1994] EU:C:1994:315, para 25.

[140] *Carbonati Apuani* (n 138) para 22.

[141] Lon Fuller, 'The Forms and Limits of Adjudication' (1978) 92 Harvard Law Review 395.

[142] On this, see also Case C-88/03 *Portugal v Commission* [2006] EU:C:2006:511.

individuals, but also subnational authorities, as it became obvious that its intrinsic goals could not be achieved without SNAs' assistance in giving effect to EU law or in refraining from taking actions that could potentially harm supranational objectives.[143] Subnational authorities for instance play key roles in realizing the goals inherent to secondary legislation, as highlighted by the references to the Water Directive and the Drinking Water Directive above. Chapter 4 will moreover highlight intriguing developments in soft legislation that confirm SNAs' insider role in the achievement of supranational objectives. EU law has long relied on the multiplication of enforcement agents to secure its objectives, famously through the doctrine of direct effect that turned individuals into such agents.[144] The examples highlighted above indicate that the EU is pursuing the same strategy in respect of local and regional authorities, realizing that they are oftentimes better placed to give effect to supranational objectives than Member States.

The example of the *Carbonati Apuani* case presents the additional benefit of underlining that the integration that now pairs subnational authorities with the EU is not necessarily a cheerful quest for ever more integration.[145] Referring to SNAs' 'connection' to the EU and the latter's polycentric nature, I do not misunderstand the relation between both actors as one of full and unconditional support and endorsement. It has indeed been observed that 'the narrative of an intimate and positive relation between law and integration is over'[146] as the contemporary EU reflects a 'lack of commitment to the idea of the EU as a whole, that is, to the idea that the Union is more than the sum of its parts'.[147] There is no reason to believe that, save for a few exceptions, SNAs are more enthusiastic about the European project than many of its Member States and citizens.[148] The intertwining between SNAs and the EU is factual, triggered by the impossibility of isolated action in the EU. Virtually all local and regional policies relate to supranational law in one way or another and EU law is equally dependent on SNAs to realize its stated objectives. In light of the imposition of the local tax, Carrara had no intention to support the borderless market when regulating, yet its fiscal scheme

143 Individuals have also come to assume a role and status not initially envisaged.

144 Case 6/64, *Costa v ENEL* [1964] EU:C:1964:66.

145 This is because the municipality had created borders in the internal market through the exercise of its autonomous competences.

146 Loic Azoulai, 'Integration Through Law and Us' (2016) 14 International Journal of Constitutional Law 449, 450 (hereafter Azoulai, 'Integration Through Law').

147 Ibid 458.

148 Regions that have a lot to gain from their continued relation to the EU and are less enthusiastic about their own States, such as Scotland, can be seen as such an exception.

nonetheless affected the EU. To say it in the words of Azoulai: '[r]esistance to further integration is just another way of relating to Europe'.[149]

It follows that the planned effort of integration set out in the Treaties has over time given rise to a parallel performative process that touches SNAs. The related changes to the structure of EU law help explain that subnational authorities perform functions not planned for by primary law. These structural changes, however, also have a second source in the form of the essence of contemporary governance challenges.

## 2. The nature of contemporary governance challenges

This section sketches local and regional authorities as essential EU allies in the realization of supranational targets. This shouldn't come as a surprise. Subnational, and in particular urban actors are increasingly identified as the geographical sites where this century's key economic, socio-cultural, and demographic challenges play out.[150] In order to tackle the corresponding governance trials, regulation is frequently issued by, or directed at, SNAs. Recent studies in other domains of the social sciences, such as governance theory, have highlighted that the role of SNAs in the European context is subject to fast and pronounced transformation.[151] Local and regional authorities indeed take on increasingly important functions in politics and governance as Europe becomes more urbanized and as our inherently interconnected world requires not only policies adopted at large but also at smaller scales. In line with that trend, considerable EU secondary and soft law at least partly addresses subnational issues and actors. The Union moreover relies on domestic authorities at all levels to implement its policies due to the feeble Brussels administrative base. SNAs' support in the realization of the corresponding objectives has accordingly become imperative. Their increased centrality in addressing contemporary governance challenges has had transformational effects on inter-level relations in the EU that explain the dynamics inherent to the insider narrative, especially the direct relation that has emerged between the Union and SNAs.

The EU's urban agenda substantiates subnational authorities' status as salient associates in the realization of supranational objectives. The agenda

[149] Azoulai, ' Integration Through Law' (n 146) 459.

[150] See generally Janne Nijman, 'The Future of the City and the International Law of the Future' in Sam Muller et al. (eds), *Law of the Future and Future of the Law* (Torkel Opsahl EPublisher 2011) (hereafter Nijman, 'The Future of the City').

[151] For an overview of the role of SNAs in governance matters, see Panara, *The Sub-National Dimension* (n 58).

constitutes a joint effort of the Commission, the Member States, and European cities networks to 'strengthen the recognition of the urban dimension by European and national policy actors'.[152] The 2016 Pact of Amsterdam recalls that the EU is one of the globe's most urbanized areas and announces that in order to realize the 'full potential of the European Union and deliver on its strategic objectives, the Urban Agenda of the EU strives to involve Urban Authorities in Achieving Better Regulation, Better Funding and Better Knowledge'.[153] The EU itself thus considers that subnational authorities' support is vital to the achievement of supranational objectives. The relation between the subnational and the supranational is not, however, one-sided. Subnational authorities indeed consider that supranational support matters for the success of their own policies. The supranational is also considered crucial for the success of SNAs, not just vice versa, given that 'EU policies also have an important role in setting the right framework within which European urban areas can tackle urban challenges and unlock their growth potential.'[154] The subnational and supranational are inherently interconnected given that they draw mutual benefits from such alliance.

Changing governance challenges engender modifications in the structure of the European legal order. According to Vincent Ostrom such adaptation constitutes a key feature of polycentric systems where 'many elements are capable of making mutual adjustments for ordering their relationships with one another within a general system of rules where each element acts with independence of other elements'.[155] The coexistence of regulation at large and small scales, sometimes termed 'glocalisation'[156] have become unavoidable given that the 'nation-state is not best equipped for dealing with many of the challenges and opportunities of the twenty-first century'.[157] The EU is part of the envisaged solution as it allows States to rule in common. Yet there is a growing awareness that oftentimes neither supranational nor national responses are suitable and local and regional impetus is required. Local and regional governments are indeed encouraged to 'develop flexible, tailored and integrated strategies to compete in an increasingly rapidly-moving and

[152] The website of the Urban Agenda is at http://urbanagendaforthe.eu/ [153] Ibid, 3.

[154] The Riga Declaration: https://ec.europa.eu/futurium/en/content/riga-declaration-0, 1.

[155] Vincent Ostrom, Polycentricity, Speech delivered at the 1972 Annual Association of the American Political Science Association: http://dlc.dlib.indiana.edu/dlc/handle/10535/3763?show=full, 57.

[156] Kim van der Leeuw, Joyeeta Gupta, and Hans de Moel, 'Climate Change: a "Glocal" Problem Requiring "Glocal" Action' (2007) 4 Environmental Sciences 139.

[157] See OECD, 'Devolution and Globalisation. Implications for Local Decision-Makers' (2001) 25 (hereafter OECD, 'Devolution and Globalisation'). Foresight for Regional Development Network Guide European Commission, 'A Practical Guide to Regional Foresight' (2001) 10.

internationally-open economic environment'.[158] There now is ample agreement that as power becomes even more diffuse a growing number of actors, including subnational authorities, will come to play pronounced governance roles. Our interconnected planet yields interconnected opportunities, such as free movement, but also trials. Climate change is often cited as the quintessential illustration of the latter as its causes and consequences are localized yet also transcend borders. This peculiarity of the climate change phenomenon is reflected in the regulatory framework developed to frame mitigation and adaptation strategies.[159]

Interconnection might well be the characterizing label of the present era.[160] Yet, interconnection is not the only phenomenon affecting SNAs' status as urbanization is transforming European countries and societies. It has been suggested that our response to the challenges of the urbanizing world will be 'crucial for the future of our planet, and marks the law of the future'.[161] Nijman has highlighted that '[q]uestions of global stability, global justice, and global governance will be in large part questions of urban stability, urban justice, and urban governance across the globe'.[162] The EU is now 'one of the most urbanised areas in the world' as 70 per cent of all individuals reside in urban areas, a number expected to increase to 80 per cent by 2050.[163] Economic forces are preceding that demographic shift as 85 per cent of European GDP is already generated in urban areas.[164] EU legislation, as recognized by the Pact of Amsterdam, frequently touches on issues that are vital to urban governance including planning, environmental protection, the delivery of public services, and transportation. [165] With the swelling centrality of the subnational more and more competences are devolved to SNAs.[166] The consequences of this state of affairs have already been documented in relation to the international legal order where subnational governments are

[158] OECD, 'Devolution and Globalisation' (n 157) 10.

[159] See Harriet Bulkeley, Vanessa Castan Broto, and Gareth Edwards, *An Urban Politics of Climate Change. Experimentation and the Governing of Socio-Technical Transitions* (Routledge 2015). For a view of the EU, see Michèle Finck, 'Above and Below the Surface: The Status of Sub-National Authorities in EU Climate Change Regulation' (2014) 26 Journal of Environmental Law 443.

[160] For a thought-provoking account, see Khanna, 'Connectography' (n 90).

[161] Nijman, 'The Future of the City' (n 150) 216.

[162] Ibid.

[163] Pact of Amsterdam (n 66) 3.

[164] European Investment Bank, Shaping Sustainable Cities (2013). Report available online: http://www.eib.org/attachments/thematic/shaping_sustainable_cities_en.pdf, 1.

[165] Pact of Amsterdam (n 66) 3.

[166] In an 'increasing number of Member States', Lenaerts and Cambien have written, 'important competences are allocated to subnational entities'. Koen Lenaerts and Nathan Cambien, 'Regions and the European Courts: Giving Shape to the Regional Dimension of Member States' (2010) 35 European Law Review 609, 609.

'transforming into objects for international regulation and are increasingly used as a means for disseminating and implementing global political programs, financial schemes, and governance strategies'.[167] SNAs also influence law-making on a transnational scale through the development of a 'European paradiplomacy' paralleling to that of the Member States and their participation in transnational networks.[168]

Whereas these evolutions denote a state of affairs noticeably different from the early days of European integration, the bi-centric Treaties have hardly caught up. The insider narrative, however, helps highlighting expressions of these changing circumstances such as polycentricity and porosity. Tripartite contracts and agreements serve to make this point.[169] These contracts are concluded between the EU, the Member State, and a regional or local authority to accommodate subnational preferences and allow SNAs to implement supranational objectives with enhanced efficiency and flexibility.[170] The resulting 'direct, active and horizontal partnership' between the three levels concerned is expected to generate results superior to the classic implementation by Member States.[171] Some have even put forward the argument that these contracts are 'solid evidence that state governments have lost control of the relations between European agencies and sub-national actors'.[172] Tripartite contracts illustrate the importance of interconnection—they are entered into as all parties involved consider that their own objectives can be best achieved through cooperation as opposed to isolation. The smart specialization agenda illustrates the same phenomenon in a different domain: because economic strength is increasingly a question of subnational economic development and transnational connection it is nonsensical to address it solely at national or supranational scale.[173]

The paradigm of interconnection is in fact key to any understanding of SNAs' contemporary role. This is recognized increasingly by various EU policy documents, such as the Committee of the Regions' 2014 Charter for Multilevel Governance in Europe, which, rather than advocating for subnational autonomies, stresses the need for, and benefit of, interconnection—between SNAs

[167] Blank, 'Localism in the New Global Order' (n 87) 263.

[168] Nikos Skoutaris, 'Comparing the Subnational Constitutional Space of the European Sub-State Entities in the Area of Foreign Affairs' (2012) 4 Perspectives on Federalism 239, 240.

[169] European Commission, 'A Framework for Target-based Tripartite Contracts and Agreements between the Community, the States and Regional and Local Authorities' COM (2002) 709 final.

[170] Martino Mazzoleni, 'The First Tripartite Agreement in the EU. An Actor-Centred Analysis of an Experimental Multi-Level Interaction' (2006) 16 Regional and Federal Studies 263, 264.

[171] Ibid, 263. [172] Ibid, 275.

[173] See by way of example Kenichi Ohmae, *End of the Nation State: The Rise of Regional Economies: How Regional Economics Will Soon Reshape the World* (Free Press 1995).

but also with other levels of public authority.[174] This underlines the necessity to revisit the opposed paradigms of exclusivity of power and separation of regulatory spheres. Rather than portraying levels of public authority as contestants for the exclusive exercise of regulatory power, as embedded in Article 5(3) TEU, the Charter highlights the need for various scales 'to work together in partnership to achieve greater economic, social and territorial cohesion in Europe'.[175] The Charter indeed portrays multi-level governance in Europe as 'based on coordinated action by the European Union, the Member States and regional and local authorities according to the principles of subsidiarity, proportionality and partnership, taking the form of operational and institutional cooperation in the drawing up and implementation of the European Union's policies'.[176] This interconnection occurs vertically between SNAs and the EU but also horizontally 'to connect regions and cities across Europe, whilst promoting multi-actorship with societal actors'.[177] It follows that the supranational and subnational levels can mutually empower another, highlighting another incentive for their increased cooperation and reason for the reshuffling of subnational regulatory competence.

The elements covered above indicate that by reason of the combined rise of the subnational and the transnational, regulation no longer operates in linear ways. Involving subnational authorities in regulation has become imperative, yet does not mean that regulatory competence is increasingly devolved to them. In fact, in order to understand contemporary urban government and its growth, norm-production, and interaction with other levels of public authority we must enrich our study of the law in keeping our minds focused on interactions, networks, and intertwining rather than sovereignty, autonomy, and spheres of competences.

174 Committee of the Regions, Charter for Multi-Level Governance in Europe (2014).
175 Ibid, 1. 176 Ibid, 1.
177 Ibid, 1.

# 2

# SNAs in the Contemporary European Union

## Introduction

This book explores the status of local and regional authorities in European Union law. Before diving deeper into that analysis, this chapter introduces the wide plethora of SNAs in the EU's various Member States. This undertaking provides an overview of the variegated power-sharing arrangements in place in the different Member States with a view to grounding further analysis. The present chapter will make seven pivotal points. It will first be seen that SNAs have radically divergent statuses and competences between, but also within, the various Member States. Second, notwithstanding such diversity, virtually all SNAs share one characteristic, which nonetheless often goes unnoticed: their jurisgenerative capacity. On a spectrum from municipal administrative decrees to regional constitutions, SNAs produce norms that coexist with norms at other levels, including EU law. Third, it will be seen that over the past decades manifold relations between SNAs and the EU have emerged, which challenge our understanding of SNAs as purely domestic phenomena. Fourth, the Committee of the Regions, the organ formally charged with representing SNAs at EU level, will be introduced. Fifth, the chapter will provide an overview of a key mechanism that allows SNAs to connect with other actors and exert influence beyond the domestic scale, namely their participation in transnational networks. Sixth, SNAs' involvement in international affairs will be documented to discard the assumption that local and regional authorities' influence does not exceed domestic boundaries. I will lastly draw attention to the increased magnitude of the subnational in contemporary governance challenges. The examination of these different dynamics serves to underline that, contrary to the prevailing constitutional imagination, local and regional authorities should not be conceived of as exclusively domestic phenomena, the influence of which does not transcend domestic borders. Rather SNAs have come to constitute nodes of public authority in a polycentric network that establishes connections irrespective of national borders.

## A. A Wide Diversity of Subnational Authorities

This section provides an overview of the convoluted diversity of local and regional authorities in the various Member States. It is almost an understatement to claim that there is a 'great deal of diversity in the territorial organisation of states'[1] as their respective internal institutional arrangements are subject to pronounced disparity.[2] States are not only divided between those that are 'decentralized' and 'unitary'. Rather each domestic structure is unique.[3] Subnational competences, however, vary not solely between but also within Member States. Such complexity has been recognized to constitute a definitional challenge as well as a deterrent effect of their study.[4]

Within a single State, devolution can be of a symmetric or asymmetric nature. In instances of symmetric devolution, such as the German variant of federalism, all SNAs of the same category (such as the sixteen German Länder) have the same competences.[5] Variation nonetheless persists in light of divergences between the competences of regional and local authorities. Such variation is even more pronounced where decentralization is of an asymmetric character. In Finland and Portugal, for example, there is no strong overall decentralization arrangement but some SNAs, the Åland and Azores islands respectively, nonetheless enjoy a special status.[6] The United Kingdom constitutes another example of potentially ever more asymmetrical devolution.[7] In addition to the devolved nations, the Greater London Authority boasts more competences than any other local government.[8] These examples

[1] John Loughlin, 'The Regional Question, Subsidiarity, and the Future of Europe' in Stephen Weatherill and Ulf Bernitz (eds), *The Role of Regions and Sub-National Actors in Europe* (Hart 2005) 157 (hereafter Loughlin, 'The Regional Question'). See also Stephen Weatherill, 'The Challenge of the Regional Dimension in the European Union' in Stephen Weatherill and Ulf Bernitz (eds), *The Role of Regions and Sub-National Actors in Europe* (Hart 2005) 9–11.

[2] Joxerramon Bengoetxea, 'Autonomous Constitutional Regions in a Federal Europe' in Elke Cloots, Geert de Baere, and Stefan Sottiaux (eds), *Federalism in the European Union* (Hart 2012) 232 (hereafter Bengoetxea, 'Autonomous Constitutional Regions in Europe').

[3] And sometimes, those Member States we think of as 'unitary' actually self-identify as of a decentralized nature. See Article 1 of the French Constitution.

[4] Bengoetxea, 'Autonomous Constitutional Regions in Europe' (n 2) 233.

[5] Articles 70–4 of the German Basic Law.

[6] On the Åland Islands, see Jaakko Husa, *The Constitution of Finland. A Contextual Analysis* (Hart 2011) (hereafter Husa, *The Constitution of Finland*).

[7] Vernon Bogdanor, *Devolution in the United Kingdom* (Oxford University Press 1999); Geoffrey Clark, 'Scottish Devolution and the European Union' (1999) 3 Public Law 505; Andrew Evans, 'UK Devolution and EU Law' (2003) 28 European Law Review 475; Jo Murkens, 'The Blunders of Brexit: Economics, Sovereignty, and the Constitution' *Law Society and Economy Working Paper Series* 14-2016 (2016).

[8] Greater London Authority Act 1999 and Greater London Authority Act 2007.

indicate that a wide panoply of decentralization arrangements can be identified as '[f]ederal states may be centralised (Austria), decentralised (Belgium), and balanced (Germany). Unitary states may be centralised (Greece, Ireland, Portugal), decentralised (Scandinavian states and the Netherlands) and regionalised (Italy, Spain, France, and, now, the UK)'.[9] In fact even formal labels such as 'federalism' do not provide any conclusive answer regarding an SNAs' autonomy. The Austrian version of federalism doesn't guarantee the Länder any pronounced independence[10] yet in Belgium, subnational competences are more pronounced than those of the federal State.[11] Belgium, it has indeed been suggested, 'has in some senses ceased to exist and has almost a residual existence', all activity taking place 'on the periphery with no centre'.[12] Matters are further complicated by the fact that SNAs are classified by diverging parameters for instance in line with their economic, administrative, constitutional, linguistic, or historic parameters.[13] A further difference resides in SNAs' self-perception vis-à-vis the EU. Oxford certainly isn't Bavaria in this regard. Formal labels have accordingly only limited value in making sense of SNAs and their status in the EU.

Beyond the definitional issue, inescapable divergences exist in relation to the scope of competences subnational authorities enjoy. The German Länder, the Italian regions, or the Spanish autonomous communities have pronounced regulatory powers and can adopt regional constitutions or constitution-like charters.[14] Other SNAs display much more limited competences, especially local governments of small size. Yet there are also powerful cities with significant regulatory competence, such as the Greater London Authority and the German City-States of Berlin and Hamburg, which are formally Länder but de facto cities.[15] The policy domains in which SNAs enjoy autonomies moreover differ between States.[16] In Germany criminal law and procedure are

[9] Loughlin, 'The Regional Question' (n 1) 157.

[10] Jan Erk, 'Austria: A Federation without Federalism' (2004) 34 Publius: The Journal of Federalism 1.

[11] Laurence Sharpe, 'The European Meso: An Appraisal' in Laurence Sharpe (ed), *The Rise of Meso-Government in Europe* (Sage 1993).

[12] Charlie Jeffrey, *The Regional Dimension in Europe: Towards a Third Level in Europe?* (Frank Cass 1997) 148, quoting Laurence Sharpe, *Decentralist Trends in Western Democracies* (Sage 1979).

[13] Bengoetxea, 'Autonomous Constitutional Regions in Europe' (n 2) 232.

[14] For Italy, see Giacomo Delledonne and Guiseppe Martinico, 'Handle with Care! The Regional Charters and Italian Constitutionalism's "Grey Zone"' (2009) 5 European Constitutional Law Review 218 (hereafter Delledonne and Martinico, 'Handle with Care!').

[15] See by way of example for London, Greater London Authority Act 1999.

[16] David Edward and Joxerramon Bengoetxea, 'The Status and Rights of Sub-State Entities in the Constitutional Order of the European Union' in Anthony Arnull, Catherine Barnard, Michael Dougan, and Eleanor Spaventa (eds), *A Constitutional Order of States? Essays in Honour of Alan Dashwood* (Hart 2011) 29.

shared between the federal level and the Länder, whereas in the UK these areas have been devolved to the Scottish Parliament, subject to the overriding legislative competence of Westminster.[17] In addition to their regulatory impact dissimilarities exist moreover in relation to SNAs' politico-economic gravity. Besides innumerable small localities, some regions are larger and more populous than small Member States like Malta or Luxembourg.[18] Greater London is one of Europe's economic powerhouses and boasts a population about as large as Austria's.[19] Nonetheless we should not lose sight of the fact that the wide majority of SNAs are not powerful regions. The EU counts only three formal federations (Austria, Belgium, and Germany), two States that recognize legislative competences to all decentralized authorities (Italy and Spain), and three States that recognize such powers to some SNAs (Finland, the UK, and Portugal).

The factors outlined above serve to clarify that no straightforward definition of a subnational authority can be provided other than that it is a level of public authority within a Member State, the competences of which diverge significantly between, as well as within, States. While such diversity encumbers the quest to make sense of SNAs' relation to the EU it should not be forgotten that Member States are qualified by diversity too. Luxembourg certainly isn't Germany. Yet the concept of State sovereignty allows us to operate abstractions with regard to States that cannot be applied to SNAs. Significantly, however, virtually all SNAs share a characteristic most relevant for the present study: they generate norms.

## B. SNAs' Norm-Generating Capacity

The focus of the present book lies on the substantive interaction between subnational and supranational normative orders. A necessary preliminary observation is that subnational authorities are generators of norms. Virtually all SNAs, no matter their size, create norms. This is evident for large regions such as Tuscany or North Rhine Westphalia that have legislative competences and sometimes also the capacity to adopt constitutions[20] or constitution-like

[17] Article 74 of the German Basic Law. Under Section 29(1) of the Scotland Act 1998 most areas of criminal law are devolved matters except for some reserved matters such as misuse of drugs, firearms, and road traffic offences.

[18] Such as some of the German Länder, for instance Nordrhein-Westfalen.

[19] Greater London boasts a population of c. 8.6 million people, Austria of 8.4 million people.

[20] Article 28(1)(1) of the German Basic Law allows for the adoption of constitutional documents by the Länder, provided that they comply with the principles of the republican, democratic, and social *Rechtsstaat*.

charters.[21] Yet, smaller SNAs, including local governments, also regulate.[22] Unlike the norm-generating activity of regions, that of localities is less documented and understood in legal scholarship, let alone in its relation to other levels of public authority.[23] When it comes to European Union law scholarly commentary is predominantly focused on regions, or even just regions with particularly pronounced autonomies.[24] In this context the norm-generating abilities of local governments, and in particular their relation to Union law, are easily overlooked.[25] In an age of urbanization and interconnection such a stance is becoming inopportune and legal scholars interested in public international law are for instance increasingly turning towards the study of urban norm-generation. While localities have been studied from the perspective of domestic constitutional law, and are increasingly examined from the perspective of public international law, EU law has not yet caught up.[26]

Localities regulate and do so ever more frequently with the rise of urbanization. A larger share of Europe's population than ever before reside in cities.[27] This number is expected to rise to 80 per cent by 2050.[28] Eighty-five per cent of European GDP is already generated in urban areas.[29] Local regulatory competence exists on a spectrum from very pronounced autonomies to the ability to enact administrative decisions. Whereas formal competences vary considerably between SNAs in various Member States, SNAs have become

[21] This is for instance the case for Italy and Spain. See further Delledonne and Martinico, 'Handle with Care!' (n 14).

[22] Article 107(3) of the Luxembourg Constitution for instance empowers local governments to create local regulations and taxes (taxes are subject to approval by the national level).

[23] There is an emergent strand of literature that examines this phenomenon from the perspective of international and transnational law. See by way of example Stacy Lozner, 'Diffusion of Local Regulatory Innovations: The San Francisco CEDAW Ordinance and the New York City Human Rights Initiative' (2004) 104 Columbia Law Review 768; Yishai Blank, 'Localism in the New Global Legal Order' (2006) 47 Harvard International Law Journal 263 (hereafter Blank, 'Localism').

[24] See for instance Bengoetxea, 'Autonomous Constitutional Regions in Europe' (n 2), who examines the role of 'constitutional regions' in the EU, or Koen Lenaerts and Nathan Cambien, 'Regions and the European Courts: Giving Shape to the Regional Dimension of Member States' (2010) 35 European Law Review 609 (hereafter Lenaerts and Cambien, 'Regions and the European Courts'), examining regions but not cities.

[25] Fernanda Nicola, 'Invisible Cities in Europe' (2012) 35 Fordham International Law Journal 1286 (arguing that cities remain 'invisible' as political communities to the EU judiciary).

[26] Janne Nijman, 'The Future of the City and the International Law of the Future' in Sam Muller et al (eds) *Law of the Future and Future of the Law* (Torkel Opsahl EPublisher 2011) (hereafter Nijman, 'The Future of the City').

[27] National Intelligence Council, *Global Trends 2030: Alternative Worlds,* www.dni.gov/nic/globaltrends (2012) 27. Neil Brenner and Roger Kreil, 'From Global Cities to Globalised Urbanization' (2014) 1 Glocalism: Journal of Culture, Politics and Innovation 1, 1.

[28] Urban Agenda for the EU, *Pact of Amsterdam* (2016) 3.

[29] European Investment Bank, 'Shaping Sustainable Cities' (2013): https://publicintelligence.net/global-trends-2030/.

very creative in making use of whatever competence they have to further their objectives. Yet, due to increased urbanization and the local nature of many contemporary governance challenges, local authorities have become important regulatory agents in recent years that often show impressive creativity in using the limited competences they have to further a policy agenda.

Virtually every local government has at least some competence relating to the provision of public services, urban planning, environmental regulation, housing, education, and crime prevention. Especially over the past few decades cities have, however, also established themselves as alternative political scales reflecting a set of preferences diverging from those endorsed at national level. Subnational governments can indeed be seen to be norm-entrepreneurs.[30] This phenomenon can be observed in light of London's pro-EU stance in Brexit Britain or major American cities' opposition to the Trump Administration in the United States.[31] This underlines that cities are not mere accumulations of buildings but socio-political spheres. National minorities can indeed be local majorities, explaining in part stark divergences between local and national politics.[32] The above-mentioned examples underline that subnational and national policies don't necessarily align. Dividing lines on certain policy matters could be pinpointed in manifold domains, suffice it to mention here the urban–rural divide in the 2016 Brexit referendum that some have captured as follows: '[t]he cities chose one future, the rest of England another. And their visions for the nation are diametrically opposed.'[33] It has indeed been argued that the two political earthquakes of 2016, the Brexit vote and the Trump election, can be understood as a backlash against 'urban liberalism'.[34] Other examples include the organization of

[30] For the origin of this terminology, see Cass Sunstein, 'Social Norms and Social Roles' (1996) 96 Columbia Law Review 903.

[31] See Speech of London Mayor Sadiq Khan at the Davos Economic Forum: https://www.london.gov.uk/press-releases/mayoral/sadiq-a-hard-brexit-is-lose-lose (2017); Liz Robbins, '"Sanctuary City" Mayors Vow to Defy Trump's Immigration Order' *New York Times*, 25 January 2017. American cities' influence on immigration policies is in no way unprecedented. See Cristina Rodriguez, 'The Significance of the Local in Immigration Regulation' (2008) 106 Michigan Law Review 567.

[32] Heather Gerken, 'Foreword: Federalism All the Way Down' (2010) 124 Harvard Law Review 4.

[33] Emily Badger, 'The Powerful Thing that Divides Britain also Divides America' *The Washington Post*, 24 June 2016: https://www.washingtonpost.com/news/wonk/wp/2016/06/24/the-powerful-thing-that-divides-britain-also-divides-america/.

[34] Andy Beckett, 'From Trump to Brexit, Power Has Leaked from Cities to the Countryside' *The Guardian*, 12 December 2016: https://www.theguardian.com/commentisfree/2016/dec/12/trump-brexit-cities-countryside-rural-voters.

local social fora in Italian cities that advocate 'globalization from below'.[35] As more citizens reside in urban areas their lives are increasingly shaped by urban norms. For urban residents local transport, housing, public services provision, and tax schemes may have just as much impact on their lives as national laws. In particular large cities are economic powerhouses, the influence of which reaches well beyond national territorial borders. At the forefront of innovation, local governments are often the sites of regulatory experimentation, another variant of subnational government's influence on policy-making beyond their own territory, and other scales frequently adopt norms inspired by such subnational experimentation.[36]

SNAs accordingly exert regulatory influence beyond their own territory and that of their State through their participation in the growing number of cross-border local government networks.[37] Such networks enable SNAs to coordinate regulatory activities, collaborate on issues of common concern, exchange experiences, and engage in a process of mutual learning. Networks moreover empower localities to pressure States and international actors into regulating.[38] Through these different channels, 'localities, from big cities to small towns, are entangled with the emerging global village'.[39] This has been understood to demonstrate that globalization 'is not only imposed on passive localities by their states or by international institutions—it is also advanced from the ground up by localities themselves'.[40] Cities' political influence appears to be continuously expanding. Their influence on national politics is well documented and can for example be seen in Dutch electoral reforms. In 1979 neighborhood councils in Rotterdam decided to allow foreign residents to vote in their elections and Amsterdam followed suit in

[35] Donatella Della Porta, 'Multiple Belongings, Tolerant Identities, and the Construction of "Another Politics": Between the European Social Forum and the Local Social Fora' in Donatella Della Porta and Sidney Tarrow, *Transnational Protest and Global Activism* (Rowman & Littlefield 2005).

[36] In relation to the phenomenon of the 'sharing economy', see Michèle Finck and Sofia Ranchordás, 'Sharing and the City' (2016) 49 Vanderbilt Journal of Transnational Law 1299.

[37] David Smith and Michael Timberlake, 'Hierarchies of Dominance Among World Cities' in Saskia Sassen (ed), *Global Networks, Linked Cities* (Routledge 2002). Helmut Philipp Aust, 'Auf dem Weg zu einem Recht der Globalen Stadt? "C40" und der "Konvent der Bürgermeister" im Globalen Klimaschutzregime' (2013) 73 Zeitschrift für ausländisches öffentliches Recht und Völkerrecht 673.

[38] Harriet Bulkeley and Kristine Kern, 'Local Government and the Governing of Climate Change in Germany and the UK' (2006) 43 Urban Studies 2237; Michele Betsill and Harriet Bulkeley, 'Cities and the Multilevel Governance of Global Climate Change' (2006) 12 Global Governance 141; Richard Stewart, 'States and Cities as Actors in Global Climate Regulation: Unitary vs. Plural Architectures' (2008) 50 Arizona Law Review 681; Harriet Bulkeley and Vanesa Broto, 'Governing by Experiment? Global Cities and the Governing of Climate Change' (2012) 38 Transactions of the Institute of British Geographers 361.

[39] Blank, 'Localism' (n 23) 263.

[40] Ibid, 268.

1981.[41] Legislation extending the right countrywide was adopted in 1985 and took effect in the 1986 local elections, illustrating how these city initiatives created a general shift in non-nationals integration into city governance. Yet today subnational authorities extend their political influence beyond the borders of their own State. The potential for such influence can even be observed with respect to the European Citizens' Initiative (ECI), the first element of direct democracy introduced at supranational level. It enables one million citizens from at least one quarter of the Member States to suggest to the Commission the enactment of new legislation.[42] In light of the nature of this novel instrument of direct democracy the subnational dimension is only apparent at second sight. Yet, there are two avenues for SNAs to rely on this mechanism to defend their own interests at EU level. First, through endorsement. This can be observed in the context of the ECI on the Right to Water which has been explicitly supported by a number of cities, including Paris, Genoa, Sevilla, Amsterdam, Vienna, and Luxembourg-City.[43] Endorsement of existing ECIs by major cities lends additional support to the objectives pursued by the Initiative and moreover allows the city to advocate its own policy preferences at EU level. Second, there is room for associations of subnational governments, or even larger SNAs on their own, to use the ECI in order to directly advocate their objectives at the supranational level. SNAs indeed have no other formal avenues to influence the EU legislative procedure individually or in small groups.[44] One could, however, imagine a scenario whereby an SNA or a group of SNAs encourages their citizens to sign an ECI in support of a subnational policy-preference they'd like to see materialize at EU level.

The above overview has indicated that subnational authorities are norm-entrepreneurs, the regulatory influence of which reaches beyond their own territorial borders, hinting at the porosity of jurisdictional borders in the contemporary European Union. This finding will be further cemented in subsequent chapters.[45] The intertwining of various levels of public authority in the polycentric EU moreover becomes obvious when considering European integration's impact on SNAs.

[41] Leslie Seidle, 'Local Voting Rights for Non-Nationals: Experience in Sweden, the Netherlands and Belgium' (2015) 16 Journal of International Migration & Integration 27, 33.

[42] Article 11(4) TEU and Regulation (EU) No 211/2011 of the European Parliament and of the Council of 16 February 2011 on the citizens' initiative (Consolidated version 01/07/2014).

[43] http://www.right2water.eu/news/luxembourg-joins-list-european-cities-support-european-citizens%E2%80%99-initiative-%E2%80%9Cwater-human-right%E2%80%9D.

[44] The Committee of the Regions, examined later in this chapter, only allows them to act collectively.

[45] See, in particular, Chapter 4.

## C. Subnational Authorities and European Integration

European integration is most commonly thought of as limiting local and regional authorities' capacity to regulate given that subnational competences have in a number of instances been transferred by the Member State to the EU.[46] In a scenario where an SNA previously had autonomous competences in a policy domain that now falls within the Union's exclusive or shared competences under Articles 3 and 4 TFEU, they may henceforth no longer regulate independently.[47] Such competence transfers can result in an 'indirect skewing of the structure of intra-state authority in favour of the central State'.[48] States are indeed formally compensated for their transfer of competences through their seat in the Council, whereas SNAs benefit of no similar compensation. In a speech at Humboldt University in 2001, the then Minister-President of North Rhine Westphalia exposed how German regions had to ring-fence their competences against EU action.[49] Many subnational competences are nowadays indeed 'shared, mixed or confused with the powers of the EU institutions'[50] and as a result subnational authorities cannot go unaffected by European integration.

The transfer of competence from the subnational to the supranational assumes numerous different shapes. Dawson documented one such facet in relation to the Open Method of Co-Ordination (OMC). While the OMC is often framed as an instrument of multi-level governance, Dawson has shown that strategic decision-making and reporting thereunder is an exclusive prerogative of the Member States.[51] This exclusivity enables Member States to reassert themselves vis-à-vis SNAs that have no active role in the OMC.[52] As a consequence of supranational integration, local and regional authorities

[46] Charlie Jeffery, 'Conclusions: Sub-National Authorities and European Domestic Policy' (1996) 6 Regional & Federal Studies 204, 316.

[47] Andrea Ross and Mayte Crespo, 'The Effect of Devolution on Implementation of EC law in Spain and the UK' (2003) 28 European Law Review 210; Jan Kottman, 'Europe and the Regions: Sub-national Entity Representation at Community Level' (2001) 26 European Law Review 161.

[48] Ibid.

[49] Wolfgang Clement, *Europa gestalten, nicht verwalten. Die Kompetenzordnung der Europäischen Union nach Nizza* (2001), cited in Charlie Jeffery, 'Regions and the European Union: Letting them In, and Leaving them Alone' in Stephen Weatherill and Ulf Bernitz (eds), *The Role of Regions and Sub-National Actors in Europe* (Hart Publishing 2005) 38 (hereafter Jeffery, 'Regions and the European Union').

[50] Bengoetxea, 'Autonomous Constitutional Regions in Europe' (n 2) 230.

[51] Mark Dawson, *New Governance and the Transformation of European Law* (Cambridge University Press 2011) 200.

[52] Ibid, 199–203.

have, furthermore, become subjected to a wide variety of obligations. They are bound to respect the supremacy and direct effect of EU law and are oftentimes in charge of the transposition and implementation of EU secondary legislation.[53] Some have also pinpointed that European integration has weakened local and regional authorities, for it empowers national executives.[54] The EU has institutionalized 'an arena within which national political elites, most prominently within the Council, have an opportunity to advance policies that might have been unfeasible had they been pursued solely within a domestic context'.[55] SNAs, it has been said, have sometimes 'been marginalised by an integration process founded on the interplay of Member States and European institutions'.[56] National parliaments have certainly lost autonomous regulatory competence as a result of the empowerment of the executive by European integration. The Barroso Initiative and the Early Warning System have, however, been designed as a mechanism to counter that trend. Subnational authorities as well as regional parliaments do not enjoy similar mechanisms.[57] This has led Weatherill to conclude that SNAs are left 'to seek protection from damage done by competence within the domestic system'.[58] It is certainly true that many Member States have created domestic procedures targeted at creating avenues for SNAs to participate in the State's EU policies but no similar procedures have been put in place for Member States. The combination of the factors introduced above has led some to argue that SNAs are in a 'plight'[59] vis-à-vis the EU as it has proven cumbersome for regional authorities to protect their own interests in the absence of support on behalf of their Member State.[60]

The relation between the EU and SNAs should not, however, be mistaken as a unidimensional phenomenon. Subnational authorities have adapted to European integration and established positive avenues of interaction with the

[53] The consequences of SNAs' failure to comply with these obligations are subject to examination in Chapter 3.

[54] Andrew Moravcsik, *Why the European Union Strengthens the State: Domestic Politics and International Cooperation*, (1994) Harvard University Center for European Studies Working Paper Series 52: https://www.princeton.edu/~amoravcs/library/strengthen.pdf, 1.

[55] Stephen Weatherill, 'Finding a Role for the Regions in Checking the EU's Competence' in Stephen Weatherill and Ulf Bernitz (eds), *The Role of Regions and Sub-National Actors in Europe* (Hart Publishing 2005) 131 (hereafter Weatherill, 'Finding a Role for the Regions in Checking the EU's Competence').

[56] Jeffery, 'Regions and the European Union' (n 49) 34.

[57] Article 6 of Protocol (No 2) on the Application of the Principles of Subsidiarity and Proportionality.

[58] Weatherill, 'Finding a Role for the Regions in Checking the EU's Competence' (n 55) 148.

[59] See Jill Wakefield, 'The Plight of Regions in a Multi-Layered Europe' (2005) 30 European Law Review 406.

[60] Ibid, 406.

EU so that the above statement at present merely illustrates one of the multiple manners in which SNAs and the EU interact. The responsibility of many infra-State bodies to implement EU law, Jeffery has claimed, has been accompanied 'by repeated attempts by some regional governments' and in particular those with legislative competences 'to engage in constitutive politics at the European level'.[61] Contemporary interactions between the subnational and the supranational can best be qualified as plurifaceted in character. A number of Member States have, for example, developed mechanisms to enable subnational participation in European matters, for instance, in obliging the national level to inform SNAs of EU matters affecting them.[62] Such obligations exist in Germany,[63] Belgium,[64] Austria,[65] Italy,[66] Spain,[67] the UK,[68] and France.[69] According to Italian law, regions and localities must for example be informed of EU draft legislation of relevance to them so that they can issue comments.[70] These initiatives seek to create an outlet for subnational concerns in respect of EU integration. In a number of Member States SNAs can also participate in EU policy-making through their upper chambers, or inter-regional or national-regional bodies.[71]

In addition to these national initiatives subnational authorities have forged mechanisms that allow them to directly relate to the European Union.

[61] Jeffery, 'Regions and the European Union' (n 49) 33.

[62] Michael Tatham, 'Devolution and EU Policy-Shaping: Bridging the Gap Between Multi-Level Governance and Liberal Intergovernmentalism' (2011) 3 European Political Science Review 53, 58.

[63] Article 23(2) of the German Basic Law.

[64] Article 168 of the Belgian Constitution.

[65] The Austrian government must inform local and regional governments both directly and indirectly through the Bundesrat in accordance with Articles 23(d)1, 23(e)1, and 23(g)1 of the Austrian Constitution.

[66] Legge 24 dicembre 2012, n. 234, Norme generali sulla partecipazione dell'Italia alla formazione e all'attuazione della normativa e delle politiche dell'Unione europea. (13G00003) (GU n.3 del 4-1-2013) (hereafter 'Law N° 234 of 24 December 2012'). For a comment see Antonio Esposito, 'La legge 24 dicembre 2012, n. 234, sulla partecipazione dell'Italia alla formazione e all'attuazione della normative e delle politiche dell'UE. Parte 1, Prime reiflessioni sul ruolo dello Camere' (2013) 9 Federalismi.it: revista di diritto pubblico italiano, comunitario e comparator 41 (available online at: http://www.federalismi.it).

[67] Article 6 of Law 24/2009 of 22 December 2009 establishes a duty for the national Parliament to transmit any EU draft legislative acts to regional parliaments.

[68] Memorandum of Understanding and Supplementary Agreements Between the United Kingdom Government, the Scottish Ministers, the Welsh Ministers, and the Northern Ireland Executive Committee (2013): http://www.gov.scot/About/Government/Inter-Governmental/Memo-of-Understanding, 9.

[69] Article 88(4) of the French Constitution.

[70] Law N° 234 of 24 December 2012 (n 66).

[71] Nikos Skoutaris, 'The Role of Sub-State Entities in the EU Decision-Making Process' in Elke Cloots Geert de Baere and Stefan Sottiaux (eds), *Federalism in the European Union* (Hart Publishing 2012) 214 (hereafter Skoutaris, 'The Role of Sub-State Entities in the EU Decision-Making Process').

SNAs have for instance eagerly established representative offices in Brussels[72] to promote the respective infra-State concerns with EU institutions.[73] The Commission is keen to communicate with subnational representatives to achieve a 'better application of its policies, to gain first-hand information and to spread its ideas'.[74] The 2016 Pact of Amsterdam proclaims that the EU henceforth 'strives to involve Urban Authorities in the design of policies, to mobilise Urban Authorities for the implementation of EU policies, and to strengthen the urban dimension in these policies'.[75] SNAs, Member States, and the Union hence relate to each other in multifaceted manners leading to the emergence of a network with multiple nodes of public authority rather than a clear hierarchical pyramid. Whereas this section has provided a brief insight into the multifaceted relations between the EU and SNAs, the most significant institutional expression thereof, the Committee of the Regions, has not yet been covered. It is the aim of the subsequent section to do so.

## D. The Committee of the Regions

The Committee of the Regions (CoR) is an EU advisory body, created by the Maastricht Treaty.[76] It advises the Commission, the Council, and the European Parliament either where the Treaty expressly provides so or where this is considered appropriate.[77] Primary law foresees that the CoR is to be consulted, inter alia, in the areas of transport,[78] education and youth,[79] economic and social cohesion,[80] the environment,[81] and infrastructure networks.[82] One of its main purposes is to ensure that SNAs 'have a political voice of their own at EU level'.[83] According to Article 300(3) TFEU, the members of the CoR

[72] Martin Nagelschmidt, 'Les relations internationales des Länder allemands et l'évolution du système fédéral dans l'Union Européenne: le cas du Bade-Wurtemberg' (1999) 30 Etudes Internationales 679, 688; Joakim Nergelius, 'The Committee of the Regions Today and in the Future—A Critical Overview' in Stephen Weatherill and Ulf Bernitz (eds), *The Role of Regions and Sub-National Actors in Europe* (Hart 2005) 124 (hereafter Nergelius, 'The Committee of the Regions').

[73] Nergelius, 'The Committee of the Regions' (n 72) 124. See also Carlo Panara, *The Sub-National Dimension of the EU* (Springer 2015).

[74] Thomas Christiansen and Pamela Lintner, 'The Committee of the Regions after 10 Years: Lessons from the Past and Challenges for the Future' (2005) EIPASCOPE 2005/1, 2 (hereafter Christiansen and Lintner, 'The Committee of the Regions after 10 Years').

[75] Urban Agenda for the EU (n 28) 5.

[76] Thomas Christiansen, 'Second Thoughts on Europe's 'Third Level': The European Union's Committee of the Regions' (1996) 26 Publius: The Journal of Federalism 93 (hereafter Christiansen, 'Europe's Third Level').

[77] Article 307(1) TFEU. [78] Articles 90–100 TFEU. [79] Article 165 TFEU.

[80] Articles 174–8 TFEU. [81] Articles 191–3 TFEU. [82] Articles 170–2 TFEU.

[83] Nergelius, 'The Committee of the Regions' (n 72) 123.

should be representatives of regional and local bodies that either hold an electoral mandate or are politically accountable to an elected assembly.[84] The name of the organ may thus lead to confusion, as it in fact not only includes representatives of regional but also of local governments. Different Member States depute rather different representatives to the Committee. While delegations from federal or regionalized States tend predominantly to represent regions, those of largely unitary States such as Denmark, Luxembourg, and Ireland are made up exclusively of representatives of local authorities.[85] The number of representatives per SNA has been subject to controversy as the representatives of 'big *Länder* in Germany, like Nordrhein-Westfalen with some 18 million inhabitants, . . . has fewer members within the committee than Luxembourg, a country which is hardly characterised by regional diversity or internal disorder'.[86]

Some have praised the CoR's strengthening of the connection between the European Commission and SNAs.[87] It has also been asserted that for local governments in particular the CoR 'provides a level of access to EU decision-making not available in the Member States'.[88] Others stressed the CoR's capacity to unite subnational voices, bringing together 'a multitude of different actors from regional, local and intermediate levels of government'.[89] This has been said to have the merit of showing that SNAs are not a homogenous category.[90] Yet overall the Committee has been subject to noticeably more criticism than praise. The Committee's opinions on draft legislation 'are somehow supposed to represent the views of the different regions throughout Europe' which is difficult given that SNAs can in no way be qualified as a homogenous unit.[91] The CoR's prerogatives are moreover to be exercised 'in the Union's general interest' rather than in that of SNAs.[92] The organ's impact on the supranational decision-making process is also considered to be 'severely limited' in light of its purely advisory voice in the legislative

[84] No additional condition is imposed regarding membership, except that the Committee of the Regions may have no more than 350 members in accordance with Article 305 TFEU.

[85] Antonio D'Atena, 'Participation of Regional and Local Authorities in the Preparatory Phase of European Policy Making—European Side' in Instituto di Studi sui Sistemi Regionali Federali e sulle Autonomie (ed), *Procedures for Local and Regional Authority Participation in European Policy Making in the Member States* (Committee of the Regions 2005) 20–1.

[86] Nergelius, 'The Committee of the Regions' (n 72) 124.

[87] Christiansen and Lintner, 'The Committee of the Regions after 10 Years' (n 74) 2.

[88] Jeffery, 'Regions and the European Union' (n 49) 39.

[89] Christiansen and Lintner, 'The Committee of the Regions after 10 Years' (n 74) 1.

[90] Peter-Christian Müller-Graff, in Stephen Weatherill and Ulf Bernitz, *The Role of Regions and Sub-National Actors in Europe* (Hart Publishing 2005) 110. See also Peter-Christian Müller-Graff, 'Die europäischen Regionen in der Verfassung der EG' (1997) Integration 147.

[91] Nergelius, 'The Committee of the Regions' (n 72) 124.

[92] Article 300 (4) TFEU.

procedure.[93] Whereas its creation 'contained the promise that lower levels would be more directly involved in decision-making processes that concerned them but from which they had been excluded'[94] it is questionable whether this goal has been achieved, as some have deplored that it 'has not established itself as an authoritative voice'.[95] What is more, the Committee is of no assistance to an SNA that wants to further its own interests vis-à-vis the EU as the Committee is a collective organ. It does thus fall short of enabling individual or even minority groups of SNAs to advocate their interests at Union level.

The most economically and politically significant regions consider the CoR a disappointment, as their economic and political weight gets lost in wider subnational concerns. In Member States such as Belgium, Austria, and Germany, the central and regional governments share the right to define the Member State's EU policy and as a consequence 'regions can get more of what they want done through Member State channels than through the CoR'.[96] Yet there seem to be no plans to change the Committee's composition and functioning. As a consequence, the larger regions particularly have sought alternative channels to cooperate with other SNAs and also the EU, notably (but not exclusively) in order to influence EU decision-making, namely through associations of local and regional authorities.

## E. Associations of Regions and Localities

The past decades have witnessed the proliferation of associations of subnational authorities. While many of these networks are of an international nature this section elaborates on those with a specific EU focus. The creation of subnational associations, which are not formally recognized under EU law, is perhaps more significant than the CoR.[97] The present section briefly introduces some of them. The Conference of European Regions with Legislative Powers (REGLEG) was created in 2001. It is the political network of EU regions with legislative power.[98] REGLEG counts seventy-three member regions from eight Member States, the population of which encompasses almost half of the

[93] Nergelius, 'The Committee of the Regions' (n 72) 125.

[94] Christiansen, 'Europe's Third Level' (n 76) 95.

[95] Jeffery, 'Regions and the European Union' (n 49) 36. [96] Ibid, 37.

[97] Stephen Weatherill, 'The Challenge of the Regional Dimension in the European Union' in Stephen Weatherill and Ulf Bernitz (eds), *The Role of Regions and Sub-National Actors in Europe* (Hart Publishing 2005) 2.

[98] The network's website is at: http://www.regleg.eu.

Union's total population.[99] The Assembly of European Regions (AER) had already emerged in 1985. Contrary to REGLEG, which accommodates only the most powerful regions, AER is open to any European SNA, irrespective of whether it has legislative competence, and even counts as members SNAs that do not form part of an EU Member State.[100] The AER actively seeks to promote inter-regional and local communication, having established an online 'Knowledge Center' that disseminates information on thematic issues.[101] One of the many topics covered is 'Smart Specialisation' a concept I will return to in Chapter 4.[102] In 2013 the association hosted a forum for cities and regions, intended to involve European and non-European stakeholders with smart specialization strategies.[103] These networks accordingly facilitate interaction and communication between subnational authorities in different Member States.[104] Such networks enable SNAs to share and compare their respective regulatory strategies on a given matter, enabling norms to travel from one scale to another notwithstanding of territorial borders. Cities networks can also form 'around global norms in order to give them local effect'.[105] An example is the Child Friendly Cities Initiative established to implement the UN Convention of the Rights of the Child.[106]

Some networks are made up exclusively of city representatives. EUROCITIES was founded in 1986 by Barcelona, Birmingham, Frankfurt am Main, Lyon, Milan, and Rotterdam and now unites over 130 cities in addition to forty partner cities in thirty-five countries, both EU and non-EU.[107] The network encourages the sharing of knowledge and exchange of ideas but also engages in lobbying work, attempting to 'ultimately shift the focus of EU legislation in a way which allows city governments to tackle strategic challenges at local level'.[108] The Council of European Municipal and Regional

[99] http://www.regleg.eu/index.php?option=com_content&view=section&layout=blog&id=2&Itemid=2.

[100] The website of the AER is at: http://www.aer.eu/en/home.html.

[101] The website of the Knowledge Centre is at: http://www.aer.eu/en/knowledge-centre/thematic-expertise-thematic-issues/economy-research-innovation.html.

[102] Ibid. [103] Ibid.

[104] See Joxerramon Bengoetxea, 'The Participation of Infra-State Entities in European Union Affairs in Spain: the Basque Case' in Stephen Weatherill and Ulf Bernitz (eds), *The Role of Regions and Sub-National Actors in Europe* (Hart Publishing 2005); Caitriona Carter and Aileen McLeod, 'The Scottish Parliament and the European Union: Analysing Regional Parliamentary Engagement' in Stephen Weatherill and Ulf Bernitz (eds), *The Role of Regions and Sub-National Actors in Europe* (Hart Publishing 2005).

[105] Nijman, 'The Future of the City' (n 26) 221.

[106] The initiative's website is at: http://childfriendlycities.org/.

[107] A current list of member cities is available at: http://www.eurocities.eu/eurocities/members.

[108] The website of EUROCITIES is online at: http://www.eurocities.eu/eurocities/about_us. See also Renaud Payre, 'The Importance of Being Connected. City Networks and Urban

Authorities (CEMR), representing local and regional authorities in forty-one countries within and outside the EU promotes exchanges between elected representatives and equally seeks to influence European policy and legislation.[109]

Specific thematic collaborations between SNAs have also emerged, for instance, with regard to climate change policy. The C40 brings together sixty-nine large cities from around the world.[110] The European Climate Alliance brings together 1,700 local and regional governments dedicated to climate action.[111] The Covenant of Mayors is a further example that is examined in additional detail in Chapter 4. Other networks group SNAs that are situated in close proximity albeit within different States. The Öresund Committee, established in 1993 between Denmark and Sweden, is composed of Swedish and Danish political office-holders at regional and local level and constitutes a loose form of cooperation within a transnational region that encompasses the cities of Copenhagen, Malmö, and Helsingborg. With the support of civil servants of the two countries, the Öresund Committee establishes policies to further economic growth and integration for the entire region.[112] The Committee's first, rather impressive, project was the construction of a bridge connecting Denmark and Sweden, which opened in 1999 to integrate and further stimulate the respective subnational economies.[113]

The Saar-Lor-Lux collaboration is another example. It groups the German Land Saarland, the French region Lorraine, and Luxembourg, and seeks to stimulate economic integration and development but also furthers other projects such as those of a cultural nature.[114] The Saar-Lor-Lux project was financed by the INTERREG III A, showing that the EU actively encourages such cooperation.[115] The Union has indeed a number of different policies

Government: Lyon and Eurocities (1990–2005)' (2010) 34 International Journal of Urban and Regional Research 260.

[109] The website of the Council of European Municipal and Regional Authorities is at: http://www.ccre.org/en/activites/index.

[110] Their website is at: http://www.c40.org/cities.

[111] http://www.climatealliance.org/home.html.

[112] More information can be found at: http://www.scandria-corridor.eu/index.php/en/alliance/politics/oeresund-committee.

[113] Linze Schaap, Casper Geurtz, Laurens de Graaf, and Niels Karsten, 'Innovations in Sub-National Government in Europe. A quick Scan' (2009) Tilburg School of Politics and Public Administration Working Paper: http://www.rob-rfv.nl/documenten/migratie/innovations_in_subnational_government_in_europe.pdf, 16 (hereafter Schaap et al, 'Innovations in Sub-National Government in Europe').

[114] See, for example, the cooperation between the German Land Saarland, the French *région* Lorraine, and Luxembourg under the Saar-Lor-Lux cooperation, the website of which is under: http://www.saarlorlux.biz/cgi-bin/cms.

[115] INTERREG III A (2000–2006) sought to foster cross-border, transnational, and interregional cooperation. Communication of 28 April 2000 from the Commission to the Member

in place that encourage transnational cooperation. Regulation 1082/2006 has, for instance, given rise to European Groupings of Territorial Cooperation (EGTC) that allows SNAs to establish an EGTC, which enjoys legal personality under EU law. The EGTC is able to act either 'for the purpose of implementing territorial cooperation or projects co-financed' by the Union, notably under the Structural Funds or 'for the purposes of carrying out actions of territorial cooperation which are at the sole initiative' of Member States or SNAs.[116] Other examples of EGTC include NOVUM, a Polish–Czech cooperation to strengthen economic and social cohesion,[117] or the SolidarCity Network between Bulgaria, Cyprus, and Greece that addresses sustainable development with a special focus on enhanced waste management.[118] These interregional and intercity networks further cooperation between different scales, allowing actors to communicate and influence beyond their own national borders. The same dynamic can be readily observed in the development of subnational international relations.

## F. SNAs and International Relations

The ability to engage in international relations is often thought of as a quintessential prerogative of the sovereign that has traditionally been 'located among the executive prerogatives of the central national State'.[119] A close look, however, reveals that the days of State-centric international relations are gone. Instead a polycentric diplomacy network has emerged in which SNAs relate to transnational, supranational, and international bodies, and sometimes also other States. Evans for instance documented 'an increasing tendency

States laying down guidelines for a Community Initiative concerning trans-European cooperation intended to encourage harmonious and balanced development of the European territory (Interreg III) [2000] OJ C 143.

116 Committee of the Regions, *The European Grouping of Territorial Cooperation* (2007) CdR 117/2007, http://cor.europa.eu/en/documentation/studies/Documents/The%20European%20Grouping%20of%20Territorial%20Cooperation%20-%20EGTC/The%20European%20Grouping%20of%20Territorial%20Cooperation%20-%20EGTC%20-%20EN.pdf; see also Davide Strazzani, 'Harmonising Trends vs Domestic Regulatory Frameworks: Looking for the European Law on Cross-Border Cooperation' (2011) 4 European Journal of Legal Studies 151.

117 The Project's website is at: https://portal.cor.europa.eu/egtc/CoRActivities/Pages/NOVUM.aspx.

118 The Project's website is at: https://portal.cor.europa.eu/egtc/CoRActivities/Pages/Efxini-Poli--SolidarCity-Network.aspx.

119 Jan Kottmann, 'Europe and the Regions: Subnational Entity Representation at Community Level' (2001) 26 European Law Review 161.

for regions to identify and pursue interests divergent from those expressed in international and European organizations by the central institutions of their States'.[120] Over the past decades, local and regional authorities have keenly diversified and multiplied the relations they entertain beyond their own national borders.[121] These developments have led Skoutaris to detect a 'European paradiplomacy' which has developed a sort of 'sub-national constitutional space' that allows local and regional authorities to participate in the international arena.[122]

SNAs' capacity to conduct their own international relations varies from one State to another. In some contexts the *in foro interno in foro externo* doctrine applies, by virtue of which an SNA can engage in international relations in its field of competence. In other contexts ad hoc formulae have been crafted. Belgian SNAs have the most expansive international relations prerogatives, as its regions and communities enjoy 'strongly developed constitutional rights to maintain autonomous foreign relations worldwide' under Article 167 of the Belgian Constitution.[123] Since the 1993 reform that transformed Belgium into a federal State, SNAs are not just entitled but even compelled to conduct their own external relations.[124] The *in foro interno in foro externo* doctrine finds application and there is an absence of hierarchy between the federal and subnational in foreign affairs.[125] The Belgian communities and regions have eagerly exercised their competences and developed 'a wide range of instruments, networks and activities via which they interact upon the international scene'.[126] By 2010 Flanders had concluded thirty-three international treaties, the Walloon Region sixty-seven, and the French-speaking community fifty-one.[127] It is noteworthy that Wallonia and Flanders have chosen different formal and informal instruments to advance their interests abroad.[128] Of particular importance for Wallonia is for instance the 'Grande Région',

[120] Andrew Evans, 'Regional Dimensions to European Governance' (2003) 52 International and Comparative Quarterly 21, 21.

[121] Bernd Gros and Peter Schmitt-Egner, *Europas Kooperierende Regionen: Rahmenbedingungen und Praxis Transnationaler Zusammenarbeit Deutscher Grenzregionen in Europa* (Nomos 1994); Silvia Raich, *Grenzüberschreitende und Interregionale Zusammenarbeit in einem 'Europe der Regionen'* (Nomos 1995).

[122] Skoutaris, 'The Role of Sub-State Entities in the EU Decision-Making Process' (n 71) 240.

[123] Ibid, 244; Stéphane Paquin, 'Paradiplomatie identitaire et diplomatie en Belgique fédérale: le cas de la Flandre' (2003) 36 Canadian Journal of Political Science/Revue canadienne de science politique 621, 627.

[124] David Criekemans, 'Foreign Policy and Diplomacy of the Belgian Regions; Flanders and Wallonia' (2010) Netherlands Institute of International Relations 'Clingendael': http://www.clingendael.nl/sites/default/files/20100300_cdsp_discussion_paper_in_diplomacy_criekemans.pdf, 2 (hereafter Criekemans, 'Foreign Policy and Diplomacy of the Belgian Regions').

[125] Ibid, 2. [126] Ibid, 3. [127] Ibid, 20. [128] Ibid, 4.

the collaboration it entertains with Luxembourg, the German Länder Saarland and Rheinland-Pfalz, and the Belgian French-speaking community and the Belgian German-speaking community.[129] In addition to conducting their own international relations the Belgian regions also determine the composition of the Belgian multilateral negotiation delegations[130] and appoint 'diplomatic representatives' placed on the diplomatic lists of the Belgian embassies.[131] In light of these vast subnational competences Criekemans concluded that the Belgian central government 'has successfully transformed itself into a coordination centre which guides all external contacts under an atmosphere of federal loyalty'.[132]

The Belgian example is certainly an extreme case. Nonetheless SNAs elsewhere also engage in their own international relations. Article 32(3) of the German Basic Law enables the Länder to conclude Treaties with other States, subject to the approval of the federal level, in domains that fall within their competences.[133] Bavaria has for example developed a number of formal relations with infra-State bodies across the EU and the wider world.[134] Not all devolved States offer similar prerogatives to their SNAs. In the UK Westminster enjoys exclusive competence over international relations.[135] The devolved territories may nonetheless conclude cooperation agreements with SNAs elsewhere, Scotland having for instance signed a treaty with the Chinese province of Shandong.[136] The meetings between Scottish Prime Minister Sturgeon and Commission President Juncker as well as the European Parliament's former President Schulz and Brexit negotiator Verhofstadt that took place just days after the June 2016 Brexit referendum are a more recent example of the region's desire to conduct independent foreign affairs in light of its disagreement with the capital.[137] Similarly, five days after his election

[129] Ibid, 27.

[130] Ibid, 7. See also David Criekemans and Timon Salomonson, 'La Belgique, la Flandre et les forums multilatéraux' (2001) 10 Bulletin d'histoire politique 125.

[131] Skoutaris, 'The Role of Sub-State Entities in the EU Decision-Making Process' (n 71) 256.

[132] Criekemans, 'Foreign Policy and Diplomacy of the Belgian Regions' (n 124) 29.

[133] See further Rudolf Hrbek, 'The Federal Republic of Germany' in Hans Michelmann (ed), *Foreign Relations in Federal Countries* (McGill-Queen's University Press 2009) 147.

[134] Skoutaris, 'The Role of Sub-State Entities in the EU Decision-Making Process' (n 71) 244.

[135] Section 3 of Schedule 2 of the Northern Ireland Act 1998.

[136] Charlie Jeffery, 'Scotland's European and International Policy' in Requejo Ferran (ed), *Foreign Policy of Constituent Units at the Beginning of the 21st Century* (Collecció Institut d'Estudis Autonòmics 2010) 116.

[137] SNP, 'Nicola Sturgeon is in Brussels Today' 29 June 2016: http://www.snp.org/nicola_sturgeon_is_in_brussels_today_get_the_facts_here.

as London mayor Khan met Paris mayor Hidalgo to discuss their cities' futures.[138]

Beyond their own international relations many SNAs have the potential to influence those of their State. Article 10(3) of the Austrian Constitution for example provides that the federal government shall consult the Länder before the conclusion of Treaties affecting their competences. The Bundesrat must moreover inform both local and regional authorities on European affairs affecting their competences.[139] The case of the Finnish Åland islands provides a possibly more unexpected example.[140] Åland has competence to determine whether an EU treaty is applicable to its territory. As a condition of its agreement to the Lisbon Treaty, it put forward four requests to the Finnish government, three of which were successful, namely, a right for the SNA to appear before the CJEU, to participate in the Early Warning System, and to participate in the meetings of the Council.[141] Its request for a seat in the European Parliament failed.[142] Åland's right to participate in the preparation and negotiation of EU Treaties is from the EU point of view an 'example of national mercy, not of European right'.[143] It is indeed imperative to note that EU law will only formally consider Finland to be a relevant actor in this scenario, not Åland. The same conclusion applies to other Member States, such as Belgium, where SNAs are also involved in the ratification of European Treaties.[144] While the relations between subnational authorities and other levels of public authority are constantly shifting, the nature and competences of SNAs is subject to fluctuation too.

## G. The Constant Evolution of Subnational Autonomies

In an 'increasing number of Member States', Lenaerts and Cambien have written, 'important competences are allocated to subnational entities. This is

[138] Ben Quinn, 'Sadiq Khan and Anne Hidalgo Rebuke Donald Trump over Muslim Ban' *The Guardian*, 10 May 2016: https://www.theguardian.com/politics/2016/may/10/sadiq-khan-anne-hidalgo-donald-trump-muslim-ban.

[139] Article 23(d)(1) of the Austrian Constitution. Municipalities are to be informed where their competences or interests are affected.

[140] On the particular constitutional status of the Åland islands, see Husa, *The Constitution of Flinland* (n 6) 121–9.

[141] Pia Alilonttinen and Savino Ruà, 'Lisbon Treaty Ratification: Will the Aland Islands Become Finland's Greenland?' (2008) The Centre for European Policy Studies 1/2008.

[142] Ibid.

[143] Niilo Jääskinen, 'The Case of the Aland Islands—Regional Autonomy versus the European Union of States' in Stephen Weatherill and Ulf Bernitz (eds), *The Role of Regions and Sub-National Actors in Europe* (Hart 2005) 98.

[144] Piet van Nuffel, 'What's in a Member State? Central and Decentralized Authorities before the Community Courts' (2001) 38 Common Market Law Review 871, 882.

true, first of all, in those Member States which are federal in structure, but the same happens to a lesser extent in those Member States with a strong unitary tradition.'[145] Others have observed that 'federalisation is increasingly common in Europe'.[146] It is true that many Member States, such as Belgium,[147] Italy,[148] Spain,[149] and the UK[150] have over recent decades decentralized competences to SNAs.[151] The current state of affairs provides a contrast to the early days of European integration when the founding States were generally more centralized and unitary, Germany being the sole Member State with a truly decentralized structure (which is the result of centralization, the Länder having founded the Federal Republic).[152]

In addition to the decentralization of competences to regions, a parallel trend has occurred according to which the local becomes a growingly important scale of regulation. The 2016 Pact of Amsterdam formalizes this in recognizing the increased importance of the urban scale and the fact that the supranational legislator needs to adapt to that evolution.[153] The localization of regulatory processes should not be underestimated. Nijman observed that '*how* the city deals with the challenges of globalisation and urbanisation is crucial for the future of our planet, and marks the law of the future'.[154] In light of the fact that the human species becomes increasingly urban in addition to economic and socio-cultural processes; 'the future of a state will be determined increasingly by the future of its cities'.[155] The Council of Europe's European Charter of Local Self-Government, ratified by forty-seven countries, catches up with that evolution and seeks to strengthen local governments. It commits the Parties:

> to applying basic rules guaranteeing the political, administrative and financial independence of local authorities. It provides that the principle of local self-government

145 Lenaerts and Cambien, 'Regions and the European Courts' (n 24) 609.

146 Schaap et al, 'Innovations in Sub-National Government in Europe' (n 113) 14.

147 See Articles 1 and 2 of the Belgian Constitution as well as the Second Gilson Act 1963.

148 Articles 116, 117, and 123 of the Italian Constitution.

149 Article 2 of the Spanish Constitution.

150 For Scotland, see Scotland Act 1998, Constitutional Reform Act 2005, and Scotland Act 2012. For Wales, see the Government of Wales Act 1998 and the Government of Wales Act 2006. For Northern Ireland, see the 1998 Belfast Agreement as well as the 2006 St Andrews Agreement.

151 Charlie Jeffery, 'Sub-national Mobilization and European Integration: Does it Make Any Difference?' (2000) 38 Journal of Common Market Studies 1; Michael Keating, 'The Regional Change in Central and Eastern Europe,' in Michael Keating and James Hughes (eds), *The Regional Challenge in Central and Eastern Europe* (Presses Universitaires Européennes 2003) 56.

152 Theodor Maunz, *Deutsches Staatsrecht* (Beck 1964) 1, 6, 9.

153 Urban Agenda for the EU (n 28).

154 Nijman, 'The Future of the City' (n 26) 216 (emphasis in original).

155 Ibid, 218.

shall be recognised in domestic legislation and, where practicable, in the constitution. Local authorities are to be elected in universal suffrage.[156]

The European Union is however formally a union of States. A dominant strand of opinion in federalism studies considers it to be common 'for systems of multi-level governance to drift power towards the centre'.[157] Bogdanor equally predicted that the State-centric nature of EU law could lead to a 'centralising effect in relations between central, regional and local government'.[158] This has not however happened—it rather seems that European integration has led to an overall fragmentation of State authority as traditional State competences are delegated to both the supranational and the subnational scale. The notion of polycentricity gives expression to that state of affairs. Keating framed this in arguing that '[a]s Europe is increasingly regionalized, regions are europeanized and the State is both regionalized and europeanized'.[159]

It is worthy of special emphasis that the dynamics documented here as well as at later stages in this book do not allude to a simple shift of increased competence to either the supranational or the national. Rather, what we are observing is an intensification of the relations between them, allowing them to exert influence on one another. This book presents various instances that can be understood as supranationalism empowering subnationalism[160] and areas where the EU actively encourages subnational regulatory experimentation.[161] At the same time, however, the supranational will not always act to increase subnational power. Kottmann understands European integration as leading to a 'loss of sub-national authorities' competence through European

[156] Council of Europe, 'European Charter of Local Self-Government' *Council of Europe Treaty Series 122* 1985.

[157] Weatherill, 'Finding a Role for the Regions in Checking the EU's Competence' (n 55) 133. See also Stephen Breyer, 'Does Federalism Make a Difference?' [1999] Public Law 651; Sandra Day O'Connor, 'Altered States: Federalism and Devolution at the Real Turn of the Millenium' (2001) 60 Cambridge Law Journal 493; George Bermann, 'Proportionality and Subsidiarity' in Catherine Barnard and Joanne Scott (eds), *The Law of the Single European Market: Unpacking the Premises* (Hart Publishing 2002).

[158] Bogdanor, *Devolution in the United Kingdom* (n 7) 279.

[159] Michael Keating, *The New Regionalism in Western Europe—Territorial Restructuring and Political Change* (Edward Elgar 1998) 183.

[160] See also Guiseppe Martinico, 'The Impact of "Regional Blindness" on the Italian Regional State' in Elke Cloots, Geert de Baere, and Stefan Sottiaux (eds), *Federalism in the European Union* (Hart Publishing 2012).

[161] Such as through the Joint Programming Initiative that encourages research coordination to transform cities into 'centres of innovation and technology.' Its website is at: http://jpi-urbaneurope.eu/.

integration'.[162] Martinico and Pierdominici have in addition illustrated that the current financial and economic crisis has led to 'centralization and compression of subnational spaces of autonomy' under the EU's impetus.[163] They note that the ECB emphasized Italy's need to showcase a 'strong commitment to abolish or merge some intermediate levels of administration (such as the provinces)'.[164] This subsequently led to domestic reform transforming the nature of the provinces,[165] establishing 'città metropolitaine' and new unions of municipalities ('unioni di communi') the competences of which overlap with those of the provinces.[166] In the austerity context supranational institutions have forced a transformation of domestic institutional arrangements despite this formally ranging far outside of the Union's conferred competences.

Intertwining exists between SNAs and other levels of public authority generally, not just the EU. In relation to public international law SNAs are equally 'transforming into objects for international regulation and are increasingly used as a means for disseminating and implementing global political programs, financial schemes, and governance strategies.'[167] These trends highlight that SNAs are no longer merely agents of their State but also of the international or transnational regulatory systems. At the same time, the subnational levels also drive globalization as new forms of 'global connectivity—along with new patterns of disconnection, peripheralization, exclusion and vulnerability' emerge.[168] Localities have indeed been described as 'prime vehicles for the dissemination of global capital, goods, work force, and images'[169] and their role as importers of international norms has been stressed.[170] Globalization should indeed not be misunderstood as a simple power shift from lower to higher levels of governance. Rather, interconnection is key. Even a former UN Secretary General admitted that '[w]hile our goals are global, they can most effectively be achieved through action at the local level'.[171] Global reordering operates at once through reterritorialization

[162] Jan Kottmann, 'Europe and the Regions: Subnational Entity Representation at Community Level' (2001) 26 European Law Review, 159, 160.

[163] Guiseppe Martinico and Leonardo Pierdominici, 'Crisis, Emergency and Subnational Constitutionalism in the Italian Context' (2014) 6 Perspectives on Federalism 116.

[164] Ibid, 126. [165] Italy: Decree-law n. 201/2011. [166] Italy: Law n. 56/2014.

[167] Blank, 'Localism' (n 23) 263.

[168] Brenner and Kreil, 'From Global Cities to Globalised Urbanization' (n 27) 2.

[169] Blank, 'Localism' (n 23) 263.

[170] Judith Resnik, 'Law's Migration: American Exceptionalism, Silent Dialogues, and Federalism's Multiple Ports of Entry' (2006) 115 Yale Law Journal 1564, 1576.

[171] Kofi Annan, UN Secretary General (2005).

and the proliferation of levels of governance and their effect on local affairs.[172] Decentralization does not mean just that the local is empowered by vis-à-vis the national but also often that it is again subdivided into different parts.[173] Urbanization coupled with decentralization and globalization will also come to affect power relations in the EU.[174]

This 'reshaping' of localities is accompanied by a 'new set of ideas about the desirable relationship between state and local governments'.[175] This becomes obvious when considering the emergence of a new rule of engagement between the subnational and the supranational documented in Chapter 4—the duty of loyal cooperation. It goes without saying that these evolutions impact on the Westphalian ideal of the State's regulatory monopoly. Glocalization erodes the assumption that 'the nation state is the primary and most appropriate locus of authority for political decision-making'.[176] It has indeed been acknowledged that the 'nation-state is not best equipped for dealing with many of the challenges and opportunities of the twenty-first century'.[177] This does not, however, entail that the State disappears, rather that it has to coexist with other scales of public authority in a polycentric Union.

The present chapter has sought to provide a brief yet informative overview of the multifaceted entities that are local and regional authorities. We have observed that subnational authorities eschew straightforward definitional exercises for their widely diverse statuses and competences as a matter of domestic law, which necessarily influence their interactions with other actors such as the European Union. Despite their large diversity many subnational authorities share an agenda of wanting to relate to the European Union in different manners. Chapters 3 and 4 underline that the resulting relations between the Union and SNAs emerge in a different light depending on whether we adopt a formal or functional perspective.

[172] Neil Brenner, *New State Spaces: Urban Governance and the Rescaling of Statehood* (Oxford University Press 2004).

[173] See also Luis Eslava, *Local Space, Global Life: The Everyday Operation of International Law and Development* (Cambridge University Press 2015) 4.

[174] By 2050, 80 per cent of all Europeans will live in cities, a number projected to increase thereafter. Urban Agenda for the EU: http://urbanagendaforthe.eu/pactofamsterdam/.

[175] Blank (n 23) 264.

[176] 'Gráinne de Búrca, 'Reappraising Subsidiarity's Significance After Amsterdam' (1999) Jean Monnet Working Paper 7/99. See also Joanne Scott, 'Member States and Regions in Community Law: Convergence and Divergence' in Carol Lyons, Neil Walker, and Paul Beaumont (eds), *Convergence and Divergence in European Public Law* (Hart Publishing 2002) 27.

[177] Foresight for Regional Development Network Guide European Commission, 'A Practical Guide to Regional Foresight' (2001) 10.

# 3

# Subnational Authorities as Outsiders of EU Law

## Introduction

The introductory chapter introduced two narratives framing the differentiated relation between subnational authorities and EU law: the outsider narrative and the insider narrative. This chapter outlines instances of the former in highlighting the outsider narrative's central dynamics throughout various domains of Union law. It will be seen that the Member States remain the sole masters of the Treaties, by virtue of which they benefit from special rights and obligations. The outsider narrative moreover perceives Member States to be monolithic entities and is deeply anchored in narratives of division and separate spheres. Its central characteristics highlight that the outsider narrative embodies a formalist understanding of European Union law.

In line with its formalist understanding the outsider narrative canvasses the EU and the Member States as the leading partners in the European project that have assumed a number of mutually enforceable rights and obligations. It confirms that the EU 'is constitutionally a Union between Member States, and arguably between their peoples'.[1] In this union there is no formal constitutional space for SNAs to directly interact with the Union and its institutions. Only the EU and the States are recognized as generators of norms, envisaging regulatory authority to be divided on a bi-centric spectrum. The existence of SNAs is acknowledged, most explicitly through Articles 4(2) and 5(3) TEU, yet these provisions establish only an indirect relation between SNAs and the Union via the Member State. Rather than being insiders to the privileged sphere of interaction between the EU and the Member States, infra-State authorities stand on the outside thereof so that they can participate merely

[1] Niilo Jääskinen, 'The Case of the Aland Islands—Regional Autonomy versus the European Union of States' in Stephen Weatherill and Ulf Bernitz (eds), *The Role of Regions and Sub-National Actors in Europe* (Hart Publishing 2005) 89 (hereafter Jääskinen, 'The Case of the Aland Islands').

indirectly via the State. The domains that give expression to the outsider narrative echo a close attachment to the origins of European integration when interconnection was less progressed and multifaceted than it is today. While SNAs are recognized to exist, contradicting any theory of pure blindness, they are seen in a light considerably different from the States. The outsider narrative hence highlights that '[t]he system established under the Treaty of Rome contemplates only two levels of government—the European [Union] and the Member States'.[2] This chapter charts various areas of EU law that substantiate the above conclusion.

## A. Manifestations of the Outsider Narrative in EU Law

This section introduces the six key characterizing features of the outsider narrative. It will be seen that (i) Member States have an exclusive status as masters of the Treaties, which (ii) gives them special rights, and (iii) obligations. Member States are (iv) seen as monolithic entities, and (v) the outsider narrative is attached deeply to narratives of division and separate spheres, representing (vi) a formalistic understanding of the European legal order. Before moving on to this analysis a word of clarification is in order. This highlights the key elements of the outsider narrative that have been highlighted in the introductory chapter, namely sovereign equality, bi-centricity, and the impossibility of assimilating Member States and SNAs. The elements listed below are not isolated manifestations of the outsider narrative but have rather been chosen to make a more general point. Similarly, the various elements of EU law covered in each section do not illustrate just one characteristic of the outsider narrative but rather all. The reason why they are not examined from the perspective of all of its characterizing features is simply rooted in concerns of space. Our analysis starts with an investigation of Member States' status as masters of the Treaties.

### 1. The Member States as masters of the Treaties

The Member States have founded the Union through the conclusion of international treaties, and continue to determine the competences, shape, and

[2] Andrea Ross and Mayte Salvador Crespo, 'The Effect of Devolution on the Implementation of European Community Law in Spain and the United Kingdom' (2003) 28 European Law Review 210, 216–17 (hereafter Ross and Crespo, 'The Effect of Devolution').

objectives thereof through treaty revision.[3] It is in this sense that the Member States are the masters of the Treaties. The conclusion of the European Treaties gave rise to a number of mutually enforceable rights and obligations between the Member States and the EU.[4] As a result of that status Member States have corresponding rights and obligations.

Primary law makes Member States' special status explicit. Article 1 TEU recognizes that they have established the EU between themselves and conferred competences on it to realize common objectives.[5] The Treaty opens with a reminder that the EU is but the product of the States' common initiative—States that continue to collectively control the fate of their supranational enterprise. According to the principle of conferral, embodied in Article 5(2) TEU, the Union shall act only 'within the limits of the competences conferred upon it by the Member States in the Treaties' to attain its stated objectives. It further declares that competences not conferred on the Union 'remain with the Member States'.[6] The EU's powers derive from those of the sovereign Member States, a transfer that enables the Union to function. Unlike many national legislatures, the Union does not dispose of a general law-making competence; rather its entire legal authority derives from the States.[7] As affirmed in the German Constitutional Court's *Maastricht* decision, each Member State has preserved 'the quality as a sovereign State in its own right and the status of sovereign equality with other States within the meaning of Article 2(1) of the United Nations Charter'.[8]

The importance of sovereign equality should not be underestimated, as 'the European Court of Justice, and Union practice generally tend to attach [importance] to state sovereignty'.[9] This position finds explicit support in primary law, for instance in the form of Article 1 TEU.[10] Beyond this opening provision, Member States' status as masters of the Treaties is repeatedly

[3] See further Gráinne de Búrca and Bruno de Witte, 'The Delimitation of Powers between the EU and its Member States' in Anthony Arnull and Daniel Wincott (eds), *Accountability and Legitimacy in the European Union* (Oxford University Press 2002).

[4] These are explored more fully in the two subsequent sections.

[5] See also Article 2 TEU.

[6] Articles 4(1) and 5(1) TEU.

[7] BVerfGE 89, 155 (Maastricht Decision) [1994] Common Market Law Review 57 (in English) (hereafter 'Maastricht Decision'). For an analysis in English, see Ulrich Everling, 'The Maastricht Judgment of the German Federal Constitutional Court and the Significance for the Development of the European Union' (1994) 14 Yearbook of European Law 1.

[8] Maastricht Decision (n 7), 91.

[9] Andrew Evans, 'Regional Dimensions to European Governance' (2003) 52 International and Comparative Quarterly 21, 21.

[10] Ibid, 21. This provision stipulates that the High Contracting Parties establish among themselves a European Union 'on which Member States confer competences to attain objectives they have in common'.

substantiated. Article 10(2) TEU determines that States are represented in the Council and Article 13(1) TEU recalls that the EU must serve the interests of 'its citizens and those of the Member States'. No reference to subnational authorities is made in these contexts, underlining that they are approached as constituent units of their Member States rather than independent actors with direct relations to the Union.

The EU's substantive objectives conversely refer only to the Union and the Member States, and now also in some respects to citizens. Article 3 TEU determines that the internal market aims at promoting 'economic, social and territorial cohesion, and solidarity among Member States'.[11] The reference to 'among Member States' is of critical importance. Chapter 4 indeed unveils that, time and time again, the question of whether the EU's economic objectives also bind SNAs has arisen. The Court has answered this in the affirmative, yet provisions such as Article 3 TEU continue to consider that the internal market exists 'among Member States' echoing a bi-centric vision of supranational law.[12] This formal account is based on the paradigms of division, disconnection, and spheres of autonomy, and neglects the reality that the market is in fact subdivided into smaller parts equally affected by economic integration.[13]

Member States' status as masters of the Treaties can be observed nowhere as lucidly as in the application of the rules on treaty revision. Whereas informal change occurs on a constant basis, inter alia via the evolving jurisprudence of the CJEU and inter-institutional arrangements, the rules on treaty revision deal with formal constitutional change.[14] The main instrument of formal constitutional change is the 'revision treaty', that is, an international agreement between the Member States of the European Union making amendments to the so-called 'founding treaties'.[15] Two procedures to amend the treaties are foreseen by Article 48 TEU, which lays out the ordinary revision procedure and the simplified revision procedures. The ordinary revision procedure is the general amendment procedure, which for instance governed

[11] Article 3 TEU.

[12] This should be contrasted with Article 26(2) TFEU: '[t]he internal market shall comprise an area without internal frontiers in which the free movement of goods, persons, services and capital is ensured in accordance with the provisions of the Treaties'.

[13] This is explicitly recognized by other areas of EU law, covered in Chapter 4.

[14] These two techniques of constitutional change of course overlap as the Treaties may codify changes previously brought about through other means, as was the case for the respect for national identities, now enshrined in Article 4(2) TEU and previously recognized by several domestic constitutional courts.

[15] Bruno de Witte, 'Treaty Revision in the European Union: Constitutional Change Through International Law' (2004) 35 Netherlands Yearbook of International Law 51, 51–2. See also Case 43/75 *Defrenne* [1976] EU:C:1976:56, para 57.

the revisions carried out under the Lisbon reform.[16] Any Member State, the European Parliament, or the Commission may submit to the Council a proposal for treaty amendment.[17] If the European Council, in consultation with the Parliament and the Commission, decides to examine the proposed amendment by a simple majority, the president of the Council convenes a Convention that comprises representatives of national parliaments, the heads of State or government, as well as Commission and Parliament representatives.[18] By consensus, the convention adopts a recommendation to a conference of Member State representatives.[19] The ordinary revision procedure's subsequent stage is the convention of a conference composed of the representatives of all Member States by the Council, which decides on the amendments to be made.[20] Every single State must give its consent for the process to move forward. The ordinary revision procedure accordingly reflects the bi-centric structure of EU law according to which two main categories of actors intervene in its shaping: the Member States and the EU itself.[21] While EU institutions certainly intervene in the process, States are the decisive actors. Every single Member State's consent is not only mandatory in the context of this conference but also domestically, as relevant amendments must be ratified by each State.[22]

Despite the formally bi-centric nature of the treaty revision process SNAs regularly intervene. Chapter 2, for instance, highlighted the involvement the Belgian and Austrian regions as well as the Finnish Åland have in this respect.[23] From the perspective of EU law such involvement is of no relevance. SNAs' contribution to treaty change is a purely domestic process that EU law is attributing no formal importance to, upholding the monolithic nature of statehood. The treaty amendment procedure indeed operates no distinction depending on whether a Member State is of a centralized or decentralized

[16] Paul Craig, *The Lisbon Treaty: Law, Politics, and Treaty Reform* (Oxford University Press 2010); Jean-Claude Piris, *The Lisbon Treaty: A Legal and Political Analysis* (Cambridge University Press 2010).

[17] Article 48(2) TEU. [18] Article 48(3) TEU.

[19] Under Article 48(3) TEU the European Council may decide to not convene a Convention 'should this not be justified by the extent of the proposed amendments'.

[20] Article 48(4) TEU.

[21] The same conclusion can be reached with respect to the simplified revision procedure enshrined in Article 48(6) TEU.

[22] Article 48(6) TEU.

[23] Pia Alilonttinen and Savino Ruà, 'Lisbon Treaty Ratification: Will the Aland Islands Become Finland's Greenland?' The Centre for European Policy Studies 1/2008, 2008; Nikos Skoutaris, 'The Role of Sub-State Entities in the EU Decision-Making Process' in Elke Cloots, Geert de Baere, and Stefan Sottiaux (eds), *Federalism in the European Union* (Hart Publishing 2012) 210 (hereafter Skoutaris, 'The Role of Sub-State Entities').

nature. It is thus the Member States as such that have exclusive control over the modification of primary law to increase or decrease the Union's competences.[24] The bi-centric spirit of the rules on treaty revision is no necessity but a choice. Legally speaking, treaty revision constitutes an amendment of an international treaty, governed by Article 39 of the Vienna Convention on the Law of the Treaties under which the contracting parties determine the rules applicable to treaty amendment.[25] It has been Member States' choice to retain a monopoly on treaty amendment. This centrality of the States could also be observed on the occasion of the Convention for the Future of Europe, the body established in 2001 to produce a draft constitution for the EU, which has since failed.[26] At this convention local and regional representatives were hardly visible. Whereas in its early stages a proposal had emerged that would have attributed a special status to 'associated regions', that is to say those regions with particularly pronounced competences, this was subsequently abandoned.[27] As a consequence, 'the Convention itself barely recognised the regional dimension to the constitutive politics of the EU'.[28] While one or two regional members 'got there by wearing non-regional hats', the Committee of the Regions (CoR) could not gain strong visibility as it was merely allowed to send six observers and these 'won the right to speak only rarely'.[29] This reflects the reality that in the European Union 'the dominant legal and political paradigm remains a Europe of the States'[30] as the paradigms of sovereign equality and Member States' status as masters of the Treaties remain very much intact. Member States are thus the sole masters of the Treaties—a status firmly anchored in the rules on treaty revision but also beyond, as the subsequent section illustrates.

[24] Article 48(2) TEU.

[25] See further Anthony Aust, *Modern Treaty Law and Practice* (Cambridge University Press 2000) 214.

[26] On the draft constitution, see Anneli Albi and Jacques Ziller (eds), *The European Constitution and National Constitutions: Ratification and Beyond* (Kluwer Law International 2007).

[27] Committee on Constitutional Affairs of the European Parliament, 'Report on the division of competences between the European Union and the Member States' (hereafter 'Lamassoure Report'), 2001/2024 (INI), 24 April 2002.

[28] Charlie Jeffery, 'Regions and the European Union: Letting them In, and Leaving them Alone' in Stephen Weatherill and Ulf Bernitz (eds), *The Role of Regions and Sub-National Actors in Europe* (Hart Publishing 2005) 39.

[29] Ibid, 39.

[30] Stephen Weatherill, 'The Challenge of the Regional Dimension in the European Union' in Stephen Weatherill and Ulf Bernitz (eds), *The Role of Regions and Sub-National Actors in Europe* (Hart Publishing 2005) 2 (hereafter Weatherill, 'The Challenge of the Regional Dimension in the European Union'). This seems to reflect the consensus at the Convention on the Future of Europe that asserted that the EU should not intervene in Member States' internal arrangements. See CONV 548/03 of 13 February 2003, 'Summary Report on the Plenary Session of 6 and 7 February 2003'.

## 2. Member States have special rights by virtue of being masters of the Treaties

The rules on treaty revision have already indicated that as masters of the Treaties Member States have exclusive rights. Two such rights are subject to more detailed examination in the present section, which engages with, on the one hand, Member States' right to standing in front of the European courts and, on the other, their involvement in closer cooperation.

### *a. Standing under Article 263 TFEU*

Member States, as masters of the Treaties, have competence to police whether the EU exceeds its conferred competence.[31] Article 263 TFEU governs the admissibility of actions challenging the legality of acts of the European institutions. [32] Its second paragraph attributes a general and unlimited right of action to the so-called privileged applicants, namely, the Member States, the European Parliament, the Commission, and the Council.[33] These actors are exempt from demonstrating an interest to bring an action; the only condition is the respect of a two-month time limit within which the action can be brought.[34]

Unlike States, local and regional governments don't qualify as privileged applicants.[35] They also don't qualify as semi-privileged applicants under Article 263(3) TFEU.[36] While a number of options remain available for SNAs to bring an action in front of the European courts, none allows them to directly and individually defend their interests—including their regulatory competence—on a supranational scale. Only Member States have that privilege. Member States' privileged status is the logical corollary of them being the masters of the Treaties by virtue of which they have an interest in safeguarding the Treaties' institutional balance and the dividing lines between

[31] As per Articles 4(1) and 5(1) TEU, the EU is an entity of conferred power, only able to exercise those competences the Member States have delegated to it.

[32] See more generally Margarita Canedo, 'L'intérêt à agir dans le recours en annulation du droit communautaire' (2000) 36 Revue Trimestrielle de Droit Européen 451.

[33] Article 263(2) TFEU reads as follows: '[i]t shall for this purpose have jurisdiction in actions brought by a Member State, the European Parliament, the Council or the Commission on grounds of lack of competence, infringement of an essential procedural requirement, infringement of the Treaties or of any rule of law relating to their application, or misuse of powers'.

[34] Case 230/81 *Luxembourg v European Parliament* [1983] EU:C:1983:32, paras 24–5; Case 131/86 *United Kingdom v Council* [1988] EU:C:1988:86 para 6.

[35] Case C-406/06 *Landtag Schleswig-Holstein v Commission* EU:C:2007:90 [2007].

[36] Article 263(3) TFEU reads as follows: '[t]he Court shall have jurisdiction under the same conditions in actions brought by the Court of Auditors, by the European Central Bank and by the Committee of the Regions for the purpose of protecting their prerogatives'.

national and supranational competence. According to Van Nuffel, Member States' privileged standing illustrates 'the responsibility that the Member States retained for themselves, at the moment of the foundation of the [EU], to see that the [EU] institutions do not overstep the powers the Member States were willing to surrender'.[37] States accordingly assume the unique role of checking that supranational institutions refrain from violating the competence division. This stance was said to reflect the States' position 'as Founding Fathers rather than their ongoing involvement with the functioning of the European Union'.[38] This relates to the temporal dimension of the insider narrative and its attachment to the early periods of European integration where interconnection did not yet prevail.

In *Commune de Differdange* a group of municipal governments from the South of Luxembourg challenged a Commission decision, addressed to the Grand Duchy's government, finding State aid granted by Luxembourg to the steel industry compatible with EU law.[39] The decision, however, required the steel industry to reduce its production capacity in return for the aid. The Commission also requested a list of the plants to be closed, including a corresponding timeline. The five municipalities in whose territory the plants were located sought a declaration that the Commission decision was void under Article 264(3) TFEU. The Court found the action to be inadmissible for the municipalities could not establish direct and individual concern.[40] The municipalities argument that, in line with principles of administrative law prevailing in a number of domestic systems, the interests of the local steel factors and in particular also the local residents should be seen as the municipality's own interests, failed.[41] The Court stressed that the decision could not be considered to be of direct and individual concern to the municipalities in light of the margin of discretion left to national authorities regarding its implementation (for instance the question of which steel plants can be closed).[42] It held that 'the decision cannot be regarded as being of direct and individual concern to the municipalities with which the undertakings affected, by virtue of the location of their factories, are connected'. The SNAs were considered outsiders to the relation between the Commission and the Member State. While the economic consequences for local governments, in

[37] Piet van Nuffel, 'What's in a Member State? Central and Decentralized Authorities Before the Community Court' (2001) 38 Common Market Law Review 871 (hereafter van Nuffel, 'What's in a Member State?'), 875.

[38] Ibid, 877.

[39] Case 222/83 *Commune de Differdange v Commission* [1984] EU:C:1984:266 (hereafter *Commune de Differdange*).

[40] Ibid, para 4. [41] Ibid, para 5. [42] Ibid, para 12.

particular a reduction in local tax revenue, went undisputed, this alone was not capable of granting *locus standi* as a matter of EU law.[43] The Commission decision occurred in a context were Luxembourg was transitioning from an industrial economy based on steel to a service economy based on financial services. Unlike steel plants, banks were established in the country's capital as opposed to the Southern part of the country. The resulting changes in tax revenue for the municipality concerned are accordingly a matter for a Member State to mediate internally. Despite EU law's interference in this matter through Article 107(1) TFEU, the consequences flowing therefrom are for the Member State to resolve internally; no matter is available as a matter of EU law.

Advocate General Léger confirmed in *Nederlandse Antillen* that Member States 'enjoy an irrebuttable presumption' that they have a legal interest in bringing proceedings, given that '[a]s parties to the Treaty, the Member States have an obvious interest in upholding the terms of an agreement to which they are parties'.[44] This privilege is reserved to States 'to the exclusion of governments of regions or of autonomous communities, irrespective of the powers they may have'.[45] The Court itself has recognized that if the contrary were true:

> it would undermine the institutional balance provided for by the Treaties, which determines the conditions under which the Member States, that is to say the States party to the Treaties establishing the [EU] and the Accession Treaties, participate in the functioning of the [EU] institutions. It is not possible for the [EU] to comprise a greater number of Member States than the number of States between which they were established.[46]

SNAs have attempted to challenge this principle time and time again, but have always been unsuccessful in doing so. In one instance, Wallonia argued that as it had taken over the responsibilities in a given domain from the Belgian government, it could bring an action for annulment in the same capacity as a Member State. The Court denied it the ability to do so. Contrary

[43] Ibid, para 5.

[44] Opinion of Advocate General Léger in Cases C-301/97 and C-452/98 *Nederlandse Antillen* [2001] EU:C:2001:623 (hereafter *Nederlandse Antillen*), para 53 (stating that as Contracting Parties to the Treaty, the Member States have an evident interest to safeguard the contents of the agreement to which they acceded).

[45] Ibid, para 56.

[46] See Case C-95/97 *Région Wallonne v Commission* [1997] EU:C:1997:184 (hereafter *Région Wallonne*), para 6, and Case C-180/97 *Regione Toscana v Commission* [1997] EU:C:1997:451, para 6. For a case comment, see Joanne Scott, 'Case C-95/97 Région Wallonne v. Commission of the European Communities [1997] ECR I-1787 (ECJ) and Case T-70/97 [1997] ECR II-1513 (CFI)' (1999) 36 Common Market Law Review 227.

to Wallonia, which claimed that the notion of 'the Member State' should be interpreted widely to encompass SNAs exercising certain competences, it held that it is apparent from 'the general scheme of the Treaties' that the terminology of 'Member State' for the purposes of *locus standi* 'refers only to government authorities of the Member States of the [EU] and cannot include the government of regions or autonomous communities, irrespective of the powers they may have'.[47]

From the perspective of EU law what matters are not an actor's actual competences but rather its formal status, more precisely the question whether it is a Member State or not. Holding otherwise, the Court argued, would upset the treaties' institutional balance.[48] Alternative options are available to SNAs wishing to challenge Union acts despite the impossibility of initiating direct actions under the privileged claimant status. These different avenues are briefly introduced in turn. SNAs can act under Article 263(4) TFEU; as an agent for their Member State; through their Member State; or through the Committee of the Regions. Whereas these various mechanisms provide SNAs with an option to engage legal proceedings, none of them allows them to individually protect their regulatory autonomy in the same way Member States can do as privileged claimants, highlighting that, as per the outsider narrative, Member States and SNAs are entities of a fundamentally different nature.

First, Article 263(4) TFEU allows any natural or legal person to institute proceedings against either an act addressed to that person which is of direct and individual concern to them, or against a regulatory act which is of direct concern to them and does not entail implementing measures.[49] Just like any other legal person, an SNA may act before the Court on this basis, provided that they dispose of legal personality under national law.[50] It is, however, well known that the Court interprets this provision strictly.[51] What is more, under this provision SNAs have, if at all, the same opportunity to challenge EU acts as any other legal person, not a special status, alike that of the Member States, to protect their regulatory competence from EU intrusion.

[47] *Région Wallonne* (n 46), para 6.

[48] Ibid.

[49] The meaning of this last category has been made clear(er) by Case T-262/10 *Microban v Commission* [2011] EU:T:2011:623 and Case T-18/10 *Inuit Tapiriit Kanatami* [2011] EU:T:2011:419.

[50] Case T-238/97 *Comunidad Autonoma de Cantabria* [1998] EU:T:1998:126, para 43; Case T-288/97 *Friuli Venezia Giulia* [1999] EU:T:2001:115, para 42; Case T-214/95 *Het Vlaamse Gewest* [1998] EU:T:1998:77, para 28.

[51] Stefan Enchelmaier, 'No-one Slips Through the Net? Latest Development, and Non-Developments, in the European Court of Justice's Jurisprudence on Art. 230(4) EC' (2005) 24 Yearbook of European Law 173.

Second, there seems to be ample agreement in legal scholarship that infra-State entities could act as agents of their State.[52] This would parallel the already existing possibility for SNAs to represent national governments in the Council.[53] If the Court were to refuse that option, it would interfere with Member States' internal institutional structure hence infringing the principle of national institutional autonomy. As an agent of their State, SNAs would however need to secure approval to bring an action, and would thus have a limited possibility to defend their own interests where these collide with those of the State, confirming the monolithic nature of statehood under the outsider narrative. Interestingly, SNAs would act as a Member State in this scenario, which would allow them to benefit from one of the privileges of membership conferred on the States, just as they do when they represent the State in the Council under Article 16(2) TEU.[54]

Third, some Member States have created additional domestic mechanisms that allow SNAs to compel the executive to defend their interests by bringing a direct action before the European Court.[55] Such arrangements exist, for instance, in Austria and Belgium. [56] In Germany, Article 52(3)(a) of the German Basic Law and Rule 45 of the Bundesrat's Rules of Procedure allow the regional chamber to compel the federal government to bring an action where it believes that competences of the Länder have been infringed.[57] In Belgium even a single region can compel the State level to act.[58] In the UK, the central government is obliged to consult the devolved administrations where it intends to bring a direct action, intervene in a direct action, or submit observations in a preliminary reference that touches on devolved matters.[59] These options are, however, purely the result of domestic arrangements,

[52] See in this regard van Nuffel, 'What's in a Member State?' (n 37) 880; Koen Lenaerts and Nathan Cambien, 'Regions and the European Courts: Giving Shape to the Regional Dimension of Member States' (2010) 35 European Law Review 609, 619.

[53] Article 16(2) TEU. For an overview of how such arrangements operate in domestic contexts, see van Nuffel, 'What's in a Member State?' (n 37) 880–1 and Article 23 (6) of the German Basic Law.

[54] On this, see further later in this chapter.

[55] See further Anne Thies, 'The *Locus Standi* of the Regions Before EU Courts' in Carlo Panara and Alexander De Becker (eds), *The Role of the Regions in EU Governance* (Springer 2011).

[56] For Austria, see Rainer Schweizer and Stephan Brunner, *Die Mitwirkung der Bundesländer an EU-Vorhaben in der Bundesrepublik Deutschland und Österreich: Ein Modell für die Mitwirkung der Kantone in der Aussenpolitik* (Stämpfli Verlag 1998) 52–3.

[57] Ibid, 33–4.

[58] For a more detailed analysis of this, see van Nuffel, 'What's in a Member State?' (n 37).

[59] See Scottish Government, Guidance for devolved administrations when considering bringing direct action before the European Court of Justice (ECJ), 13 December 2011, http://www.gov.scot/Topics/International/Europe/Our-Focus/UK-Gov/GuidanceECJ.

as from the point of view of EU law, the Member State acts on its own. As such, the Member States' legal indivisibility remains intact.

Fourth, the Treaty of Lisbon has elevated the Committee of the Regions to the status of a semi-privileged applicant, enabling it to bring actions to protect its own prerogatives.[60] Under Article 8(2) of Protocol No 2, the Committee may in addition act where legislative acts for which it must be consulted are suspected to infringe the subsidiarity requirement.[61] While these prerogatives allow the Committee to initiate direct actions, they are not tools that SNAs could individually rely on to protect their respective regulatory prerogatives.

In light of the above we can conclude that SNAs can rely on a number of options to bring actions in the supranational courts. Their ability to do so is, however, significantly more limited than that of the Member States as SNAs have no possibility of defending their competences against EU intrusion. According to Jääskinen the current rules can be justified given that legally, SNAs:

> do not have a sphere of competence that is protected by [EU] law and that could directly be infringed by new [EU] legislation. In this respect, the position of the regions is different from that of the Member States. The latter possess a general exclusive competence in all matters regarding which the EU has not been attributed special powers by the Treaties.[62]

Because subnational authorities are not masters of the Treaties, their rights diverge from those of the Member States. The rules on closer cooperation equally illustrate that Member States and subnational authorities have considerably different rights under EU law.

### b. *Only Member States can engage in closer cooperation*

As a general rule, all twenty-eight Member States participate in the creation of EU secondary legislation. This statement does not, however, account for the enhanced cooperation procedure.[63] Article 20 TEU authorizes enhanced cooperation that furthers the aims of the EU, protects its interests, and reinforces the integration process subject to certain conditions.[64] Under the enhanced cooperation procedure, a group of at least nine Member States can commonly legislate if agreement among all twenty-eight States has proven

[60] Article 263(3) TFEU allows the CoR to bring for instance an action where supranational institutions disregard their obligation to consult the Committee.

[61] Article 307 TFEU.

[62] Jääskinen, 'The Case of the Aland Islands' (n 1) 100.

[63] See more generally, Filip Tuytschaever, *Differentiation in European Union Law* (Hart 1999) and Alexander Stubb, *Negotiating Flexibility in the European Union: Amsterdam, Nice and Beyond* (Palgrave 2002).

[64] Article 20(1) TEU.

impossible.[65] The enhanced cooperation procedure can indeed only be relied on if the Council has established that the pursued objectives cannot be attained through the collaboration of all States within a reasonable time frame.[66] Article 328 TFEU provides that the enhanced cooperation initiative adopted must be open to any Member State at any time. The acts adopted, however, only bind those States that participate. It further follows from Article 326 TFEU that enhanced cooperation has to comply with the treaties and EU law and shall not undermine the internal market or economic, social, and territorial cohesion. Enhanced cooperation must also 'respect the competences, rights and obligations of those Member States which do not participate in it'.[67] Unlike opt-outs such differentiation takes place through secondary law, explaining why it has been labelled as a form of 'secondary law differentiation'.[68]

The enhanced cooperation procedure has for instance been considered in the context of a European financial transaction tax, a common consolidated corporate tax base, and a European company statute.[69] Should a region with extensive fiscal and regulatory autonomy have desired to join any of these initiatives it would have been barred from doing so as a matter of EU law given its lack of sovereign statehood. SNAs joining a closer cooperation mechanism would certainly raise a number of issues, such as the fragmentation of legal regimes. This in itself is not, however, a prohibitive reason against closer cooperation as fragmentation also reigns between participating and non-participating Member States. In Member States that operate fiscal decentralization, fragmentation is moreover accepted; the only difference would be that the autonomous regime adopted by one SNA would be aligned with that of other Member States. Despite the merely formal obstacle of statehood, SNAs are prevented from participating in the closer cooperation mechanism.

Article 20 TEU's reference to the 'Member States' underlines that the Treaties consider the division of regulatory authority in the EU to be bi-centric.[70] Similar dynamics can also be observed in other areas of EU law

[65] Article 328 TFEU. [66] Article 20(2) TEU.

[67] Article 327 TFEU, which further provides that non-participating Member States 'shall not impede its implementation by the participating Member States'. The CJEU has made clear in Joined Cases C-274/11 and C-295/11 *Spain and Italy v Council* [2012] EU:C:2013:240 that it applies a very soft standard of review to the decisions of the Member States to engage in enhanced cooperation, allowing generous space for such coordination in the future.

[68] Daniela Kroll and Dirk Leuffen, 'Enhanced Cooperation in Practice. An Analysis of Differentiated Integration in EU Secondary Law' (2014) 3 Journal of European Public Policy 353, 353.

[69] For an overview, see ibid.

[70] Article 20(1) TEU reads as follows: 'Member States which wish to establish enhanced cooperation between themselves within the framework of the Union's non-exclusive competences may

that allow Member States to cooperate, such as Article 73 TFEU according to which Member States may 'organize between themselves and under their responsibility such forms of cooperation and coordination as they deem appropriate' in the context of national security. This confirms local and regional authorities' outsider status, as, notwithstanding the competences that they have under domestic arrangements, these are not recognized by EU law to the effect that they could participate in enhanced cooperation, a prerogative reserved to the Member States. The engagement in closer cooperation is accordingly a prerogative only Member States enjoy by virtue of their status as masters of the Treaties.

### *c. Member States have special obligations by virtue of being masters of the Treaties*

As masters of the Treaties the Member States not only have special rights but also special obligations, as evidenced by the rules on direct and indirect responsibility that underscore that, notwithstanding which national organ is responsible for a breach of EU law, the Member State is always liable. This reflects that Member States are considered as monolithic entities, every breach occurring within their territory being attributed to the central State as a matter of EU law.

### *d. Direct responsibility*

An examination of the rules on direct responsibility reveals that if SNAs fail to implement EU norms correctly, the Member State will be responsible vis-à-vis EU law.[71] This is more than a mere hypothetical question. Oftentimes SNAs are in charge of the transposition and implementation of supranational norms, especially where their autonomous competences are affected.[72] With regard to Spain it has been argued that the 'implementation of EU law by the regions is common practice'.[73] The same is true in almost all other Member

make use of its institutions and exercise those competences by applying the relevant provisions of the Treaties, subject to the limits and in accordance with the detailed arrangements laid down in this Article and in Articles 326 to 334 of the Treaty on the Functioning of the European Union.'

[71] See by way of example Case C-302/97 *Konle* [1999] EU:C:1999:271, para 62; Case C-424/97 *Haim* [2000] EU:C:2000:357, paras 61–62; Case C-224/01 *Köbler* [2003] EU:C:2003:513, paras 44–7 and 50.

[72] Article 23(6) of the German Basic Law attributes responsibility for the implementation of European directives to the Länder wherever they concern an area of their competence.

[73] Maite Zelaia Garagarza, 'The Spanish State Structure and EU Law: The View of the Spanish Constitutional Court' in Elke Cloots, Geert de Baere, and Stefan Sottiaux (eds), *Federalism in the European Union* (Hart Publishing 2012) 386.

States.[74] While SNAs must, as agents of EU law, implement and observe supranational obligations, they are not direct interlocutors of the EU—this function being reserved to the masters of the Treaties. This spirit is apparent in Article 258 TFEU that enables the Commission to initiate actions against a Member State that has 'failed to fulfil an obligation under the Treaties'. If the Member State does not comply with the Commission's opinion, the latter may trigger infringement proceedings.

As masters of the Treaties, Member States have consented to being bound by the obligations inherent to primary law. The obligations arising under the Treaties are indeed addressed to the States, which consequently bear sole responsibility for their breach. This state of affairs corresponds very much to orthodox conceptions of public international law, reflecting the maxim of *pacta sunt servanda*. It also reflects a concern for the *effet utile* of EU law as automatically addressing infringement proceedings to Member States responds to efficiency concerns, as the EU need not concern itself with the question of which domestic authority is at fault. We can moreover understand this as a reflection of the principle of Member State equality enshrined in Article 4(2) TEU, as it prevents differentiated treatment between Member States of a centralized and decentralized structure. The present section illustrates the legal rules of responsibility in the context of the implementation of EU law. It will be seen that whereas SNAs are frequently charged with the implementation of EU secondary legislation the Member States always bear responsibility for their possible shortcomings.

Union law recognizes subnational authorities as implementers of supranational norms. SNAs are 'part and parcel of a Member State' and as such bound by the Treaties.[75] It follows that where SNAs are tasked by their State to implement EU secondary legislation they must do so in the manner required by EU law. According to Article 288(2) TFEU, a regulation 'shall have general application' and 'be binding in its entirety and directly applicable in all Member States'. No transposing measures are needed for regulations to produce legal effects.[76] Directives, however, are per Article 288(3) TFEU 'binding, as to the result to be achieved, upon each Member State to which it is addressed, but shall leave to the national authorities the choice of form and

[74] Jääskinen, 'The Case of the Åland Islands' (n 1) 89 (noting that the Finnish Åland islands are 'obliged to implement [EU] legislation falling within its competence without having direct [EU] law-based access to decision-making processes and adjudication at the EU level').

[75] Koen Lenaerts, 'EU Federalism in 3-D' in Elke Cloots, Geert de Baere, and Stefan Sottiaux (eds), *Federalism in the European Union* (Hart Publishing 2012) 16.

[76] This is not merely unnecessary but also impermissible as transposition would cast doubt on 'both the legal nature of the applicable provisions and the date of their coming into force'. See Case 39/72 *Commission v Italy* [1973] EU:C:1973:13, paras 16–17.

methods'. Article 288 TFEU recognizes that 'national authorities' determine how to achieve the results formulated in the directive while at the same time clarifying that they formally bind the Member State. This already indicates that while SNAs are tolerated implementers, Member States bear responsibility for any connected shortcomings.

Advocate General Capotorti recognized in 1982 that the implementation of directives 'by means of legislative measures of a regional nature' is 'acceptable from the [EU] point of view' as 'each Member State is free to distribute legislative powers within its territory as it thinks best'.[77] Under this principle of national institutional autonomy Member States are free to allocate domestic implementing capacity as they wish. This principle has been affirmed time and time again. In *Hansa Fleisch*, a dispute had arisen between a private company and a German local authority.[78] It concerned fees payable after health inspections had been carried out on the premises of the company, a slaughterhouse. Under EU secondary legislation, administrations are authorized to collect fees related to such inspections.[79] Whereas guidelines for the calculation of the fees were provided, Member States were explicitly allowed to depart from the predetermined level.[80] Under German law, the Länder had competence to calculate their amount. The company argued that the fees set by Schleswig-Holstein were unlawful because they exceeded the amount provided by EU law. The Court invoked the principle of national institutional autonomy, recalling that:

> each Member State is free to allocate powers internally and to implement [EU] acts which are not directly applicable by means of measures adopted by regional or local authorities, provided that that allocation of powers enables the [EU] legal measures in question to be implemented correctly.[81]

Member States can accordingly delegate their implementing authority to an SNA. In addressing the compatibility of regional fee levels and EU law, the Court stressed that the directive left discretion to national authorities to adapt the amounts provided in secondary legislation to their real costs. No

[77] Opinion of Advocate General Capotorti in Case 68-73/81 *Belgium v Commission* [1982] EU:C:1982:30, para 162.

[78] Case C-156/91 *Hansa Fleisch v Landrat des Kreises Schleswig-Flensburg* [1992] EU:C:1992:423 (hereafter *Hansa Fleisch*).

[79] Council Directive 85/73/EEC of 29 January 1985 on the financing of health inspections and controls of fresh meat and poultry meat [1985] OJ L 32.

[80] Article 2(2) of Council Decision 88/408/EEC of 15 June 1988 on the levels of the fees to be charged for health inspections and controls of fresh meat pursuant to Directive 85/73/EEC [1988] OJ 1988 L 194.

[81] *Hansa Fleisch* (n 78), para 23.

provision of EU law, the Court stated, prevents Member States 'from entrusting to regional or local authorities the powers to derogate from the standard levels of fees, under the conditions and within the limits' set by EU law.[82] The German government added that the decentralized implementation of EU secondary law presents benefits, as 'the fixing of fees at the level of the individual Länder is the most appropriate way of ensuring ... that fees correspond to real inspection costs'.[83] While the decentralized implementation of supranational norms is accordingly tolerated and recognized to present benefits, the question of responsibility takes us back to Member States' exclusive status as masters of the Treaties by virtue of which they bear exclusive responsibility for any breach of EU law.

Whereas EU law recognizes SNAs as key implementers of supranational norms it also holds that only Member States can incur direct liability under Union law. Time and time again, the Court has affirmed that when an SNA fails to implement EU law correctly, the State is responsible for its failure.[84] Member States cannot hide behind their internal structure to escape responsibility[85] or to avoid ending an infringement.[86] States are equally prevented from arguing in their defence that they have no competence to bring an SNA's infringement to an end.[87] The principle of exclusive Member State responsibility is readily illustrated by a number of cases relating to the implementation of supranational standards into domestic law.

*Commission v Belgium* (1981) concerned a directive aimed at protecting human health and the environment through the adoption of measures encouraging the prevention, recycling, and processing of waste.[88] When Belgium had to defend itself in front of the CJEU for having failed to fully implement the directive, it argued that it was prevented from doing so because of difficulties arising from its internal devolutionary process. Important institutional

[82] Ibid, para 24.

[83] Opinion of Advocate General Jacobs in Case C-156/91 *Hansa Fleisch v Landrat des Kreises Schleswig-Flensburg* [1992] EU:C:1992:423, para 28.

[84] See by way of example Case C-358/03 *Commission v Austria* [2004] EU:C:2004:824, para 13; Case C-87/02 *Commission v Italy* [2004] EU:C:2004:363, para 38.

[85] See by way of example Case 69/81 *Commission v Belgium* [1982] EU:C:1982:26, para 5; Case C-247/98 *Commission v Spain* [2000] EU:C:2001:4, para 20; Case C-383/00 *Commission v Germany* [2002] EU:C:2002:289, para 18; Case C-388/01 *Commission v Italy* [2003] EU:C:2003:30, paras 25–6; Case C-357/03 *Commission v Austria*, EU:C:2004:681, para 10; Case C-358/03 *Commission v Austria* [2004] EU:C:2004:824, para 13.

[86] Case 96/81 *Commission v Netherlands* [1982] EU:C:1982:192, para 12; Joined Cases 227–230/85 *Commission v Belgium* [1988] EU:C:1988:6, paras 9–10.

[87] Case C-323/96 *Commission v Belgium* [1998] EU:C:1998:411, paras 40–2; Case C-236/99 *Commission v Belgium* [2000] EU:C:2000:374, para 22.

[88] Case C-69/81 *Commission v Belgium* [1982] EU:C:1982:26.

reforms concerning the redistribution of powers between national and regional institutions had been initiated but not yet completed. The federal government put forward the argument that as long as these reforms had not been finalized, subnational governments were not in a position to exercise their powers and to implement secondary legislation.[89] The Court held that although these circumstances may explain the difficulty of implementation, 'they do not expunge the failure of the Kingdom of Belgium to fulfil its obligations'. [90] It went on to recite its *locus classicus* in responsibility cases, namely that 'a Member State may not plead provisions, practices or circumstances in its internal legal system to justify failure to comply with obligations under [EU] directives'.[91] Internal arrangements, no matter their nature, may not lead to the exemption of responsibility of a Member State that fails to comply with its obligations. As masters of the Treaties, States are accountable. This was confirmed in *Commission v Netherlands* (1982) where the Netherlands was found to have failed to transpose a directive on the quality of bathing water.[92] In the Netherlands, the supervision of water quality was operated in a decentralized manner even if SNAs were under the control of national authorities.[93] The Court announced that 'each Member State is free to delegate powers to its domestic authorities as it considers fit and to implement the directive by means of measures adopted by regional and local authorities'.[94] This, however, does not 'release it from the obligation to give effect to the provisions of the directive by means of national provisions of a binding nature'.[95] Similarly, where the Italian Abruzzo region fell short of carrying out environmental impact assessments that were mandated by secondary legislation, the Italian State was found to have failed to comply with its obligations under EU law.[96]

Where a State fails to comply with a supranational judgment, it is equally prevented from blaming such lack of compliance on domestic arrangements.[97] In one instance, Belgium had argued that the delay in remedying its omission to transpose a directive was 'the result of special difficulties arising out of the transfer of a substantial number of powers to the new regional institutions in Belgium'.[98] Belgian legislation did not empower the federal executive to compel regional authorities to implement the directive, and the federal government found itself unable to independently transpose it.[99] The

[89] Ibid, para 4. [90] Ibid, para 5. [91] Ibid, para 5.

[92] Case 96/81 *Commission v Netherlands* [1982] EU:C:1982:192. [93] Ibid, para 11.

[94] Ibid, para 12. [95] Ibid, para 12.

[96] Case C-87/02 *Commission v Italy* [2004] EU:C:2004:363.

[97] Joined Cases 227–230/85 *Commission v Belgium* [1988] EU:C:1988:6.

[98] Ibid, para 6. [99] Ibid, para 8.

Court considered that this practical impossibility could not exempt Belgium from formal responsibility. While Member States are free to delegate powers internally as they see fit, issues arising from devolution do not release States 'from the obligation to ensure that the provisions of the directive are properly implemented in national law'.[100] It is worth noting that Member States' direct responsibility extends to financial responsibility. Where a Member State omits to rectify its failure to comply with EU law after a judgment has been issued against it, it is financially liable, notwithstanding which organ caused the failure.[101]

In some scenarios, States transpose directives but impose on SNAs the task to ensure compliance therewith. This happened in Spain in the context of a directive on water pollution.[102] The Directive had been transposed at national level by a law that attributed competence to the autonomous regions to establish the required action programmes.[103] When some autonomous communities failed to establish such programmes, Spain was declared to be in breach of its obligations under EU law, including the duty of loyal cooperation.[104] Spain's argument that it was unable to ensure the creation of action programmes was rejected as internal domestic arrangements cannot be relied on to justify a failure to comply with obligations under EU law.[105] Indeed, 'neither the division of powers as between the State and the autonomous regions nor the obligation to comply with directions given in the national legislation transposing the directive into national law can serve to justify failure to comply with the obligations imposed by the directive'.[106] Even if a failure to comply with EU law can be explained, this will not prevent the Court declaring the State to have infringed EU law or to hold that the State is obliged to bring such an infringement to an end.[107] States may accordingly not rely on internal constitutional arrangements to justify breaches of EU law.

[100] Ibid, para 9.

[101] Under Article 260 TFEU the Member State will be financially liable to pay a lump sum or penalty payment. This provision, inserted by the Maastricht Treaty, was first deployed by the Court in Case C-387/97 *Commission v Greece* [2000] EU:C:2000:356.

[102] Council Directive 91/676/EEC of 12 December 1991 concerning the protection of waters against pollution caused by nitrates from agricultural sources [1991] OJ L 375/1.

[103] Case C-274/98 *Commission v Spain* [2000] EU:C:2000:206.

[104] Ibid, para 12. See also Article 4(3) TEU.

[105] Case C-274/98 *Commission v Spain* [2000] EU:C:2000:206, paras 17–19.

[106] Ibid, 20.

[107] Case C-69/81 *Commission v Belgium* [1982] EU:C:1982:26, para 5. Case 96/81 *Commission v Netherlands* [1982] EU:C:1982:192, para 12. Joined Cases 227–230/85 *Commission v Belgium* [1988] EU:C:1988:6, paras 9–10; Case C-274/98 *Commission v Spain* [2000] EU:C:2000:206, para 20, Case C-383/00 *Commission v Germany* [2002] EU:C:2002:289, para 18, and Case C-358/03 *Commission v Austria* [2004] EU:C:2004:824, para 13.

As the fields of competence addressed by a directive do not necessarily reflect domestic divisions of competences, a single directive often has to be transposed by a number of actors. A directive on the prevention of major accidents which involve dangerous substances was for instance implemented by the federal level and the German Länder.[108] When some Länder failed to implement correctly, Germany was declared to be in failure of its obligations under EU law.[109] The Court did not accept that 'by reason of the number and complexity of the implementing measures necessary both at the federal and the Länder level, there were special circumstances which the Commission should have taken into account in accordance with the principle of cooperation'.[110] As a State may not plead internal arrangements 'including those resulting from its federal organisation' to justify failures to comply with EU law, Germany was responsible.[111] The Court has indeed affirmed time and time again that States cannot evade responsibility in claiming that they are unable to compel SNAs to transpose or adopt transposition measures on their behalf.[112] The fact that the central State has attempted to compel SNAs to end existing infringement is similarly irrelevant.[113] EU law goes further than merely holding Member States responsible for breaches committed by public authorities within its territory. It has in addition imposed an obligation on States to watch over SNAs implementing secondary legislation, and this even where States are not competent to do so under domestic power-sharing arrangements. The *Suckler Cow Premium* case established that Member States must watch over SNAs' implementation of supranational obligations.[114] Pursuant to the duty of loyal cooperation, enshrined in Article 4(3) TEU, States must supervise the application of EU law in their respective territory and bring possible infringements to an end.[115]

[108] Council Directive 96/82/EC of 9 December 1996 on the control of major-accident hazards involving dangerous substances [1997] OJ L 10/13.

[109] Case C-383/00 *Commission v Germany* [2002] EU:C:2002:289.

[110] Ibid, para 15. [111] Ibid, para 18.

[112] This was confirmed in Case C-358/03 *Commission v Austria* [2004] EU:C:2004:824 (the Court rejected Austria's argument that in light of domestic law it could not compel the regional government of Carinthia to adopt the measures necessary to transpose a European directive).

[113] Case C-103/01 *Commission v Germany* [2003] EU:C:2003:301 (the German Länder were in charge of transposing a directive dealing with protective equipment for fire fighters but failed to do so adequately as some of them added requirements not foreseen by the directive. Germany was found to be in violation of EU law despite proving its efforts that the SNA align its legislation with the directive).

[114] Case C-8/88 *Germany v Commission* (Suckler Cow Premium) [1990] EU:C:1990:241, para 3.

[115] See also: Case C-33/90 *Commission v Italy* [1991] EU:C:1991:476 where the Court held that Italy has a duty to supervise the correct implementation of EU legislation concerning toxic waste in the region or Calabria; Case 96/81 *Commission v Netherlands* [1982] EU:C:1982:192, para 12; Joined Cases 227–230/85 *Commission v Belgium* (1988) EU:C:1988:6, paras 9–10.

Member States' responsibility for their SNAs' shortcomings of course extends beyond the implementation of secondary law. Italy was for instance found to have engaged in discrimination on the basis of nationality and to have infringed Article 56 TFEU when some cities, including Florence, Venice, and Padua, set preferential rates to access museums, parks, and galleries for nationals of a Member State or residents above a certain age (hence excluding those of the same age living abroad).[116] Similarly, when the Flemish Parliament did not respect EU public procurement law in the context of the construction of its own premises, Belgium was liable notwithstanding the fact that according to domestic legislation, it could not adopt decisions concerning the conclusion and performance of contracts with regard to legislative bodies in light of the independence and supremacy of legislative authority under the Belgian constitution.[117]

It is, however, imperative to note that even though from the perspective of supranational law the Member State alone incurs liability for breaches of EU law, States are free to fashion domestic procedures to hold SNAs to account. Member States have indeed formulated various avenues that allow the State to claim damages from a local or regional authority subsequent to the CJEU's finding of responsibility. Numerous domestic mechanisms allow States to internally hold SNAs liable for their failure to comply with EU law and the subsequent finding of responsibility and financial loss the State suffered.[118] From the perspective of EU law the existence of such processes is however invisible and irrelevant.

The States' direct responsibility for breaches of EU law underlines that as masters of the Treaties they have special responsibility to ensure that obligations undertaken under the Treaties are carried out properly. This formalistic understanding of responsibility looks towards the result of the implementation process rather than modalities thereof.[119] This echoes *pacta sunt servanda* and the *effet utile* of EU law and further prevents supranational mingling with domestic power-structures. It also ensures the equality between Member States with different institutional structures, as making available an excuse to those of a decentralized nature would result in 'severe inequality in the treatment of States were one to admit the opening up of the unitary façade on which the law currently insists'.[120] The Court has indeed warned that 'it is not the task of the [EU] institutions to rule on the division of powers by the

[116] Case C-388/01 *Commission v Italy* [2003] EU:C:2003:30. [117] Ibid, para 40.

[118] See Article 169 of the Belgian Constitution, Article 117 (5) of the Italian Constitution and Article 23d (5) of the Austrian Constitution.

[119] Sacha Prechal, *Directives in EC Law* (Oxford University Press 1995) 69.

[120] Weatherill, 'The Challenge of the Regional Dimension in the European Union' (n 30) 2.

institutional rules proper to each Member State'.[121] The complete and effective implementation of EU law can indeed be 'more difficult in those Member States where power is shared or devolved to one or more sub-national bodies'[122] and can even be a 'source of conflict' in these States.[123] In treating the State as a monolithic entity EU law stays clear of intervening in that process. The section below examines the rules on indirect responsibility and reaches the conclusion that also in this domain Member States are subject to special obligations by virtue of their masters of the Treaties status.

### *e. Indirect responsibility*

The study of indirect responsibility under EU law unveils the same absence of a direct relation between SNAs and the EU as direct responsibility. Under the influence of the doctrine of monolithic statehood any breach of EU law by a national public authority is attributable to the State. The doctrine of indirect responsibility was initially crafted in *Francovich* and subsequently refined through cases such as *Brasserie du Pêcheur* and *Köbler*.[124] Indirect responsibility arises whenever 'the State' breaches a provision of EU law that confers rights upon individuals if the breach is sufficiently serious and there is a direct causal link between the breach and the harm. Under this doctrine, domestic courts must entertain suits for financial compensation that individuals bring against a State that fails to comply with EU law. Indirect responsibility is said to safeguard individual rights and the efficiency of the Treaties in ensuring that failures to comply with EU law are rectified.[125] In holding the masters of the Treaties responsible, the Treaties' institutional balance is safeguarded as the objectives pursued under EU law are achieved.

*Brasserie du Pêcheur* affirmed that the State is financially liable, 'whatever be the organ of the State whose act or omission was responsible for the

[121] Case C-95/97 *Région Wallonne v Commission* [1997] EU:C:1997:184, para 7. See also Case C-8/88 *Germany v Commission* [1990] EU:C:1990:241, para 13; Case C-33/90 *Commission v Italy* [1991] EU:C:1991:476, para 24.

[122] Ross and Crespo, 'The Effect of Devolution' (n 2) 210.

[123] Ibid, 212.

[124] Joined Cases C-6/90 and 9/90 *Francovich & Bonifaci v Italy* [1991] EU:C:1991:428; Joined Cases C-46/93 and 48/93, *Brasserie du Pêcheur/Factortame III* [1996] EU:C:1996:79; Case C-224/01 *Gerhard Köbler v Austria* [2003] EU:C:2003:513. For an overview of the literature on State liability, see Carol Harlow, 'Francovich and the Problem of the Disobedient State' (1996) 2 European Law Journal 199; Georgios Anagnostaras, 'The Allocation of Responsibility in State Liability Actions for Breaches of Community Law' (2001) 26 European Law Review 138 (hereafter Anagnostaras, 'The Allocation of Responsibility').

[125] This rationale was already present in Case 26/62 *Van Gend en Loos* [1963] EU:C:1963:1, para 13 where the Court found that 'the vigilance of individuals concerned to protect their rights amounts to an effective supervision in addition to the supervision entrusted by Article 169 and 170 to the diligence of the Commission and the Member States'.

breach'.[126] The notion of 'organ of the State' is understood to have 'both a horizontal and a vertical dimension. It encompasses all three branches of government but also decentralised entities and public emanations.'[127] In actions for indirect responsibility, the Member State will invariably be the defendant, notwithstanding whether the administration, the legislature, or the judiciary are at the origin of the breach.[128] States must ensure that individuals obtain reparation for damage caused to them due to non-compliance with EU law, no matter which organ is at the origin of that breach. For the purposes of this determination, it does not matter, from the perspective of EU law, which public authority is responsible for the breach and which public authority is, according to domestic arrangements, responsible for providing reparation for the damages flowing from the breach.[129] As a corollary of their direct responsibility under Article 258 TFEU, States alone are liable. This monolithic conception of the State, its legal indivisibility, has been amply reaffirmed where a subnational authority was at the origin of the breach.

*Konle* reaffirmed that Member States are subject to an obligation to make good damages caused by the unlawful actions of decentralized authorities.[130] The Court held that the State cannot 'plead the distribution of powers and responsibilities between the bodies that exist in its national legal order to free itself from liability on this basis'.[131] As a consequence, '[i]t is for each Member State to ensure that individuals obtain reparation for damage caused to them by non-compliance with [EU] law, whichever public authority is responsible for the breach and whichever public authority is in principle, under the law of the Member State concerned, responsible for making reparation'.[132] By virtue of their capacity as masters of the Treaties, States must ensure that the Treaties are respected on a domestic level. *Haim* and *Fuß* confirmed that, as a matter of EU law, Member States' obligation to provide reparation holds true notwithstanding which public authority is at the origin of the breach and responsible for providing reparation under national provisions.[133] Whereas the obligation to ensure that individuals obtain reparation lies exclusively with the State, the pecuniary funds do not necessarily have to stem from the latter. Rather, subject to the principles of equivalence and effectiveness, States can delegate the execution of their obligation to provide compensation to SNAs. A number of Member States dispose of mechanisms that allow the

[126] Ibid, para 32. [127] Anagnostaras, 'The Allocation of Responsibility' (n 124) 139.

[128] Case C-5/94 *Hedley Lomas* [1996] EU:C:1996:205.

[129] Case C-302/97 *Konle* [1999] EU:C:1999:271, para 62 (hereafter *Konle*); Case C-424/97 *Haim* [2000] EU:C:2000:357, paras 61–2 (hereafter *Haim*).

[130] *Konle* (n 129) para 62. [131] Ibid, para 62. [132] Ibid, para 62.

[133] *Haim* (n 129); Case C-429/09 *Günter Fuß* [2010] EU:C:2010:717.

national government to act against the SNA committing the breach of EU law on a domestic scale.[134] From the perspective of EU law, however, they are outsiders incapable of being direct interlocutors of the EU in this respect.

In *Haim* Advocate General Mischo recommended that SNAs be seen as insiders in the context of claims for indirect responsibility. He argued that in a democratic system liability should be the corollary of power and that there is a paradox in holding the State responsible for entities whose autonomy it must respect under national law.[135] This is interesting as the underlying assumption of this proposition is that SNAs are, just as the Member States, insiders. The Court, however, has never endorsed this view. As a matter of EU law, the corollary between power and responsibility is not given effect due to the attachment to the monolithic conception of statehood and practical effectiveness. Adopting Advocate General Mischo's conception would indeed have compelled the Commission and the Court to intervene in domestic power-sharing arrangements. As a consequence it seems fair to conclude that EU law maintains 'the traditional rule of international law that the Member States must be regarded as entities as regards to the fulfilment of obligations deriving from European law, as they are party to the treaties'.[136] Just as under the rules on direct responsibility, those on indirect responsibility reflect the special status Member States have as masters of the Treaties. This status is indeed a central characteristic of a Member State under the outsider narrative, as is the monolithic nature of statehood.

## 3. Member States are monolithic entities

The above examination of the rules on direct and indirect responsibility has already confirmed that Member States are monolithic entities given that any breach of supranational obligations by a domestic public authority is automatically attributed to the State. This section highlights additional instances illustrating the monolithic nature of the Member States, which constitutes a key characteristic of the narrative of SNAs as outsiders of EU law. The monolithic nature of statehood is of course a corollary of the principle of sovereign equality enshrined in Article 4(2) TEU, as a consequence of which EU law does not differentiate between Member States on the basis of their respective

[134] See in this regard Article 169 of the Belgian Constitution, Article 117 (5) of the Italian Constitution and Article 23d (5) of the Austrian Constitution.

[135] Opinion of Advocate General Mischo in Case C-424/97 *Haim* [2000] EU:C:1999:253.

[136] Maartje Verhoeven, 'The 'Costanzo Obligation' and the Principle of National Institutional Autonomy: Supervision as a Bridge to Close the Gap?' (2010) 3 Review of European Administrative Law 23, 25.

structure. This extends to Member States' acquisition or loss of territory. In the context of German reunification, the 'absorption' of the Eastern German Länder by what was then the Federal Democratic Republic was considered to fall under the 'moving treaty boundaries' rule by the European institutions.[137] Similarly when Algeria seceded from France in 1962 and Greenland withdrew from the EEC in 1985 France and Denmark's status as EU Member States went unaffected.[138] This section looks towards the doctrine of purely internal situations, the ordinary legislative procedure, and the Court's attachment to the State's legal indivisibility to underline the monolithic nature of statehood under EU law.

### a. *The doctrine of purely internal situations*

Pursuant to the doctrine of purely internal situations, the rules on the fundamental freedoms cannot be applied to activities that have no cross-border element.[139] This entails that subnational norms that discriminate against individuals, products, or services from other SNAs in the same Member State are not caught by EU law unless they also impact on other Member States. Scottish tuition fees serve as an example: Scottish universities distinguish fees depending on whether the student is a Scottish or EU student (lower fees) or an international student (higher fees). Whereas students from EU Member States must be charged the local rate as doing otherwise would be contrary to the principle of non-discrimination under Article 18(1) TEU and the Charter of Fundamental Rights, students from England, Wales, and Northern Ireland are subject to international fees.[140] While the principle of purely internal situations is well-established in the Court's adjudicative practice it has been subject to increased criticism.

The operation of this doctrine can be observed in *Flemish Care Insurance* the Flemish government argued that the consequences of its policies (an insurance scheme) were of a purely internal nature and thus outside the scope of EU law.[141] Under the doctrine EU law cannot be applied 'to activities which have no factor linking them with any of the situations governed by [EU]

[137] Jochen Frowein, 'The Reunification of Germany' (1992) 1 American Journal of International Law 86, 157–9.

[138] Merijn Chamon and Guillaume van der Loo, 'The Temporal Paradox of Regions in the EU Seeking Independence: Contraction and Fragmentation Versus Widening and Deepening?' (2014) 20 European Law Journal 613, 621.

[139] The doctrine of purely internal situations was first uttered in Case 175/78 *R v Saunders* [1979] EU:C:1979:88, para 11.

[140] Catherine Barnard, *The Substantive Law of the EU* (Oxford University Press 2010) 238.

[141] Case C-212/06 *Government of the French Community and Walloon Government v Flemish Government* [2008] EU:C:2007:398. On this case, see further Chapter 4.

law and which are confined in all relevant respects within a single Member State'.[142] The consequence of this doctrine, which has been subject to considerable criticism in recent years, is that subnational norms that discriminate against individuals, products, or services from other SNAs in the same Member State are not caught by EU law unless they also impact on other Member States.[143] The doctrine can be read as a corollary of the principle of national institutional autonomy, according to which EU law does not involve itself in matters purely internal to a State. This reflects the outsider narrative as there is a presumption that subnational and EU norms exist in different spheres and that, as a result, subnational policies cannot impact upon, and undermine, EU objectives, contrary to Member State measures. Under this doctrine subnational measures are treated unlike those of the Member States, as EU law does not apply to them. In *Flemish Care Insurance*, Advocate General Sharpston criticized the doctrine openly,[144] stating that:

> I must confess to finding something deeply paradoxical about the proposition that, although the last 50 years have been spent abolishing barriers to freedom of movement between Member States, decentralised authorities of Member States may nevertheless reintroduce barriers through the back door by establishing them within Member States. One might ask rhetorically, what sort of a European Union is it if freedom of movement is guaranteed between Dunkirk (France) and De Panne (Belgium), but not between Jodoigne and Hoegaarden?[145]

Despite such vivid criticism the Court decided not to abandon the doctrine of purely internal situations in *Flemish Care Insurance* but simply to hold that the situation at hand was not of a purely internal nature.[146] This illustrates that, while the doctrine is increasingly controversial, the Court is not ready to abandon it. It is nonetheless very exceptional for a situation to be qualified as purely internal. A recent illustration thereof can be found in an opinion of

[142] Para 33, citing Case 20/87 *Gauchard* [1987] EU:C:1987:532, paras 12–13; Case C-18/95 *Terhoeve* [1999] EU:C:2006:703, para 26.

[143] Miguel Poiares Maduro, 'The Scope of European Remedies: The Case of Purely Internal Situations and Reverse Discrimination' in Tonia Novitz, Claire Kilpatrick, and Paul Skidmore (eds), *The Future of European Remedies* (Hart Publishing 2000); Niamh Nic Shuibhne, 'Free Movement of Persons and the Wholly Internal Rule: Time to Move on?' (2002) 39 Common Market Law Review 731; Alina Tryfondiou, 'Reverse Discrimination in Purely Internal Situations: An Incongruity in a Citizen's Europe' (2008) 35 Legal Issues of Economic Integration 43.

[144] As Advocate General Tesauro had previously done in his opinion in Joined Cases C-363, 407–411/93 *Lancry & Others v Direction Générale des Douanes & Others* [1994] EU:C:1998:179, para 28.

[145] Opinion of Advocate General Sharpston in Case C-212/06 *Government of the French Community and Walloon Government v Flemish Government* [2008] EU:C:2007:398, para 116 (hereafter 'Opinion of Advocate General Sharpston').

[146] On this, see further Chapter 4.

Advocate General Szpunar. In *Gibraltar Betting and Gaming Association* the question of the Treaties' territorial scope of application was raised explicitly in the context of Article 56 TFEU.[147] In 2014 the UK had adopted a new fiscal regime on gambling duties that requires gambling providers to pay a duty in respect of services provided to 'UK persons' regardless of whether the provider is established in the UK or another State.[148] Gibraltar is a British Crown Colony that does not form part of the United Kingdom.[149] The Gibraltar Betting and Gaming Association (GBGA) challenged this decision, given that gambling services offered from Gibraltar to the UK were henceforth subject to such a fiscal burden, arguing that they breach Article 56 TFEU. The question for the Court was thus whether the UK and Gibraltar count as a single Member State, and, consequently, whether the doctrine of purely internal situations would apply.

Gibraltar put forward the argument that by virtue of its distinct constitutional status the provision of services between its territory and the UK should fall within the ambit of Article 56 TFEU so that any restrictions thereto must be justified.[150] Advocate General Szpunar suggested that 'for the purposes of Article 56 TFEU, Gibraltar and the UK are to be treated as one entity'.[151] As a consequence of the application of the doctrine of purely internal situations, Article 56 TFEU should not be triggered. He justified this stance in drawing on the monolithic nature of the Member States and their status as masters of the Treaties.

Article 28 of the Act concerning the Conditions of Accession and the Adjustments to the treaties holds that Gibraltar is not part of the Union's customs territory.[152] His analysis started with a reminder that by virtue of Article 52(1) TEU the Treaties apply to 28 Member States, drawing analogies with principles of public international law such as Article 29 of the Vienna Convention on the Law of Treaties.[153] The outsider narrative and its expressions are indeed firmly rooted in public international law, which had a particularly strong impact in the early decades of European integration. The Advocate General then drew attention to Article 355(3) TFEU

[147] See generally Eileen Denza, *British Overseas Territories Law* (Kluwer 2012) and Keith Azopardi, *Sovereignty and the Stateless Nation: Gibraltar in the Modern Legal Context* (Hart 2009).

[148] Opinion of Advocate General Sharpston, (n 145) para 1 of the opinion.

[149] Ibid, para 32 of the opinion.

[150] Ibid, para 21 of the opinion.

[151] Opinion of Advocate General Szpunar in Case C-591/15 *Gibraltar Betting and Gaming Association* [2017] EU:C:2017:32, para 4 (hereafter 'Opinion of Advocate General Szpunar').

[152] Act concerning the Conditions of Accession and the Adjustments to the Treaties of the Kingdom of Denmark, Ireland, and the United Kingdom of Great Britain and Northern Ireland [1972] OJ L73/14.

[153] Opinion of Advocate General Szpunar, (n 151) para 24 of the opinion.

according to which the Treaties apply to the European territories for whose external relations a State is responsible—as is the case with the UK and Gibraltar. Declaration No 55, although not legally binding, moreover states that 'the Treaties apply to Gibraltar as a European territory for whose external relations a Member State is responsible'.[154] As a consequence there was no doubt that there is a solid treaty basis for the application of the Treaties to Gibraltar. The Advocate General subsequently highlighted the United Kingdom's status as a master of the Treaty, stating that '[i]t is the UK and not Gibraltar that has assumed obligations towards the other Member States in ratifying the Treaties'.[155]

The above led the Advocate General to conclude that 'Article 355(3) TFEU does not add a new Member State. Ergo, Gibraltar and the UK cannot be other than a single Member State for the purposes of applying Article 56 TFEU'.[156] While the Court itself has not yet pronounced on the matter this expression of the outsider narrative is likely to have implications beyond the case at hand given that as a result of the 2016 Brexit vote, Gibraltar, where 96 per cent of those voting voted in favour of remaining in the EU, has attempted to identify avenues to stay within the internal market while the UK leaves.[157] While such claims would always have been anchored in shaky grounds, the opinion in *Gibraltar Betting and Gaming Association* casts even more doubt on such an option. We now move on to an illustration of the outsider narrative's grounding in bi-centricity.

### *b. The bi-centric nature of the ordinary legislative procedure*

This subsection provides a brief overview of the bi-centric structure of the ordinary legislative procedure. The institutions that participate in the making of EU secondary legislation represent either the Member States or the European Union, upholding the Treaties' bi-centric division of public authority. What is more, Member States are in this context always considered as monolithic entities speaking with a single voice. As a consequence, only the Member States and the EU are perceived as active makers and shakers of

[154] Ibid, para 26 of the opinion. [155] Ibid, para 37 of the opinion.

[156] Ibid, para 56 of the opinion.

[157] Adam Withnall, EU Referendum: 'Gibraltar Backs Remain in First Result of the Night' *The Independent* (London, 23 June 2016): http://www.independent.co.uk/news/uk/politics/eu-referendum-results-live-gibraltar-result-latest-remain-brexit-turnout-a7098626.html; Agence France Presse, 'Gambling Tax Blow as Gibraltar is Deemed 'One Entity' with UK' *The Guardian* (London, 20 January 2017): https://www.theguardian.com/world/2017/jan/20/britain-eu-politics-gibraltar-gambling-tax-brexit.

supranational law. While they consequently emerge as insiders, SNAs are passive outsiders to this decision-making process.

The ordinary legislative procedure governs supranational law-making and involves, on the one hand, the EU's various institutions as well as its Member States.[158] Under this procedure the Commission submits a legislative proposal to the European Parliament and the Council that must reach consensus on the proposal.[159] The European Commission represents the supranational interest and the European Parliament represents European citizens.[160] The Council, however, represents the Member States.[161] Its character is profoundly intergovernmental. Article 16(2) TEU provides that the Council 'shall consist of a representative of each Member State at ministerial level, who may commit the government of the Member State in question and cast its vote'.[162] The reference to representatives 'at ministerial level' was introduced by the Maastricht Treaty. The German Länder had pressed for such change so that regional ministers could participate in Council meetings.[163] We must wonder whether the option for supranational actors to participate in Council meetings elevates SNAs from an outsider to an insider status. According to Skoutaris, 'it is difficult to overstate the constitutional significance of this amendment that has survived all subsequent Treaty modifications. In essence, it questions—at least partially—the "federal blindness" thesis'.[164] When examined from the insider/outsider divide the provision doesn't, however, strike as revolutionary given that subnational representatives do not sit in the Council in their subnational capacity but rather as representatives 'of the Member State'. Article 16(2) TEU indeed allows regional officials to attend Council meetings but the crucial point is that, from the point of view of EU law, they do not sit as representatives of the SNA but of the State also engaging the State as a whole. This confirms the monolithic conception of statehood. No direct relation between the EU and SNAs emerges that would transform the latter into insiders as EU law views them as representing the Member State, upholding bi-centricity.

158 Article 13 TEU establishes a number of EU institutions, which create, execute, and arbitrate EU law.

159 Article 294 TFEU.

160 See Article 14(2) and 17(1) TEU respectively.

161 For a general overview of the Council's functioning, see Article 16 TEU.

162 Article 16(2) TEU.

163 The Council's rules of procedure also foresee that ministers may be accompanied by 'officials who assist them' which allows subnational representatives to travel with them. Also in this scenario, what is visible at EU level is the representative of the Member State. See Article 5(3) of Annex to Council Decision 2009/937/EU adopting the Council's Rules of Procedure [2009] OJ L325/35.

164 Skoutaris, 'The Role of Sub-State Entities' (n 23) 219.

We conclude that where the Member States are represented in the ordinary legislative procedure, they are perceived as monolithic units, speaking with a single voice, and this even under Article 16(2) TEU, which was intended to make room for subnational representation. In accordance with the outsider narrative, Member States have a particular status in the EU institutional framework, including privileges of representation to which SNAs cannot aspire. The consequence of this institutional configuration is that local and regional authorities cannot directly intervene in the supranational law-making process and they are not active contributors to its normative development.[165]

The monolithic conception of statehood under EU law has been said to entail a strengthening of the national level in internal power-relations. De Witte stressed that European integration leads 'to a reinforcement of the central State in its relation with autonomous sub-national institutions' given that all public authorities witness an erosion of their competences by the EU, but only Member States can compensate for this through their role in EU decision-making 'while the regions are excluded from the institutional structure of the [EU] and yet have to accept the consequences flowing from [EU] acts which they did not help to shape'.[166] Member States' insider status allows them to compensate for competence-transfers to the EU whereas this option is not available to SNAs. While the bi-centric nature of supranational policy-making can lead to a weakening of subnational authority, justifications have been brought forward. Weatherill has stressed that the main argument for denying SNAs any formal role in EU policy-making is that it 'would slow the process down and that it would create a risk of driving particular local preoccupations into the heart of a system that is meant to function on behalf of all European citizens'.[167] From the perspective of EU law, SNAs are thus comprised in the monolithic State structure, preventing them from independently contributing to the shaping of EU law. In this bi-centric structure, there is no room for subnational involvement, which is upheld by the CJEU's procedure.

[165] Daniel Wincott, 'The Governance White Paper, the Commission and the Search for Legitimacy' in Anthony Arnull and Daniel Wincott (eds), *Accountability and Legitimacy in the European Union* (Oxford University Press 2002) 379.

[166] Bruno de Witte, 'Community Law and National Constitutional Values' (1991) 18 Legal Issues of Economic Integration 1, 13.

[167] Stephen Weatherill, 'Finding a Role for the Regions in Checking the EU's Competence' in Stephen Weatherill and Ulf Bernitz (eds), *The Role of Regions and Sub-National Actors in Europe* (Hart Publishing 2005) 149.

### c. *The Court adheres to the monolithic nature of statehood under EU law*

As a corollary of monolithic statehood the Court doesn't investigate domestic institutional structures. This entails that it refrains from engaging with the specificities of domestic arrangements. In *Bero* (2014), for instance, the Court recalled that obligations arising under EU secondary legislation are 'imposed upon the Member States as such, and not upon the Member States according to their respective administrative or constitutional structures'.[168]

The monolithic nature of statehood can also be observed readily in those cases that compelled the Court to assess an SNA's regulatory measure without enquiring into the respective domestic context. In *Scotch Whisky* (2015), the ECJ had to assess whether planned Scottish legislation that would have imposed a minimum pricing scheme per unit of alcohol on alcoholic beverages was compatible with the free movement of goods under Article 34 TFEU.[169] It considered that while, in general, public health concerns are capable of justifying limitations on the free movement of alcoholic goods within the Union's internal market under Article 36 TFEU, the minimum pricing scheme would have hindered the market access of foreign producers, whose competitive advantage is low pricing.[170] As a result the Court suggested that Scotland should further its public health objectives through different measures that are less restrictive of trade.[171] In this context, the ECJ recommended that Scotland rely on the 'increased taxation' of alcoholic beverages.[172] Scotland, however, does not hold fiscal competence over alcoholic goods, making this option unavailable to it. This is indeed one of Westminster's reserved matters.[173] This results in a situation where the Court assesses subnational measures under the assumption that it is a Member State, a sovereign equal that has unlimited competence (except for those competences delegated to the EU). While this results in problematic situations for units such as Scotland, the same can be imagined in a scenario where the Court examines a Member State measure assuming that the Member State is in possession of all regulatory competence except for that delegated to the EU, whereas in fact, on a domestic scale, only an SNA and not the Member State can exercise the said competence. By virtue of treating Member States as monolithic black boxes, the Court accordingly doesn't take into consideration domestic subdivisions of power that reveal whether a given actor has or doesn't have regulatory competence over a given issue.

[168] Joined Cases C-473/13 and C-514/13 *Bero and Bouzalmate* [2014] EU:C:2014:2095, para 28.

[169] Case C-333/14 *Scotch Whisky* [2015] EU:C:2015:845.

[170] Ibid, para 46.

[171] Ibid, paras 39–41.

[172] Ibid, para 49.

[173] See Schedule 5 of the Scotland Act 1998.

This left the referring domestic court with a tough choice when deciding the case. The Scottish Court of Session ultimately decided that while the minimum pricing measure fell within the ambit of Article 34 TFEU, it could be justified under Article 36 TFEU.[174] The domestic court indeed disagreed with the ECJ's proportionality assessment in holding that minimum pricing achieves the targeted objective. When examining whether a tax scheme would, as put forward by the Luxembourg court, pursue the same objective, it considered that 'the elephant in the room is the fact that the Scottish Government has no power to raise taxation on alcohol. That is a matter reserved to the United Kingdom Government'.[175] The Scottish court thus openly addressed the ECJ's blindness regarding domestic institutional structures and concluded that the domestic measure was allowed to stand.[176] We now turn to the outsider narrative's attachment to paradigms of division and separate spheres of public authority.

### *d. The outsider narrative is characterized by the paradigms of division and separate spheres of public authority*

The outsider narrative is characterized by traditional notions of division and separate spheres of public authority. These paradigms are reflected nowhere as clearly as in the Treaties' rules on the division of regulatory competence. The Treaties consolidate the EU as a Union of conferred powers that can only exercise those competences that the Member States have conferred upon it.[177] The Treaty framework indeed maps regulatory authority as divided between two scales: the Member States and the EU. In the resulting scheme, States and the Union emerge as the only two scales of public authority with norm-generating abilities of relevance to the EU, leaving out any consideration for SNAs' regulatory autonomies. It follows that the outsider SNAs' competences are considered to bear no impact on European integration. An analysis of the Treaty provisions on the allocation of regulatory competence corroborates that finding.[178] Enumerations of competence in constitutional documents are common practice, and, since the Lisbon Treaty revision, such an enumeration also forms part of EU primary law.[179] This cataloguing of competences was

[174] *The Scotch Whisky Association and Others v The Lord Advocate and the Advocate General (2016)* [2016] CSIH 77 P762/12.

[175] Ibid, para 192.

[176] Ibid, para 205.

[177] See Articles 4(1), 5(1) and 5(2) TEU.

[178] The connected but separate issue of the exercise of such competence is examined later in this chapter.

[179] Articles 70–4 of the German Basic Law enumerate the competences of the federal government and the Länder respectively. See also Chapter 46 of the Scotland Act 1998.

considered necessary to counter the gradual acquisition of increased power by the EU in areas where competence had not unequivocally been conferred to it, also known as 'competence creep'.[180] The effort is also symptomatic of the current climate of competence as some States wish to ring-fence their own competences against those of the EU.[181]

From the perspective of EU law, regulatory competence can be divided alongside two static lines dividing the States and the Union. This creates two separate spheres of competence: the national and the supranational as underlined by Article 4(1) TEU, which recalls that competences not conferred on the Union remain with the Member States. This simplification of reality neglects that in many circumstances subnational authorities have regulatory competence under domestic arrangements—or at least presumes that the existence of these competences bears no influence on the supranational legal order. This is amply confirmed by the various provisions on the Union's exclusive, shared, coordinating, and complementary competence.[182] The distribution of public power between the Union and the States varies in these different constellations, yet the bi-centric nature of the provisions remains unaltered. In instances of exclusive competence Member States have (temporarily) ceded the exercising of public authority so that only the EU can regulate.[183] Spheres of exclusive EU competence, as defined by Article 3 TFEU, include the customs union, the establishment of competition rules in the internal market, and the common commercial policy. The EU is empowered to regulate in these domains whereas the Member States are excluded from doing so.[184]

The 'ordinary' mode of competence division is that of shared competence. Shared competence encompasses the internal market, social policy, environmental and consumer protection, as well as the area of freedom, security, and justice.[185] Article 2(2) TFEU provides that in instances of shared competence 'the Union and the Member States may legislate and adopt legally binding

[180] Mark Pollack, 'Creeping Competence: The Expanding Agenda of the European Community' (1994) 14 Journal of Public Policy 519; Stephen Weatherill, 'On Competence Creep and Competence Control' (2004) 23 Yearbook of European Law 1.

[181] For a general description of that climate, see Loic Azoulai, '"Integration Through Law" and Us' (2016) 14 International Journal of Constitutional Law 449.

[182] See Article 2 TFEU.

[183] Article 2(1) TFEU. On exclusive competences, see further Robert Schütze, 'Dual Constitutionalism Constitutionalised: the Emergence of Exclusive Competences in the EC Legal Order' (2007) 32 European Law Review 3.

[184] This does not however, at least in theory, deny Member States' status as masters of the Treaties as, pursuant to Article 48 TEU, they may revoke any of the EU's competences at any point.

[185] Also referred to as 'concurrent competences', these competences are governed by Article 4 TFEU.

acts'.[186] The Member States, however, shall 'exercise their competence to the extent that the Union has not exercised its competence' or when the Union has decided to cease exercising its competence. The text of primary law portrays competence as being divided in an either–or fashion between the supranational and national domains of public power.

The same spirit governs coordinating competences, which are defined by Article 2(3) TFEU to include economic, employment, and social policy.[187] In these domains, the EU has competence only to provide 'arrangements' for the Member States to exercise their competences in a coordinating manner. The exact scope of the coordinating competences is still somewhat unclear.[188] Notwithstanding the scope to be allocated to coordinating competences it is apparent that there is no space for any consideration of subnational competences as only the Member States and the Union are portrayed as regulators. Article 6 TFEU moreover refers to areas where the EU can 'support, coordinate or supplement' Member States' competences, such as culture, tourism, vocational training, youth, and administrative cooperation. Here, the EU has 'competence to carry out and to support, coordinate or supplement the actions of the Member States'.[189] Such complementary competence cannot, however, lead to the harmonization of national laws.[190] Again, regulatory competence is fashioned in a bi-centric manner and enshrines a presumption that clear lines between national and supranational regulatory power can be drawn.

This brief overview signals that the division of competences inherent to the EU Treaties is bi-centric. In accordance with the outsider narrative only the States and the Union are recognized norm-generators.[191] Any regulatory autonomy exercised within a Member State is considered to be that of the State—underlining the monolithic nature of statehood as well as the principle of national institutional autonomy. This ignores that, on a domestic scale, regulatory competence may be fragmented and that SNAs are important regulators.

[186] See also Protocol (No 25) on the Exercise of Shared Competence.

[187] See further Article 5 TFEU.

[188] Craig has situated them somewhere between shared and complementary competences. Paul Craig, 'Competence: Clarity, Conferral, Containment and Consideration' (2004) 29 European Law Review 338.

[189] Article 6 TFEU. [190] Article 2(5) TFEU.

[191] Articles 4(3) and 4(4) TFEU provide a somewhat more nuanced version of that principle. They provide that with regard to research, technological development, and space as well as development cooperation and humanitarian aid, the exercise of EU competence 'shall not result in Member States being prevented from exercising theirs'. This principle is, however, limited to individual thematic spheres and it is somewhat uncertain how it applies in practice.

The first section of the present chapter has examined a number of areas of EU law to reveal the predominance of two actors in EU law: the Member States and the EU. It is true that EU law acknowledges the existence of local and regional authorities, proving wrong any presumption of regional blindness. Crucially, however, SNAS are not acknowledged in the same capacity as Member States. The States are the masters of the Treaties that hold a privileged position. It will, however, be seen in Chapter 4 that some provisions of EU primary law make explicit reference to subnational autonomies. The next section will enquire whether such recognition has the potential to contradict the conclusions that have thus far been offered.

## 4. Explicit references to SNAs in the EU Treaties

The preceding analysis has highlighted that under the outsider narrative subnational authorities have a status significantly divergent from that of the States. Most expressions of the outsider narrative can be located in the EU Treaty framework. The next part of the present chapter engages with explicit references to SNAs in the Treaties. The central question that is explored is whether the explicit acknowledgement of local and regional authorities by primary law changes their outsider status to that of an insider.

The Treaties repeatedly refer to SNAs. The Preamble for instance provides that one of the objectives underlying the EU's creation is to reduce the differences between the EU's various regions.[192] Article 13 TFEU declares the EU's aim to protect 'cultural traditions and regional heritage'. Pursuant to Article 167(1) TFEU the EU shall moreover contribute to the flowering of common cultural heritage while respecting 'national and regional diversity'. Article 191(3) TFEU obliges the EU to account for 'environmental conditions in the various regions of the Union' when formulating environmental policy. Article 39(2)(1) TFEU embodies the same logic in providing that when the EU formulates its common agricultural policy, it shall account for 'structural and natural disparities between the various agricultural regions'. The Union shall moreover encourage cooperation with respect to natural or man-made disasters and support national, regional, and local efforts of risk prevention.[193] Under Article 170(1) TFEU, the EU shall contribute to the establishment of trans-European networks in the areas of transport, telecommunications, and energy infrastructures to allow citizens, economic operators, but also 'regional and local communities' to derive the full benefit of the internal market.

[192] Emphasis added. [193] Article 196(1)(a) TFEU.

Such references clearly illustrate that the EU is not blind towards the existence of SNAs. It is, however, unequivocal that they are unable to challenge SNAs' outsider status. The above provisions recognize the existence of the local and regional but not as an independent regulatory scale entertaining direct relations to the European Union. It is striking that most, albeit not all, of the provisions outlined refer to the regional, but not the local level. This is likely another sign that the Treaties are anchored in earlier stages of European integration where regions were more significant than localities. This is however subject to modification, as evidenced by the Pact of Amsterdam, which will be further discussed in Chapter 4.[194]

There are, however, two particular provisions of EU primary law, Articles 4(2) and 5(3) TEU, which seem more far-reaching in their recognition of local and regional authorities than the provisions enumerated above. As such they deserve more detailed attention. This chapter investigates whether the express references to SNAs in Articles 4(2) and 5(3) TEU contest the inference that SNAs are outsiders of the European legal order. It will be seen that this interrogation must be answered negatively. While both provisions are an attempt to recognize SNAs more fully in EU law, they fall short of recognizing them as insiders.

### a. *Article 4(2) TEU*

The first sentence of Article 4, paragraph 2 TEU, which was inserted into the framework of EU primary law in 2009, is phrased as follows:

> [t]he Union shall respect the equality of Member States before the Treaties as well as their national identities, inherent in their fundamental structures, political and constitutional, inclusive of regional and local self-government.

It is obvious that Article 4(2) TEU refers to subnational autonomies in a different manner from the provisions of primary law envisaged just above. Rather than portraying SNAs in a purely passive capacity Article 4(2) TEU recognizes that regions and localities 'self-govern', an activity that entails independent policy and law-making capacities. The Charter of Fundamental Rights of the European Union reproduces another version of what seems to be the same principle. According to the Charter's preamble the EU contributes to the preservation and development of common values 'while respecting the diversity of the cultures and traditions of the peoples of Europe as well as the national identities of the Member States and the organisation of their public authorities at national, regional and local levels ...'.

[194] Urban Agenda for the EU, *Pact of Amsterdam* (2016).

Article 4(2) TEU and the Charter mandate that the EU respect Member States' national identities, inclusive of regional and local self-government. These two provisions certainly contradict any theory of regional blindness.[195] From a terminological perspective, both clauses are particularly interesting as, unlike the provisions examined above, they recognize infra-State bodies as sites of self-government, rather than just as subjects affected by EU law. While definitions of 'self-government' may vary, it indeed seems plausible to assume that it can be understood to encompass regulatory autonomy. We must consequently wonder about the legal implications of SNAs' recognition as sites of self-government. Kingston noted that Article 4(2) TEU 'represents a considerable strengthening of emphasis' compared to its pre-Lisbon form that simply obliged the EU to respect Member States' national identities 'with no specific mention of regional and local self-government'.[196] The explicit reference to SNAs is noteworthy as a simple reference to 'national identity' could on its own have been understood to encompass domestic institutional structures, at least in those Member States with a constitutionally protected decentralized structure. The explicit reference to local and regional self-government accordingly puts a strong, and maybe stronger than needed, emphasis on SNAs. From my perspective the relevant question is whether SNAs are, as elsewhere in the Treaties, recognized as outsiders, or alternatively whether Article 4(2) TEU turns SNAs into insiders forming an integral part of the EU and its legal order and actively contributing to the latter's development.

A textual and contextual reading of Article 4(2) TEU indicates that the provision cannot be understood as transforming subnational authorities into insiders. The reference to subnational self-government forms part of a potentially open list of elements that constitute a Member State's national identity. By virtue of this new identity clause, EU law is compelled to respect Member States' identities—as expressed through their political and constitutional structures, and also 'regional and local self-government'. This is quite different from a direct respect for SNAs and their regulatory autonomies. Under Article 4(2) TEU, the recognition of SNAs is of a merely indirect nature, devolutionary arrangements being considered one of various characteristics that form part of national identity. This finding also seems to be confirmed by the reference to national identity in the Charter as this provision more clearly

[195] Ingolf Pernice, 'The Treaty of Lisbon: Multilevel Constitutionalism in Action' (2009) 15 Columbia Journal of European Law 349, 394 (stating that the reference to local and regional in Article 4(2) is a sign that the EU is no longer *landesblind*).

[196] Suzanne Kingston, 'The European Court of Justice and the Devolution of Taxation Powers' in Elke Cloots, Geert de Baere, and Stefan Sottiaux (eds), *Federalism in the European Union* (Hart Publishing 2012) 250.

supports such an interpretation.[197] Under this interpretation SNAs' outsider status remains intact, for their recognition by EU law is indirect through the Member State. No direct relation between SNAs and the EU is established.

Mandrino has advanced a different interpretation of Article 4(2) TEU, arguing that 'the new Treaty considers the regional and local dimension as an integral part of the complex institutional building of the EU'.[198] Recognizing SNAs as integral components of the EU's constitutional setting would mean that they are recognized as Member States' equals and thus insiders. Mandrino's interpretation does not, however, attract consensus. According to Lenaerts, Article 4(2) TEU should be understood as imposing 'a general obligation on the Union to respect Member States' fundamental political and constitutional structures as regards "regional and local self-government", which are an inherent part of their national identity'. [199] This, he goes on to argue, signifies that EU law does not as such oppose internal devolutions of power to SNAs.[200] This principle of non-interference is of a very different nature from the insider status. Whereas Article 4(2) TEU does not interfere with domestic institutional arrangements it falls short of modifying their status as defined elsewhere in the Treaties. While the modifications to the provision's text signal a willingness to acknowledge the existence of SNAs in the EU, Article 4(2) TEU should be read as 'a duty to respect national identity, including regional and local autonomy' rather than as a direct recognition of SNAs. [201] SNAs are not elevated to the same status as the Member States—they are recognized and respected—but they remain on the outside of the bipolar relationship between the Member States and the EU.

The position that Article 4(2) TEU recognizes SNAs only indirectly through the Member State's domestic arrangements finds support in two elements of its drafting history: first, its initial formulation under the draft Constitutional Treaty; and second by the Court's first application of Article 4(2) TEU's subnational dimension. The first draft of the Constitutional Treaty, published in early 2003, stated in its Article 9 that:

[197] It is unlikely that the framers of the Treaty of Lisbon would have intended to insert two references to national identity into the Treaties that carry a divergent interpretation.

[198] Claudio Mandrino, 'The Treaty of Lisbon and the New Powers of Regions' (2008) 10 European Journal of Legal Reform 519.

[199] Koen Lenaerts, 'EU Federalism in 3-D' in Elke Cloots, Geert de Baere, and Stefan Sottiaux (eds), *Federalism in the European Union* (Hart Publishing 2012) 16 (referring to Article 4(2) TEU).

[200] Ibid.

[201] Joxerramon Bengoetxea, 'Autonomous Constitutional Regions in a Federal Europe' in Gaert De Baere, Elke Cloots, and Stefan Sottiaux (eds), *Federalism in the European Union* (Hart 2012) 238 (hereafter Bengoetxea, 'Autonomous Constitutional Regions in a Federal Europe').

[t]he Union shall respect the national identities of its Member States, inherent in their fundamental structures and essential State functions, especially their political and constitutional structure, including the organisation of public administration at national, regional and local level.[202]

The reference to 'public administration' confirms SNAs to be largely passive implementers rather than active creators of norms. This interpretation is confirmed by the Court's first application of Article 4(2) TEU's subnational dimension in *Digibet*. Whereas this case is examined in further depth in Chapter 4, it should be noted that the Court considered that 'the division of competences between the [German] *Länder* cannot be called into question, since it benefits from the protection conferred by Article 4(2) TEU'.[203] The Court accordingly interprets Article 4(2) TEU as preventing EU intrusion into domestic power-sharing arrangements as expressed through its national identity.

Many questions related to the interpretation of Article 4(2) TEU remain unanswered, including the conceptualization of national identity in Member States devoid of a singular constitutional identity, such as (and maybe only) Belgium.[204] If the Court were to accept the lack of a common Belgian constitutional identity it would have to determine whether the identity of a region can be understood as that of the State.[205] Such questions can only be answered by future adjudication, if at all. While only time will tell how Article 4(2) TEU, and in particular its subnational dimension, will be given judicial meaning, it appears unlikely that SNAs' outsider status will be altered. SNAs are recognized indirectly, as component parts of the Member States whose special status is not called into question. It is imperative to note that doing so would bear the risk of infringing another component of Article 4(2) TEU: the 'equality of Member States'. Sovereign equality indeed mandates that Member States be treated as monolithic and abstract entities notwithstanding their decentralization formulae. It follows that while the reference to subnational authorities in Article 4(2) TEU has to be understood as an attempt to recognize the existence of localities and regions in EU law, it falls

[202] CONV 528/03 of 6 February 2003, Draft to Articles 1 to 26 of the Constitutional Treaty: http://www.whi-berlin.de/documents/cv00528.en03.pdf.

[203] Case C-156/13 *Digibet* [2014] EU:C:2014:1756, para 34.

[204] Stefan Graziadei, 'Belgian Constitutional Court Upholds the "Essential Elements" of Power Sharing Deal' (*I-CONnect Blog*, 28 January 2015), http://www.iconnectblog.com/2015/01/belgian-constitutional-court-upholds-the-essential-elements-of-power-sharing-deal/

[205] Ibid.

short of granting them an insider status. The subsequent section examines the reference to subnational autonomies in Article 5(3) TEU.

### *b. Article 5(3) TEU*

Subsidiarity is frequently cast as the posterchild of local and regional autonomies, and the coexistence of different scales of public authority, in the EU.[206] This is in particular so since the recognition of subsidiarity in primary law has been revised by the Lisbon Treaty to include a reference to SNAs. Again, the question that emerges is whether local and regional authorities are portrayed as insiders or outsiders of EU law. Article 5(3) TEU reads as follows:

> [u]nder the principle of subsidiarity, in areas which do not fall within its exclusive competence, the Union shall act only if and in so far as the objectives of the proposed action cannot be sufficiently achieved by the Member States, either at central level or at regional and local level, but can rather, by reason of the scale or effects of the proposed action, be better achieved at Union level.

Subsidiarity, especially its post-Lisbon formulation, can be understood as an attempt to move away from the bi-centric treaty framework that represents the public international law roots of EU law. Some have asserted that with the entry into force of Article 5(3) TEU, 'subsidiarity now penetrates below the Member State level, and requires examination of the regional issues'.[207] Yet, even in its newly revised form subsidiarity fails to establish SNAs as insiders of EU law. Subsidiarity intervenes as a pre-legislative device the primary role of which consists in the regulation of the exercise of regulatory competence.[208] In areas of non-exclusive EU competence, such as customs policy and competition policy, subsidiarity unveils which level of public authority should realize a given objective.[209] Despite its limited practical role, the spirit of subsidiarity has acquired an almost mythical existence in EU circles.[210] The normative considerations attached to subsidiarity, for instance that it can be 'a way of enhancing pluralism and the diversity of national values',[211] are seen to have a wider meaning in EU law. Subsidiarity has also been labelled as 'a principle constitutive

[206] This is not least reflected by Article 5(3) TEU which henceforth refers also to the local and regional levels of government.

[207] Bengoetxea, 'Autonomous Constitutional Regions in a Federal Europe' (n 201) 238.

[208] Vlad Constantinesco, 'La subsidiarité comme principle constitutional de l'intégration européenne' (1991) 46 Aussenwirtschlaft 411.

[209] Article 3 TFEU.

[210] See inter alia Gráinne de Búrca, 'Reappraising Subsidiarity's Significance After Amsterdam' (2000) Harvard Jean Monnet Working Paper 7/99.

[211] Paul Craig, 'Subsidiarity: A Political and Legal Analysis' (2012) 50 Journal of Common Market Studies 72, 73.

of a multilevel governance in Europe',[212] an 'opponent' to sovereignty[213] that 'works as an element connecting the different levels of governance and government and as a technique of making flexible the map of competences drawn by the treaties or the constitutions'.[214] These descriptions appear to indicate that subsidiarity signals a distancing from some key features of the outsider narrative such as the division of regulatory spheres and bi-centricity. As de Búrca has, however, noted Member States' attempt to set competence boundaries in the Treaties 'reflects a more fundamental wish to protect the integrity of the boundaries of the state polity'.[215] Subsidiarity was indeed not designed to orchestrate the collaboration between various actors in multi-level Europe but rather to designate which actor, to the exclusion of others, has regulatory competence. When making that assessment no formal attention is given to SNAs as sites of regulatory authority despite Article 5(3) TEU's reference to the local and regional levels. This envisages the isolation rather than fusion of the various levels of public authority in the EU.

This conclusion is anchored in the fact that Article 5(3) TEU establishes a two-part, not a three-part test. It enquires whether the goals of the proposed action can be sufficiently achieved by the Member States (either at central, regional, or local level) and determines that if this is not the case it is for the EU to regulate. Article 5(3) TEU does *not* enquire whether (i) the objectives can be best achieved at subnational level, (ii) if not at national level, and that if that is not so then (iii) the case for supranational legislation is made.[216] The local and regional level are recognized to exist, but only indirectly, as it is for the Member States to decide whether they should regulate. This choice is, however, purely for the Member States to operate on a domestic scale and the EU is indifferent to the States' choice.

We must thus conclude that under Article 5(3) TEU either the national or the supranational is the appropriate scale of regulation. In the former

[212] Ken Endo, 'Subsidiarity and Its Enemies: To What Extent is Sovereignty Contested in the Mixed Commonwealth of Europe?' (2001) EUI Working Paper RSC 2001/24, 24 (hereinafter Endo, 'Subsidiarity and Its Enemies').

[213] Ibid.

[214] Guiseppe Martinico, 'Dating Cinderella: On Subsidiarity as a Political Safeguard of Federalism in the European Union' (2011) 6 European Public Law 652.

[215] Gráinne de Búrca, 'Setting Constitutional Limits to EU Competence?' (2001) Faculdade de Direito da Universidade Nova de Lisboa, Francisco Lucas Pires Working Paper Series on European Constitutionalism, Working Paper 2001/02, 12.

[216] This gives rise to a presumption that the Member State should in principle regulate unless there are compelling reasons for the EU to do so. As seen further below, this is not, however, how the principle operates in practice. See also Adam Cygan, 'The Parliamentarisation of EU Decision-Making? The Impact of the Treaty of Lisbon on National Parliaments' (2011) 36 European Law Review 478, 481 (hereafter Cygan, 'The Parliamentarisation of EU Decision-Making?').

scenario, it is for the State to decide whether to regulate in a centralized or decentralized manner. This maintains the monolithic conception of statehood inherent in the outsider narrative as from the perspective of EU law the Member State is the regulating instance. While the State may designate SNAs as regulators, EU law does not directly engage with their norm-generating capacity, as, from its perspective, it does not matter whether the Member State legislates at central, regional, or local level. Any such regulation is considered to be that of the State. This sketches a division of public authority alongside two centres: the national and the supranational. Article 5(3) TEU admits the existence of SNAs but only recognizes them in a passive vein, as outsiders, as it is does not itself designate them to constitute norm-generating scales. Article 5(3) TEU indeed leaves it to the Member States to 'decide according to their own constitution whether to apply the principle domestically as well'.[217]

The preceding conclusion of course does not deny that Article 5(3) TEU's altered textual formulation could be seen as an attempt to move away from the State-centric, public international law dominated, outsider narrative paradigm. It is true that the very motivation behind the introduction of the principle into primary law was to safeguard the autonomy of smaller units[218] and to counter the fear of over-centralization.[219] The German Länder indeed played a prominent role behind the insertion of subsidiarity into the Maastricht Treaty.[220] Subsidiarity has not, however, been able to change the status of SNAs from that of outsiders to insiders of EU law. A similar conclusion emerges from the examination of the Protocol No 2 on the application of the principles of proportionality and subsidiarity.

### 1) Protocol No 2 on the application of the principles of subsidiarity and proportionality

The new formulation of Article 5(3) TEU is not the sole innovation brought about by the Lisbon Treaty with regard to subsidiarity. Henceforth there is also a revised version of Protocol No 2 on the application of the principles of subsidiarity and proportionality, which leads to a procedural thickening

[217] Reimer von Borries and Malte Hauschild, 'Implementing the Subsidiarity Principle' (1999) 5 Columbia Journal of European Law 374 (hereafter von Borries and Hauschild, 'Implementing the Subsidiarity Principle').

[218] Antonio Estella, *The EU Principle of Subsidiarity and Its Critique* (Oxford University Press 2002) 80.

[219] Endo, 'Subsidiarity and Its Enemies' (n 212) 25.

[220] Von Borries and Hauschild, 'Implementing the Subsidiarity Principle' (n 217) 371–2.

of the principle.[221] This reinforcement of subsidiarity's procedural dimension has been said to be 'giving new shape to the principle of subsidiarity after Lisbon'.[222] Protocol No 2 refers, on a number of occasions, to SNAs.[223] Its Article 2 provides that before proposing legislative acts, the Commission 'shall consult widely. Such consultation shall, where appropriate, take into account the regional and local dimension of the action envisaged'.[224] This requirement mandates that the Commission consult various actors, including SNAs, in the context of its own legislative activity. This should not be confused with an acknowledgement of SNAs as insiders: the regulating authority remains the Commission and SNAs are seen as outsiders upon which EU legislation has an impact, not actors that actively contribute to the shaping of EU legislation.

Article 5 of Protocol No 2 establishes that EU directives must contain an assessment of 'the rules to be put in place by Member States, including, where necessary, the regional legislation'.[225] This requirement seeks to ascertain the impact of EU legislation on domestic authorities in their implementing capacity. SNAs are seen as passive outsiders giving effect to supranational rules rather than as independent regulators. Article 5 of Protocol No 2 further provides that EU draft legislative acts shall account for financial and administrative burdens 'falling upon the Union, national governments, regional or local authorities, economic operators and citizens, to be minimized and commensurate with the objective to be achieved'. Also in this context SNAs are seen as actors subject to EU law and supranational institutions are required to be sensitive to the effects supranational regulation has on them without creating any direct rights of SNAs vis-à-vis the EU.

Under Protocol No 2, the Committee of the Regions has moreover been granted the power, in some circumstances, to bring actions before the Court for the infringement of Article 5(3) TEU.[226] This has already been examined in the section on *locus standi* and it has been seen that, under some circumstances, this provision allows SNAs to collectively challenge an EU legislative act. It does not, however, assimilate SNAs to the insider Member States. We conclude that these various provisions recognize SNAs' existence and EU law's impact on them. The relationship between SNAs and the EU is, however, of a purely indirect nature and does not elevate SNAs to an insider

[221] Sanja Bogojevíc and Xavier Groussot, 'Subsidiarity as a Procedural Safeguard of Federalism' in Loic Azoulai (ed), *The Question of Competence in the European Union* (Oxford University Press 2014) 234.

[222] Ibid.

[223] Protocol (No 2) on the Application of the Principles of Subsidiarity and Proportionality [2008] OJ C115/206 (hereafter referred to as 'the Subsidiarity Protocol' or 'Protocol No 2').

[224] Article 2 of Protocol No 2.

[225] Article 5 of Protocol No 2.

[226] Article 8 of Protocol No 2.

status. The same conclusion will be reached after an examination of the Early Warning System, an additional innovation enshrined in Protocol No 2.

### 2) The early warning system

Article 4 of Protocol No 2 obliges the Commission, the European Parliament, and the Council to forward draft legislative acts to national Parliaments.[227] The 'Early Warning System' (EWS) is a 'pre-legislative constitutional intervention device'[228] designed to give national Parliaments, which have lost power as a result of European integration, a say in the EU legislative process.[229] A looser form of cooperation with national parliaments had already entered into force in 2006 after the Commission declared in its Barroso Initiative that it would welcome letters from national parliaments as part of a wider political dialogue.[230] The EWS allows national parliaments to issue a reasoned opinion when they believe that an EU draft legislative act violates subsidiarity. If more than one-third of national parliaments raise a reasoned opinion, a 'yellow card' is triggered and the proposal must be reviewed.[231] The initiating institution can, however, decide to maintain, amend, or withdraw the draft and must provide reasons for its decision.[232] If the reasoned opinions represent at least half of all votes assigned to national Parliaments, an 'orange card'[233] is triggered and the Commission must review the draft legislative act, and may decide to maintain, amend, or withdraw the draft. If it decides to maintain the draft, it must issue a reasoned opinion on the draft's compliance with Article 5(3) TEU.[234] The reasoned opinion is subsequently forwarded to the European Parliament and Council who have the final word on the matter.[235]

[227] Article 4 of Protocol No 2 moreover imposes an obligation on the Commission and the European Parliament to forward their amended drafts to national Parliaments.

[228] Cygan, 'The Parliamentarisation of EU Decision-Making?' (n 216) 481.

[229] The EWS has been described as a 'sugar-coating' for the bitter process that is EU integration for national parliaments. Philipp Kiiver, 'The Treaty of Lisbon, the National Parliaments and the Principle of Subsidiarity' (2008) 15 Maastricht Journal of European and Comparative Law 77, 77.

[230] 'Communication from the Commission to the European Council—A citizens' agenda—Delivering results for Europe' COM (2006) 211 final.

[231] Jean-Victor Louis, 'The Lisbon Treaty: The Irish "No": National Parliaments and the Principle of Subsidiarity—Legal Options and Practical Limits' (2008) 4 European Constitutional Law Review 429, 438 (hereafter Louis, 'The Lisbon Treaty: The Irish "No"').

[232] See Article 7(2) of Protocol No 2. According to Article 6 of the Protocol, national Parliaments have eight weeks from the date of transmission of a draft legislative act to send a reasoned opinion. The threshold is one-quarter in the case of a draft legislative act based on Article 76 TFEU.

[233] Louis, 'The Lisbon Treaty: The Irish "No"' (n 231) 438 (arguing that the orange card owes its name to the Dutch name of the complementary mechanism).

[234] Article 7(3) of the Protocol No 2.

[235] The legislative proposal can be halted by a vote of 55 percent of the votes in the Council or a majority in the Parliament.

The EWS gives effect to Article 12 TEU, pursuant to which national parliaments contribute actively to the good functioning of the Union.

Article 6 of Protocol No 2's reference to 'national' parliaments leads us to enquire whether, and if so to what extent, regional parliaments participate in the EWS' operation. Regional parliaments are indeed just as likely as national parliaments to lose some of their decision-making abilities as a consequence of European integration. Five distinct avenues for subnational involvement in the EWS can be pinpointed. First, Article 6 of Protocol No 2 provides that it is for each national parliament 'to consult, where appropriate, regional parliaments with legislative powers'. This reflects that European integration not only affects national, but also subnational political power. Subnational competence is, however, merely recognized in an indirect manner.[236] It is through the State that regional parliaments are consulted, not directly by the EU, and States have discretion whether they wish to do so. No direct relation between the subnational and supranational scales emerges. Second, SNAs may participate in the EWS in those Member States with a bicameral parliamentary system in which one chamber is composed of regional representatives. In this case this chamber will have one of the two votes attributed to each national parliament. This is for instance the case in the German and the Austrian Bundesrat.[237] The EWS allows regional parliaments to intervene in EU decision-making. From the perspective of EU law, however, such parliaments are 'national' parliaments acting on behalf of the State. Third, regional parliaments can be considered as national parliaments by specific provision. Declaration 51 specifies that

> Belgium wishes to make clear that, in accordance with its constitutional law, not only the Chamber of Representatives and Senate of the Federal Parliament but also the parliamentary assemblies of the Communities and the Regions act, in terms of the competences exercised by the Union, as components of the national parliamentary system or chambers of the national Parliament.

Belgium has created an explicit avenue for its regional parliaments to be recognized as 'national parliaments'. This allows regional legislatures to directly intervene in the EWS without the need to pass through a second chamber at national level. Just as under Article 16(2) TEU, which allows regional

[236] On this, see also Bengoetxea, 'Autonomous Constitutional Regions in a Federal Europe' (n 201) 238.

[237] See also Philipp Kiiver, 'The Conduct of Subsidiarity Checks of EU Legislative Proposals by National Parliaments: Analysis, Observations and Practical Recommendations' (2012) ERA Forum 535, 544; Josu Osés Abando, 'Early Warning and Regional Parliaments: In Search of a New Model. Suggestions from the Basque Experience' (2013) 5 Perspectives on Federalism 74 (hereafter Abando, 'Early Warning and Regional Parliaments').

ministers to act as Member State ministers in the Council, Declaration 51 allows the involvement of regional parliaments not, however, in their own capacity but representing the State. Fourth, a number of domestic procedures enable SNAs to transmit concerns related to EU draft legislative acts to a national parliament, which may then include them in its own reasoned opinion. Some of the Spanish regions' statutes of autonomy for example provide for participation in subsidiarity control.[238] Abando has noted that this has allowed the Basque chamber to make 'specific contributions' with regard to subsidiarity monitoring but also that this mechanism 'does not guarantee the taking into account of the contributions by the regional parliaments'.[239] From the perspective of EU law, such procedures are invisible: what the EWS sees is solely the final reasoned opinion submitted by the national Parliament. The former Commission President Barroso in fact recognized in 2012 that the Commission 'has no information as to the involvement of the respective regions in the elaboration and adoption of these opinions'.[240] In 2011, the Commissioner for Interinstitutional Relations and Administration stated that 'the Commission does not take account of the extent to which opinions of the regions are reflected in reports forwarded by the Member States'.[241] While all of these evolutions are of much interest, they occur within a State, which EU law continues to see as a monolithic entity. SNAs remain outsiders, only involved in EU legislative affairs indirectly through their Member State.

Finally, SNAs participate in subsidiarity review indirectly and collectively through the Committee of the Regions (CoR), which can initiate actions against legislative acts for the adoption of which the Treaties provide that it is to be consulted.[242] This avenue, which has already been examined, does not form part of the EWS but it is worth briefly mentioning it since it also engages with subsidiarity review.[243] However, as has already been seen, SNAs can only act collectively and indirectly through this mechanism, as they need to agree on the action with the other members of the CoR and then act as the CoR, not individual SNAs.

[238] Abando, 'Early Warning and Regional Parliaments' (n 237) 78.

[239] Ibid, 74.

[240] Question for written answer by MEP Izaskun Bilbao Barandica (ALDE) on the statistics on the early warning process, no. E-5865/2010, at http://www.europarl.europa.eu/sides/getDoc.do?pubRef=-//EP//TEXT+WQ+E-2010-5865+0+DOC+XML+V0//EN.

[241] Question for written answer E-009555/2011 on the Committee of the Regions and early warning system: http://www.europarl.europa.eu/sides/getDoc.do?pubRef=-//EP//TEXT+WQ+E-2011-009555+0+DOC+XML+V0//EN.

[242] Article 8 of Protocol No 2.

[243] Adam Cygan, 'The Regions Within Multi-Level Governance: Enhanced Opportunity for Improved Accountability?' (2014) 21 The Maastricht Journal of European and Comparative Law 265, 274.

The overview of the above provisions has confirmed that Protocol 2 is a 'state-centric process of subsidiarity review whose objective is to improve the accountability of, and inject democratic legitimacy into, what continues to be an equally state-centric legislative process'.[244] It is not, however, a mechanism that allows SNAs to directly interact with the supranational level as insiders. While the EWS offers a number of options for SNAs to indirectly participate in subsidiarity review, these avenues differ greatly from those available to Member States. This lack of direct intervention has been criticized by associations representing SNAs. Especially regions with legislative competence consider the current state of affairs to be unsatisfactory. The Conference of European Regional Legislative Assemblies (CALRE) demanded that regional parliaments with legislative competences be able to take legal action before the CJEU in areas falling within the scope of their competences.[245] The CoR has also repeatedly called for an extension of SNAs' standing,[246] both indirectly through the Committee but also through granting SNAs with legislative powers standing before the Luxembourg Court. For the time being, SNAs, however, cannot aspire to the privileged status that Member States hold as masters of the Treaties.

This section has revealed that while subsidiarity can be seen as a mechanism supposed to recognize SNAs in EU law, they in fact remain outsiders. Article 5(3) TEU mandates that the Member States—either at central or subnational level—achieve the objectives of the proposed action, and that, if this proves impossible, it is for the Member States to fulfil that task. This formulation underscores that there are two levels at which objectives can be achieved: the Member State and the EU. When the Member State is considered the appropriate scale, it is for the latter to decide the modalities of such action, and evaluate whether it should do so in a centralized or decentralized manner. Article 5(3) TEU merely recognizes the Member State's choice rather than SNAs' ability to participate. The same conclusion has been reached with regard to the EWS, which, while creating a number of options for SNAs to

[244] Ibid, 265.

[245] CALRE, Declaration of Innsbruck (2009) 5, available under http://www.calrenet.eu/index.php/documents/declarations.

[246] Opinion of the Committee of the Regions on the Revision of the Treaty on European Union and of the Treaty establishing the European Community (1996) OJ C100/1, Opinion of the Committee of the Regions on The 2000 Intergovernmental Conference (2000) OJ C156/6, para 5.13; Opinion of the Committee of the Regions on the Draft Report of the European Parliament on the Division of Powers between the European Union and the Member States (2002) OJ C192/31, para 3.11; Opinion of the Committee of the Regions on the Treaty establishing a Constitution for Europe (2005) OJ C71/1, para 1.28.

intervene in this process indirectly, offers no direct avenues of participation to them—they remain outsiders.

This chapter has exposed a number of areas of EU law in which local and regional authorities emerge as outsiders of the EU legal order. This does not mean that EU law is blind towards the existence of SNAs. Rather, the notion of outsider reflects that SNAs do not form part of the privileged relationship between the Member States and the European Union, the structure that the Member States have created and continue to control. In accordance with the outsider narrative, Member States are sovereign equals, a status deriving from their capacity as masters of the Treaties. Each State has the same status, rights, and obligations irrespective of their geographical and demographic size, economic magnitude, and internal structure. They are perceived as monolithic entities. It follows that the EU and the Member States are the only two levels of public authority the existence of which is integrally acknowledged by EU law. EU law emergences as a bipolar structure in which there is no space for SNAs. As a consequence of SNAs' outsider status, they are primarily conceived of as actors that implement—and are subject to—EU norms. Unlike Member States, EU law does not consider the regulatory autonomies that SNAs have to constitute a limit of EU law worthy of protection. SNAs are outsiders to the institutional balance between the EU and the Member State; they are passive recipients of EU law. The subsequent chapter, however, illustrates that this conclusion is not valid for all areas of EU law.

# 4

# The Insider Narrative

## Introduction

The insider narrative captures that beyond the formal letter of EU law a parallel yet distinct narrative can be identified according to which SNAs are insiders of supranational law and its substantive development. This narrative becomes apparent if we shift our attention away from formal status and towards the manifold functional interconnections that have emerged between various levels of public authority over the past decades. Despite the absence of any formal space for them to do so, SNAs have, via the relations they entertain, taken on a pivotal role in the administration of EU law and the development of the supranational legal order. As a result they have in some respects acquired an insider status that is in many manners analogous to that of the Member States. Chapter 1 has already indicated that this insider status modifies not merely the status of SNAs in Union law but also the nature of the European legal order itself, which is characterized by ever more polycentricity and porosity. Polycentricity indicates that the Union is made up and shaped by a plurality of nodes of public authority rather than just two, whereas porosity denotes that the borders delimitating these spheres are porous, permitting mutual cross-fertilization and intertwining to occur.

This chapter traces polycentricity and porosity in various areas of EU law and moreover charts four distinct dynamics that frame SNAs' insider status. First, that SNAs are capable of influencing EU law's substantive development. Numerous examples highlight that the interaction between subnational and supranational norms is capable of modifying EU law's substantive core. It will be seen, second, that subnational authorities have become allies in the achievement of supranational objectives. Third, we will observe how porosity allows subnational norms to influence EU law and it will be documented; fourth, that polycentricity emerges as the most accurate description of the structure of EU law. Fifth, the chapter will illustrate the assimilation between Member States and SNAs in many domains of Union law, and we will lastly see that, in their capacity as market participants, SNAs are insiders for they cannot merely be equated with private market participants. Before embarking on that venture a word of caution in relation to the structure of the present chapter is in order. This chapter examines case law and policy initiatives that underline local and regional authorities' insider status. To this end, it has been subdivided into various sections and sub-sections that each portray a particular characteristic of the insider narrative that plays out most strongly in that respective area. Yet, as we will see, the instruments covered, however, embody more than one illustration of the insider narrative so that this chapter's form is explained as a matter of structuring ample material rather as a substantive imperative. We shall commence with an overview of SNAs' capacity to contribute to the substantive development of supranational law.

## A. SNAs as Contributors to EU Law's Substantive Development

The outsider narrative takes for granted that only Member States contribute to EU law's substantive development. The modalities of treaty-making and the ordinary legislative procedure allocate a central role to the masters of the Treaties but do not provide any room for the involvement of SNAs. From a formal perspective local and regional authorities are thus at the outside of the generation of EU norms. Once our perspective shifts to that of EU law's informal development through the Court's case law a different conclusion emerges. In its adjudicative practice the Luxembourg Court indeed doesn't distinguish between norms of national and subnational origin. Given that it treats both sets of norms in the same manner, subnational norms can, just like national norms, contribute to supranational law's substantive development. This can be readily observed in the *Omega* case. This case will be examined in more detail than all other cases subject to analysis here. While a lengthy analysis of multiple cases would be unfeasible, the isolation of a single judgment enables us to survey the Court's analysis for its significance for the subnational dimension in detail.

### 1. The *Omega* case

*Omega* is one of those cases known to any student of EU law.[1] When the Court decided in 2004 that the freedom to provide services, a cardinal

[1] Case C-36/02 *Omega Spielhallen-und Automatenaufstellungs-GmbH v Oberbürgermeisterin der Bundeststadt Bonn* [2004] EU:C:2004:614 (hereafter *Omega*).

principle of market integration, could be restricted by a national measure that aims at the protection of public policy and human dignity, scholarly ink was flowing eagerly.[2] Different authors explored the case from different perspectives. Some were concerned with its implications for the fundamental economic freedoms, others with the classification of human dignity as a general principle, and yet others were interested in the status of national constitutional identities in EU law.[3] *Omega,* however, also allows us to pinpoint SNAs' contributions to EU law's substantive development. It is well known that SNAs are creators of norms that affect their own territory, and receivers and implementers of national and supranational norms. *Omega,* however, reveals that SNAs moreover generate norms, the impact of which exceeds the national territory. It allows us to observe that in the polycentric Union the borders between scales of public authority are porous, allowing subnational norms to influence those at supranational level.

Omega, a German company, operated a laserdrome in the city of Bonn, which is located in North Rhine Westphalia. Laserdromes are installations in which 'laser sport' takes place, an activity where players use targeting devices to hit sensory tags fixed on the installations and also the jackets of other players. Following demonstrations by the local population Bonn's mayor prohibited the operation of the game on the ground that it involved 'playing at killing' individuals. The city issued this prohibition on the basis of legislation of North Rhine Westphalia that entrusted localities with averting risks to public order.[4] Bonn had operated an independent normative assessment given that at the time (and still today) there was no consensus in Germany regarding the

[2] As the Court explained, the order prohibiting Omega from operating its laserdrome affected both the freedom to provide services and the free movement of goods. It is settled case law that in such scenarios the measure will be examined in relation to just one of the fundamental freedoms if one of them is entirely secondary in relation to the other. In *Omega*, the freedom to provide services prevailed over the free movement of goods (paras 24–8 of *Omega* (n 1)).

[3] For an overview of the literature see Alberto Alemanno, 'À la recherche d'un juste équilibre entre libertés fondamentales et droits fondamentaux dans le cadre du marché intérieur. Quelques réflexions à propos des arrêts « Schmidberger » et « Omega »' (2004) Revue du Droit de l'Union Européenne 709; Jürgen Bröhmer, 'Anmerkung zum Urteil des EuGH vom 14.10.2004 in der Rechtssache C-36/02, Omega Spielhallen und Automatenaufstellungs-GmbH' (2004) Zeitschrift für Europäisches Wirtschaftsrecht 755 (hereafter Bröhmer, 'Omega'); Thomas Ackermann, 'Case C-36/02, *Omega Spielhallen- und Automatenaufstellungs-GmbH v. Oberbürgermeisterin der Bundesstadt Bonn*, Judgment of the Court of Justice (First Chamber) of 14 October 2004, nyr' (2005) 42 Common Market Law Review 1107 (hereafter Ackermann, 'Omega'); Herke Kranenborg and Miele Bulterman, 'What If Rules on Free Movement and Human Rights Collide? About Laser Games and Human Dignity: The Omega Case' (2006) 31 European Law Review 93 (hereafter Kranenborg and Bulterman, 'Free Movement and Human Rights').

[4] Paragraph 14(1) of the Ordnungsbehördengesetz Nordrhein-Westfalen. For a commentary see Klaus Schönenbroicher, *Ordnungsbehördengesetz Nordrhein-Westfalen* (Verlag Reckinger 2011).

regulation of lasergames. The Federal Ministry of Justice had even announced that a federal law prohibiting lasergames was undesirable.[5] Numerous cities nonetheless banned the game; some considering that there was only a minimal leap from lasergames to 'real killing in Yugoslavia'.[6] Beyond the German borders, lasergames were operated in many Member States.[7] It is crucial to note that in banning Omega's activity, Bonn did not follow federal or regional legislative orders but autonomously evaluated the desirability of such a ban.

Following the local order, a British provider could no longer deliver equipment to Omega. From the perspective of EU law the question hence was whether the municipal order had infringed the freedom to provide services.[8] Raising this question in the context of a reference for preliminary ruling, the Federal Administrative Court alerted the ECJ that the respect for human dignity constitutes a cardinal constitutional principle in Germany.[9] That court was unequivocal that, as a matter of domestic law, the protection of human dignity could justify Bonn's decision. Whereas the ECJ had already recognized that fundamental rights can restrict fundamental freedoms, it was unclear whether there needed to be agreement between the Member States on status of the fundamental right.[10]

The question for preliminary ruling was reformulated as follows: 'the referring court asks, first, whether the prohibition of an economic activity for reasons arising from the *protection of fundamental values laid down by the national constitution*, such as, in this case, human dignity, is compatible with [EU] law'.[11] In light of such formulation one could be tempted to believe that the ECJ was unaware of *Omega*'s subnational dimension. That would, however, be an over-hasty conclusion, as it seems that the Court knew that there was no domestic agreement on the matter.[12] It had further been brought to the Court's attention that in domestic proceedings Omega had argued that the principle of equality before the law had been infringed as it had been 'put

[5] Der Spiegel 13/1994 'Ewiger Streit' (1994), 93–5, available online: http://www.spiegel.de/spiegel/print/d-13686882.html.

[6] Ibid (referring to Munich).

[7] AG opinion in *Omega* (n 1), para 14.

[8] Article 56 TFEU.

[9] *Omega* (n 1) para 12.

[10] AG opinion in *Omega* (n 1), para 20. See also Case C-112/00 *Eugen Schmidberger v Austria* [2003] EU:C:2003:333 (hereafter *Schmidberger*). For other instances where the CJEU balances economic freedoms with fundamental rights, see Case C-341/05 *Laval un Partneri Svenska byggnadsarbetareförbundet* [2007] EU:C:2007:809; Case C-438/05 *International Transport Workers' Federation v Viking* [2007] EU:C:2007:772. For a scholarly comment, see Sybe de Vries, 'Balancing Fundamental Rights with Economic Freedoms According to the European Court of Justice' (2013) 9 Utrecht Law Review 169.

[11] *Omega* (n 1) para 23 (my own emphasis).

[12] This conclusion is not obvious from the case itself. I take this information from private correspondence with Omega's lawyer (on file with the author).

at a disadvantage compared to other laserdrome operators in Germany'.[13] Notwithstanding its awareness that the measure at hand was that of a city, the Court treated it, as it usually does, as if it were that of a State. The consequences of such assimilation between national and subnational norms are evaluated further later in this chapter.

The Court unsurprisingly identified that the municipal measure negatively affected the freedom to provide services.[14] This brought the matter within the scope of EU law. Such a finding might have been avoided had the Court treated the ban as a national rather than subnational measure as it is not obvious that foreign service providers were at a greater disadvantage than domestic providers.[15] Treating the measure as one of a subnational nature might accordingly have shielded it from the application of EU law.[16] In assimilating the subnational measure to that of a Member State the Court could easily declare it to conflict with Article 56 TFEU and swiftly move to the justification stage of its analysis. In examining possible justifications, it engaged in a confusing blending of principles. The Court examined the measure from the point of view of the public order exemption in *Van Duyn,*[17] the limitation of fundamental freedoms by a fundamental right as seen in *Schmidberger,*[18] and arguably also constitutional identity. The Court recalled that:

> the competent authorities took the view that the activity concerned by the prohibition was a threat to public policy by reason of the fact that, in accordance with the conception prevailing in public opinion, the commercial exploitation of games involving the killing of human beings infringed a fundamental value enshrined in the national constitution, namely human dignity.[19]

Pursuant to that reasoning, *public order* had been infringed because, in accordance with *public opinion,* lasergames infringed human dignity, understood to be a fundamental value enshrined in the *national constitution.* This reasoning merges considerations operating at different levels into a whole. The public opinion was that of a subset of Bonn's population (those that had protested against the laserdrome), whereas its mayor produced a public policy assessment on the basis of regional legislation. Bonn had moreover expressly

[13] AG opinion in *Omega* (n 1) para 14 (acknowledging that Omega 'is claiming that the principle of equality before the law has been infringed by the fact that it has been put at a disadvantage compared to other laserdrome operators in Germany as well as operators of other games such as "Paintball" or "Gotcha").

[14] AG opinion in *Omega* (n 1) paras 25 and 33.

[15] The Court refrained from determining the discriminatory nature of this ban, not engaging with the cross-border element. *Omega* (n 1) para 25.

[16] This will be observed and examined throughout this chapter.

[17] Case C-41/71 *Van Duyn v Home Office* [1974] EU:C:1997:300 (hereafter *Van Duyn*).

[18] *Schmidberger* (n 10). [19] *Omega* (n 1) para 32.

mentioned 'that the activity concerned constitutes a danger to public policy'.[20] Article 52 TFEU allows for restrictions of the free movement on the basis of public policy, a justification that must be interpreted strictly.[21] The Court recalled that the specific circumstances that justify recourse to the public policy exemption vary in time and space and national authorities therefore enjoy a wide margin of discretion.[22] It concluded that 'the contested order did not go beyond what is necessary in order to attain the objective pursued by the competent national authorities'.[23] It concerned merely one variant of lasergames, those that involve shooting individuals, and the prohibition 'corresponds to the level of protection of human dignity which the national constitution seeks to guarantee'.[24] Bonn's order was accordingly compatible with supranational law. The remainder of the present section examines the Court's assessment of the various grounds of derogation to illustrate that in assimilating the subnational prohibition to that of a Member State it could impact supranational law's substantive development. It highlights that subnational norms have the same potential as those of a Member State to influence the substantive development of EU law and thus provoke informal constitutional change—in this case through the discovery of the general principle of the respect of human dignity.

### *a. Omega and the protection of national identities under EU law*

*Omega* established that a ground does not need to reflect a legal conception common to all Member States to justify derogation under EU law.[25] It was 'the first case in which a Member State relies upon a value enshrined in its constitution to justify a derogation from the free movement provisions'.[26] Whereas the respect for human dignity is a value common to the EU and all Member States, it enjoys a particularly prominent standing in Germany's post-WWII constitutional order.[27] Article 1(1) of the German Basic Law enshrines the respect for human dignity,[28] which is considered 'the most basic and foundational of rights'.[29] The German Federal Constitutional Court defined it as

[20] *Omega* (n 1) para 28 (also noting that public policy also appears in the North Rhine Westphalia law that empowered Bonn to issue the order.)

[21] *Omega* (n 1) paras 28–30, citing Case C-54/99 *Église de Scientologie* [2000] EU:C:2000:124 (hereafter *Église de Scientologie*).

[22] *Omega* (n 1) para 31. [23] *Omega* (n 1) para 39. [24] Ibid.

[25] AG opinion in *Omega* (n 1) para 20.

[26] Kranenborg and Bulterman, 'Free Movement and Human Rights' (n 3) 97.

[27] AG opinion in *Omega* (n 1) para 12 (describing human dignity as a 'fundamental value' in Germany).

[28] Article 1(1) of the German Basic Law.

[29] Vicki Jackson, 'Constitutional Dialogue and Human Dignity: States and Transnational Constitutional Discourse' (2004) 65 Montana Law Review 15, 18.

the 'highest value of the constitutional order',[30] as 'the Basic Law erected a value-oriented order that limits public authority'.[31] This value system, which 'centers upon the dignity of the human personality developing freely within the community' amounts to a 'fundamental constitutional decision affecting all spheres of law'.[32] In Germany the respect for human dignity is moreover a fully justiciable right.[33]

The ECJ treated *Omega* as raising the question whether *Germany's* interpretation of human dignity in relation to lasergames was compatible with supranational law[34] given that the German variant of human dignity differed from that espoused in other legal orders, including EU law.[35] Human dignity was hence understood as a component of Germany's national constitutional identity, now protected by Article 4(2) TEU. According to the Advocate General it is indeed impossible 'to equate the substance of the guarantee of human dignity under the German Basic Law with that of the guarantee of human dignity as recognized in [EU] law'.[36] It follows that while the *principle* of human dignity is protected by EU law the *standard* to which it is applied in Germany takes the form of an expression of national identity.[37]

*Omega* established for the first time that it 'is not indispensable' for a restrictive measure 'to correspond to a conception shared by all Member States as regards the precise way in which the fundamental right or legitimate interest in question is to be protected'. [38] The fact that the German standard of protection was stronger than those found elsewhere in the EU accordingly did not, per se, preclude its ability to restrict the fundamental freedom.[39] This implies that Member States can pursue objectives not shared by other Member States without this, as such, being contrary to EU law. The difficulty with such analysis from my perspective lies in the fact that the *standard* of protection

[30] BVerfGE 45, 187, *Lebenslange Freiheitsstrafe* (1977) (1 BvL 14/76).

[31] BVerfGE 6, 32 *Elfes* (1957) (1BvR 253/56).

[32] BVerfGE 7, 198, *Lüth* (1958) (1BvR 400/51). For an English version of these decisions, refer to Donald Kommers, *The Constitutional Jurisprudence of the Federal Republic of Germany* (Duke University Press 1997) 305, 315, 363.

[33] Kranenborg and Bulterman, 'Free Movement and Human Rights' (n 3) 97.

[34] AG opinion in *Omega* (n 1) para 2.

[35] *Omega* (n 1) para 34 and AG opinion in *Omega* (n 1) paras 82–91. See Walter Frenz, 'Menschenwürde und Dienstleistungsfreiheit' (2005) Neue Zeitschrift für Verwaltungsrecht 48, 50 ('Menschenwürde setzt sich also nicht als nationale Verfassungsnorm durch, sondern im Gewande des Gemeinschaftsrechts'); Eric Carpano, 'Droits fondamentaux et libertés communautaires de circulation: brèves remarques sur le développement du système communautaire de protection des droits fondamentaux' (2005) 120 Les Petites Affiches 27.

[36] AG opinion in *Omega* (n 1) para 92.

[37] See also Jürgen Schwarze, 'Der Schutz der Grundrechte durch den EuGH' (2005) 48 Neue Juristische Wochenschrift 3457, 3461 (hereafter referred to as Schwarze, 'Grundrechte').

[38] *Omega* (n 1) para 37.

[39] Schwarze, 'Grundrechte' (n 37) 3461.

was not that of Germany but rather that of Bonn. In the absence of domestic consensus as to human dignity's relation to lasergames, we must, however, wonder to what extent Bonn's assessment can be construed as an expression of national identity. The city's decision merely constituted a particular, localized, conception of a fundamental constitutional value. The absence of agreement whether lasergames infringe human dignity begs the question whether Bonn's interpretation of human dignity is really so fundamental to the German constitutional system that it justifies restrictions to a fundamental freedom.

What is striking from my perspective is that the Court's non-differentiation between subnational and national norms allowed Bonn's norm to affect the substantive core of EU law. The conflict between the municipal ban and economic freedom indeed provided an opportunity for the ECJ to clarify that elements of national constitutional law not shared by other Member States can limit a fundamental economic freedom. *Omega* further developed EU law in recognizing the protection of human dignity to be constitutive of a general principle of EU law. The Court did not enquire whether the standard of dignity applied was that of the Member State or the SNA. In omitting to operate a distinction on this point, it effectively treats any decision from within the Member State as that of the Member State. *Omega* appears to indicate that when an SNA creates a norm and the referring court endorses that norm as representing that Member State's national identity it does not matter whether it is homogeneously applicable. The ECJ indeed entrusts the referring court with the determination whether Bonn's standard 'corresponds to the level of protection of human dignity which the national constitution seeks to guarantee in the territory of the Federal Republic of Germany'.[40] This confirms Besselink's claim that it is up to the domestic courts to 'decide the particular national constitutional rights involved; next it is the ECJ which determines the consequences of this state of affairs under [EU] law'.[41] As a consequence, the ECJ did not enquire further—despite its awareness of internal regulatory fragmentation.

### *b. The protection of human dignity as a general principle of EU law*

*Omega* served as an opportunity to clarify human dignity's status in EU law.[42] The ECJ proclaimed that EU law 'undeniably strives to ensure respect for human dignity as a general principle of law'.[43] Advocate General Stix-Hackl

[40] *Omega* (n 1) para 39.

[41] Leonard Besselink, 'National and Constitutional Identity Before and After Lisbon' (2010) 6 Utrecht Law Review 46; Vassilios Skouris, 'Die Zusammenarbeit zwischen BVerwG und EuGH—eine positive Bilanz' (2013) Neue Zeitschrift für Verwaltungsrecht 33.

[42] *Omega* (n 1) para 34 and AG opinion in *Omega* (n 1) paras 82–91.

[43] *Omega* (n 1) para 34.

agreed that 'protection of human dignity is afforded recognition as a general principle—and therefore forms part of primary legislation'.[44] *Omega* is rightly remembered as the case that confirmed that the protection of human dignity amounts to a general principle.[45] This conclusion itself remains unaltered by the case's subnational dimension. Awareness of the subnational dimension, however, confirms that SNAs have the capacity to influence EU law's substantive development.

The legal dispute was triggered by a city's exercise of regulatory autonomy, which ultimately and indirectly led to the discovery of the general principle. Bonn's declaration of human dignity's heightened importance—of course indirectly and through a chain of events—led to the recognition of the general principle. Subtle as it may be, the relation between the local claim and the EU principle points towards the interconnection and intertwining of the European and municipal legal orders in the polycentric EU. This can be framed as a manifestation of porosity. The importance that Bonn attributes to human dignity results—through the Court's classification of a general principle—in an increased gravity of human dignity in EU law, and therefore indirectly in other Member States. These dynamics could even be construed as an instance of performativity, a concept that helps us to understand why local measures, even if devoid of legal force, can pollinate legal change at other scales.[46] It would indeed not have mattered had the referring court later found Bonn's measure to be unlawful. The declaration of a general principle would have, and has, continued to enshrine the heightened importance of human dignity in EU law.

The Court seems to operate on the assumption that any norm originating within a Member State is that of the Member State.[47] From this we might then conclude that the ECJ treats any measure from *within* a Member State as that *of* the Member State. At first glance, this might appear like a disempowerment of SNAs—the Court simply ignores the fact that it was the city that created the norm in the first place. This is, however, not necessarily so. If an action from within a Member State is equated with that of a Member

[44] AG opinion in *Omega* (n 1) para 93.

[45] The Court had already affirmed in Case C-377/98 *Netherlands v Parliament and Council* [2001] EU:C:2001:523 that '[i]t is for the Court of Justice, in its review of the compatibility of acts of the institutions with the general principles of Community law, to ensure that the fundamental right to human dignity and integrity is observed.' This case, however, concerned EU secondary law which itself protected human dignity.

[46] I discuss this further in Michèle Finck, 'The Role of Localism in Constitutional Change: A Case Study' (2014) 15 The Journal of Law and Politics 53.

[47] This also reflects the principle of national institutional autonomy. As will be seen later, however, the *Digibet* case took a somewhat different stance on this matter.

State, SNAs are placed on the same footing as States, and secure derogations from EU law that allow them to further independent policy goals. SNAs are treated in the same manner as the masters of the Treaties, and, provided that the referring court endorses their stance, can define informal constitutional change in the EU. One could frame the absence of engagement with the subnational dimension as an 'immunity' of EU law towards subnational norms. This would, however, be mistaken, as EU law is in fact receptive to them. Even though the ECJ does not engage with the subnational dimension, the result of *Omega* was that, rather than being declared incompatible with EU law, the local norm is allowed to stand despite its limiting effect on the freedom to provide services. Moreover, in being treated as an act of the Member State, the local order, indirectly and through a chain of events, impacts on the substance of EU primary law by giving rise to the recognition of a general principle of EU law. In being treated as the measure of a Member State, the local measure has the same effects as those that have been observed for Member State (constitutional) norms, leading to the creation of a general principle of EU law.[48]

### c. *The public policy exemption*

Articles 52 and 62 TFEU allow Member States to derogate from the free movement of services on grounds of 'public policy'. Ackermann stressed that what the CJEU refused to expressly acknowledge in *Schmidberger* 'has now been unequivocally stated in *Omega*: the protection of fundamental rights belongs to the concept of public policy to which the relevant provisions of the Treaty refer'.[49] Since it proved impossible to equate the protection of human dignity under the German Basic Law with dignity as recognized in EU law,[50] the Advocate General argued that the 'circumstances of public policy invoked by the Member State by way of justification' should be examined.[51] The public policy analysis enables the Court to account for circumstances specific to a given State.[52] *Omega* was one of the first cases in which States invoked the public policy derogation to restrict the economic activity of private firms.[53] The Court had, however, already established that public policy 'may vary

[48] Article 6(3) TEU. [49] Ackermann, 'Omega' (n 3) 115.

[50] Para 92 of the AG opinion in *Omega* (n 1).

[51] Ibid, para 93. See also Kranenborg and Bulterman, 'Free Movement and Human Rights' (n 3) 97 ('[a]s it is impossible to equate the protection of human dignity under the German constitution as a justiciable fundamental right with the protection offered by EC law, Stix-Hackl makes a plea to evaluate the measure of the Bonn authorities under the public policy exception').

[52] Kranenborg and Bulterman, 'Free Movement and Human Rights' (n 3), 97.

[53] Catherine Barnard, *The Substantive Law of the EU. The Four Freedoms* (Oxford University Press 2013) 509 (hereafter Barnard, *The Substantive Law of the EU*).

from one country to another and from one period to another' and Member States enjoy a corresponding degree of discretion.[54] EU law indeed does not impose 'a uniform scale of values' on States in this context.[55] *Omega* illustrates that SNAs benefit from the same margin of discretion. This is noteworthy as derogations develop on a case-by-case basis and thereafter form an integral part of the European legal order. The case subject to analysis here illustrates that in this regard local and regional authorities have the same capacity to shape the direction of EU law as the Member States.

The Advocate General argued that it must be possible 'to admit under the public policy exception those considerations that relate to a right the protection and observance of which [EU] law itself demands'.[56] In this context, 'national authorities' have a discretion in assessing whether lasergames amount to a 'genuine and sufficiently serious threat to a fundamental interest of society',[57] an interest which is determined in the light of 'national value judgments'.[58] Bonn itself had relied on public policy to prohibit lasergames and the regional law granting it competence to do so was also concerned with public policy.[59] It added that this ground of derogation must be strictly interpreted[60] as 'public policy may be relied on only if there is a genuine and sufficiently serious threat to a fundamental interest of society'.[61]

Accounting for the subnational origin of the ban we must wonder whether the public policy exemption makes sense. It is true that the lasergame activity had 'aroused public displeasure'[62]—yet such displeasure was expressed by merely a subset of Bonn's population, a minuscule proportion of the country's 80 million inhabitants. *Omega* establishes that for social opposition to justify the invocation of public policy, it need not be felt nationwide. One may, however, wonder whether a 'sufficiently serious' threat to a fundamental interest of society exists where a measure is taken by a single locality. As a consequence municipalities enjoy the same margin of discretion as Member States. *Omega* exhibits that local objectives can outweigh European objectives—but only where the local objective is recognized as valid by EU law. The main motivation behind Bonn's order was the desire to safeguard public order in its territory.[63] In recognizing the compatibility of the local order with EU law, the ECJ allowed the local concern to limit a goal that ranks high on

[54] *Van Duyn* (n 17) paras 18–19. [55] Case 268/99 *Jany* [2001] EU:C:2001:616.

[56] AG opinion in *Omega* (n 1) para 93. [57] AG opinion in *Omega* (n 1) paras 100–1.

[58] AG opinion in *Omega* (n 1) para 105. [59] *Omega* (n 1) para 28.

[60] *Omega* (n 1) para 30. [61] Ibid, citing *Église de Scientologie* (n 21).

[62] AG opinion in *Omega* (n 1) para 108.

[63] It has been seen that Bonn explicitly referred to public policy in its order and that the regional law, which provided the basis of the order, was indeed also concerned with public order.

the agenda of European integration. Precisely because EU law treats a local measure as that of a Member State, SNAs are afforded the same discretion as the Member States in creating public policy.

### *d. The justification of the local measure*

Decided merely a year after *Schmidberger, Omega* confirmed that fundamental rights can limit fundamental freedoms.[64] *Omega* however goes further, as due to the generic character of human dignity, State interference with the four freedoms is more difficult to control than in respect of a 'conventional fundamental right'.[65] Once a derogation is invoked the Court (in theory the referring court but in practice often the ECJ) determines whether the means chosen are suitable to attain the aim and whether they do not go beyond what is necessary.[66] In *Omega*, however, the Court omits to engage with this aspect. This has been subject to criticism as it failed to determine whether the measure was 'really necessary to protect human dignity as guaranteed in the German constitution'.[67] While *Omega* clearly raised a number of sensitive questions, Kranenborg and Bulterman stressed that in other sensitive areas, such as gambling, the Court conventionally examines whether imperative requirements in the general interest 'serve to limit betting activities in a consistent and systematic manner'.[68] As a consequence a test assessing 'whether the measure at stake forms part of a wider policy to restrict or prohibit games simulating the killing of human beings, such as violent video games or paint ball' could have been employed.[69]

Necessity seems to be of particular importance as the judgment 'does not indicate any other criteria that could help us to find any limits for the protection of human dignity under [EU] law'.[70] As the Advocate General herself recognized, '[t]here is hardly any legal principle more difficult to fathom in law than that of human dignity'.[71] Bröhmer has even argued that the ECJ gave Member States carte blanche to restrict economic freedoms in the name of dignity,[72] the content of which, as protected by EU law, remains obscure.[73] The neglect of the necessity test seems all the more surprising as the Court

[64] *Schmidberger* (n 10). For a comment, see Christopher Brown, 'Case C-112/00, *Eugen Schmidberger, Internationale Transporte und Planzuge v. Austria*. Judgment of 12 June 2003, Full Court' (2003) 40 Common Market Law Review 1499.

[65] Ackermann, 'Omega' (n 3) 1114.

[66] Barnard, *The Substantive Law of the EU* (n 53) 534.

[67] Kranenborg and Bulterman, 'Free Movement and Human Rights' (n 3).

[68] Case C-243/01 *Gambelli* [2003] EU:C:2003:597.

[69] Kranenborg and Bulterman, 'Free Movement and Human Rights' (n 3) 100.

[70] Ackermann, 'Omega' (n 3) 116.

[71] AG opinion in *Omega* (n 1) para 74.

[72] Bröhmer, 'Omega' (n 3) 756.

[73] Ibid 755–6.

was aware of the nature of lasergame regulation in Germany. Taking into account *Omega*'s subnational dimension would have compelled the Court to engage with these aspects more assiduously to determine whether a measure is truly 'necessary' if applied by a single city. What is more, if a justification is invoked, in theory, one of the requirements is that it is uniformly applicable.[74] In *Omega*, the Court mentioned the criterion without discussing its application to the facts. Advocate General Stix-Hackl simply asserted that the public order notice 'undoubtedly constitutes a uniformly applicable measure',[75] and the ECJ proclaimed that the contested municipal order was not motivated 'by any consideration linked to the nationality of the providers or recipients of the service'.[76] This is somewhat confusing as both Court and the Advocate General were aware that Omega had been subject to differentiated treatment.[77] One would thus have expected the Court to engage with this issue more openly. Had it done so it would have had to answer some challenging questions, for instance, whether Omega was subject to the same rules as other lasergame operators. As Omega asserted that lasergames are similar to paintball, and that it was put at a disadvantage compared to paintball operators,[78] as well as video games and contact sports,[79] these claims should also have been examined. This would in turn have compelled the CJEU to clarify whether such fragmentation *within* a Member State is approached from the same angle as fragmentation *between* Member States.[80] The Court's silence can only be read as implying that SNAs have the same discretion as Member States to formulate policies that stand in tension with prescriptions of EU law. This entails that SNAs enjoy the same regulatory freedom as Member States as a matter of EU law. The norms thus created can, due to porosity, equally affect EU law's substantive development, showing that SNAs are, just as the Member States, insiders of the European legal order. The subsequent section evaluates an additional aspect of SNAs' insider status, namely their status of internal market participants.

[74] See by way of example Case 3/88 *Commission v Italy* [1989] EU:C:1989:606. The contours of these requirements are, however, subject to controversy.

[75] Para 109 of *Omega* (n 1).

[76] Para 29 of *Omega* (n 1).

[77] AG opinion in *Omega* (n 1) para 14.

[78] This is not mentioned in the opinion or the judgment. I take this information from private correspondence with Omega's lawyer (on file with author).

[79] Para 40 of the AG opinion in *Omega* (n 1) ('Omega argues that the simulation of killing and violence in films as well as in the visual arts and in contact sports and children's games is widespread and accepted in society; "Lasersport" is no different from those activities.')

[80] On this, see further Case C-156/13 *Digibet v Westdeutsche Lotterie* [2014] EU:C:2014:1756 (hereafter *Digibet*).

## B. Polycentricity

The introductory chapter already introduced the notion of polycentricity, which indicates that the Union is made up of and shaped by a plurality of nodes of public authority. This mutation of the structure of the supranational legal order highlights the emergence of networks of governance between public actors that cannot be comprehensively grasped through the Treaties' bi-centric lens. This section looks into additional examples of the said phenomenon, including CJEU case law, the Covenant of Mayors, the Pact of Amsterdam, and the Committee of the Region's Charter on Multi-Level Governance, as well as the European Citizens' Initiative. It starts with an analysis of the *Horvath* case that exemplifies the challenges and opportunities inherent to polycentric regulation and engages with the interrogation of whether subnational authorities' regulatory autonomies benefit from the same supranational protection as those of the Member States.

### 1. *Horvath*

*Horvath* concerned the degree of autonomy that SNAs enjoy in the implementation of regulations, and the relation between such autonomy and the imperative of non-discrimination.[81] While regulations need not be transposed into domestic legislation, national authorities are nonetheless required to take enforcement action.[82] Sometimes a significant degree of autonomy exists with respect to such enforcement. As a result, in a Member State with a decentralized structure where multiple authorities act as implementers, a single regulation can be interpreted and implemented differently in various parts of the national territory.

*Horvath* arose in the specific context of the Common Agricultural Policy (CAP). A regulation on import support schemes for farmers was implemented in a decentralized fashion in the UK and as a result farmers in England were subject to different rules than those elsewhere in the UK. This begged the question whether the treatment of English farmers was discriminatory. An English farmer indeed claimed that he was in a less favourable position than farmers in Scotland, Northern Ireland, and Wales for the sole reason of his geographical location. The Grand Chamber was called upon to determine whether this difference in treatment, which resulted directly from

[81] Case C-428/07 *Horvath* [2009] EU:C:2009:458 (hereafter *Horvath*).

[82] See further Article 288 TFEU.

the decentralized implementation of the regulation, amounted to discrimination. Answering this question in the affirmative would have entailed that the decentralized implementation of EU secondary law is, as such, contrary to EU law unless all authorities apply it in the exact same manner, rendering devolution arrangements somewhat redundant.

The Court and the Advocate General first invoked the principle of national institutional autonomy, emphasizing that EU law does not per se oppose the decentralized implementation of EU standards if they are implemented correctly.[83] This conclusion was reinforced by the fact that the regulation itself stated that 'Member States shall define, at national or regional level, minimum requirements for good agricultural and environmental condition'.[84] The Advocate General interpreted this flexibility as a sign that the EU legislature 'did not consider a uniform regulatory approach within each Member State to be necessary, but instead wished to leave each Member State to choose the appropriate regulatory level within its own political system'.[85] As a consequence, 'the rules adopted by those authorities may differ as between the regions concerned'.[86] The Court even stressed that the definition of minimum requirements 'at national or regional level' must, as stipulated by the regulation, account for 'the specific characteristics of the areas concerned'.[87] This underlines that, as is often the case, secondary legislation recognized polycentricity and its benefits.[88] Whereas Member States are bound by the requirements of the regulation 'it nevertheless leaves them, by using general concepts and terms, a certain discretion with regard to the actual determination of those requirements'.[89] From this it follows that, as a general matter, EU law doesn't oppose national choices regarding the decentralized exercise of public authority, validating polycentricity.

[83] *Horvath* (n 81) paras 48–50, citing Joined Cases 51/71 to 54/71 *International Fruit Company and Others* [1971] EU:C:1971:128 and Case C-156/91 *Hansa Fleisch Ernst Mundt* [1992] EU:C:1992:423.

[84] Article 5(1) of Council Regulation (EC) No 1782/2003 establishing common rules for direct support schemes under the common agricultural policy and establishing certain support schemes for farmers and amending Regulations (EEC) No 2019/93, (EC) No 1452/2001, (EC) No 1453/2001, (EC) No 1454/2001, (EC) No 1868/94, (EC) No 1251/1999, (EC) No 1254/1999, (EC) No 1673/2000, (EEC) No 2358/71 and (EC) No 2529/2001 [2003] OJ L270/269 (hereafter referred to as the 'Direct Support Schemes Regulation').

[85] *Horvath* (n 81) AG opinion, para 91.

[86] *Horvath* (n 81) para 53.

[87] Ibid, para 25.

[88] Article 5(1) of the Direct Support Schemes Regulation (n 84) ('Member States shall define, at national or regional level, minimum requirements for good agricultural and environmental condition on the basis of the framework set up in Annex IV, taking into account the specific characteristics of the areas concerned, including soil and climatic condition, existing farming systems, land use, crop rotation, farming practices, and farm structures.')

[89] *Horvath* (n 81) para 26.

Turning to the examination of whether the decentralized implementation had resulted in discrimination, the Court recalled that 'divergences existing between the legislation of the various Member States' are acceptable 'so long as that legislation affects equally all persons subject to it'.[90] *Horvath,* however, didn't raise the question of regulatory fragmentation *between* but rather *within* Member States. The Grand Chamber assimilated SNAs to Member States in this respect, holding that they can make use of the same interpretative autonomy. As long as the various minimum standards applied throughout the UK are compatible with the regulation, no discrimination can be established.[91] As a consequence 'divergences between the measures provided for by the various administrations cannot, alone, constitute discrimination'.[92] EU law hence approaches regulatory fragmentation within a Member State in the same manner as regulatory fragmentation between Member States, assimilating SNAs to the insider Member States.[93] Secondary legislation indeed recognizes that agricultural policy is best governed in a polycentric fashion and the Court highlights subnational actors' pivotal contribution thereto.

The assimilation between Member States and SNAs finds a particularly strong expression in the opinion of Advocate General Trstenjak who relied on *Azores*, a State aid case examined below, which was previously thought of as being specific to State aid law.[94] She justified her reliance on the *Azores* test in stating that the criteria the Court employs when assessing the compatibility of subnational norms with EU law are, irrespective of 'sector-specific terminology' ultimately 'no more than a difference in treatment between economic operators'.[95] The Advocate General went on to argue that:

> [a] devolved organisation of agricultural law takes account not least of the increased importance of the regions within the European Union, which finds expression, for example, in the principle of subsidiarity being enshrined by the Treaty of Maastricht, the creation of the Committee of the Regions, the responsibility of the regions for the implementation of [EU] law and the possibility of representation in the Council under Article 203 EC. In addition, it takes into consideration the present moves towards decentralisation in the Member States, such as in the United Kingdom, largely following a similar political logic, which suggests a convergence in developments at [EU] level and at national level.[96]

The Advocate General's reference to the 'convergence' of the increased fragmentation of public authority and EU law's effort to accommodate these

[90] Ibid, para 55. [91] Ibid, paras 47–57. [92] Ibid, para 47.

[93] Save for the application of the doctrine of purely internal situations, which was not at issue here.

[94] Opinion of Advocate General Trstenjak in *Horvath* (n 81).

[95] Ibid, para 106.

[96] Ibid, para 94.

evolutions relates to porosity, as evolutions occurring at one scale trigger change at another. She further engaged with polycentricity in acknowledging that SNAs are significant actors in the CAP, which was said to benefit from 'devolved and differentiated implementation'.[97] The devolved organization of agricultural law 'takes account of the fact that regional differentiation is entirely necessary' given that 'account is to be taken of the structural and natural disparities between the various agricultural regions'.[98] The insider SNAs are actively involved in the delivery of the CAP and can fulfil roles Member States fall short of. The margin of discretion that the regulation accorded to domestic decision-makers moreover 'contributes to a differentiation corresponding to the needs of each region'.[99] Agricultural policy doubtlessly is a polycentric challenge that is best addressed in a polycentric fashion.

The Court joined its Advocate General in underlining the benefits of decentralized implementation. It noted that regulations leave room for interpretative freedom to account for 'regional differences'.[100] Decentralized implementation is indeed considered to present benefits that cannot be achieved through centralized action, showcasing that SNAs fulfil functions Member States cannot achieve. SNAs' supplementing function for the States' shortcomings in achieving supranational aims is indeed a key feature explaining their insider status. The resulting polycentric structure is considered beneficial for EU substantive law as it for instance allows for a 'greater closeness of national, regional and local decision-makers to the situation and to the citizen, the simplification of legislation and the easing of the burden on the administration'.[101] Not only are SNAs seen as integral components of the European legal space but there is an additional recognition that subnational implementation can fulfil objectives that decentralized implementation cannot. Polycentricty consequently not solely accounts for decentralized Member State structures but also presents benefits for EU law itself. Determining whether EU law approaches fragmentation *between* Member States to the same extent as fragmentation *within* Member States was also at the centre of the *Digibet* case.

## 2. *Digibet*

*Digibet* presented the Court with questions it already had to pronounce itself on in *Horvath* and in *Omega* in the context of gambling.[102] Gambling is a sensitive issue regulated in different manners by the various Member States.

97 Ibid, para 89. 98 Ibid, para 92. 99 Ibid, para 92.

100 *Horvath* (n 81) para 48.

101 Opinion of Advocate General Trstenjak in *Horvath* (n 81) para 93.

102 *Digibet* (n 80).

Such regulatory fragmentation is permissible as a matter of EU law in light of the absence of a harmonized gambling framework at supranational level. Given that 'significant moral, religious and cultural differences between the Member States' persist and in the absence of harmonization, it is for each State to determine in accordance with its 'own scale of values, what is required in order to ensure that the interests in question are protected'.[103] In reality, not only Member States but also SNAs have regulatory competence in respect to gambling. In Germany the Länder regulate games of chance in accordance with the Basic Law, highlighting the polycentric nature of this regulatory framework.[104]

In 2008 all sixteen German Länder adopted a Treaty on games of chance that expired in 2011.[105] In 2012 a new Treaty entered into force and was ratified by fifteen Länder, with the exception of Schleswig-Holstein, which adopted its own legislative regime. Schleswig-Holstein's liberalizing law established rules less restrictive than those foreseen by the Treaty.[106] A key divergence resided in the fact that advertising was in principle authorized under the regional law but not under the Treaty.[107] In 2013 Schleswig-Holstein discontinued the application of its law and ratified the Treaty. This triggered litigation between the Land and a public lottery company in the context of which the compatibility of the Treaty with EU law was questioned.[108]

The *Digibet* case begged pertinent questions regarding the relation between subnational gambling laws and Article 56 TFEU such as whether the fragmented nature of gambling regulation influences its compatibility with EU law. As a matter of supranational law gambling regulations must be justified by legitimate public interest objectives and the referring court suspected that if the public interest prevailing within a State genuinely mandates restrictive gambling legislation it should be perceived homogeneously throughout the national territory. Despite the fact that no Advocate General opinion was deemed necessary, *Digibet* accordingly addresses a number of important questions regarding the relation between SNAs and EU law. The relevance of polycentricity is particularly pronounced here in light of the polycentric nature of the online gambling market itself.

*Digibet* raised the question of the framework to be applied to the public interest criterion. The referring court had explicitly enquired whether Schleswig-Holstein's adoption of independent legislation had impacted on the availability of the public interest justification. The question to be answered

[103] Ibid, para 24.
[104] In accordance with Articles 70 and 72 of the German Basic Law.
[105] *Digibet* (n 80) paras 4–5. [106] Ibid, paras 5–6. [107] Ibid, paras 7–9.
[108] Ibid, paras 11–14.

was hence whether a public interest must be perceived homogeneously within a Member State to be valid under EU law—a question that was left implicit in *Omega.* As a matter of principle, national legislation that restricts access to gambling can be justified by requirements in the public interest including the prevention of addiction, consumer protection, or the prevention of fraud and incitement to squander money.[109] In *Digibet*, the order for reference explicitly enquired whether the fact that betting regulation is heterogeneous within rather than just between Member States affects the availability of such justification. The German Federal Supreme Court indeed suspected that 'the different legal position in one Land as compared with the others' could result in an infringement of the freedom to provide services, as 'a ban on the facilitation and organisation of games of chance on-line would be without foundation'.[110] If the public interest is assessed by reference to the national territory the consistency of the public interest argument must be questioned if part of the national territory temporarily doesn't perceive this interest to exist. In *Omega*, the ECJ had chosen not to engage with this sensitive question in ignoring that Bonn's interpretation of human dignity was not that of Germany. As the referring court in *Digibet* explicitly put its finger on the consequences of such fragmentation, the Court was unable to evade the issue. The referring Court had stressed that requiring that a public interest be felt homogeneously in a State would prevent SNAs from determining 'whether it is appropriate to ban certain gaming activities' and thus severely limit their autonomy.[111] The ECJ confirmed that the German Treaty restricted the freedom to provide services and evoked the possibility to justify such restrictions in the presence of overriding reasons in the public interest as long as the corresponding measures are proportionate and non-discriminatory.[112] Due to porosity domestic regulation impacts the EU objectives of the unhindered circulation of services in the internal market, explaining why EU law imposes checks on such measures.

The Court questioned in particular whether the proportionality of the Treaty was called into question by the existence of more liberal legislation in Schleswig-Holstein for a limited period of time.[113] Digibet argued that the temporary regional regime was barred by *Carmen Media Group*, which established that regional and federal authorities are jointly required to fulfil Germany's obligation under Article 56 TFEU.[114] The Court invoked 'the

[109] Ibid, para 23. [110] Ibid, para 15.

[111] Cited at para 16 of the judgment, referring to Case C-46/08 *Carmen Media Group* [2010] EU:C:2010:505, para 58.

[112] *Digibet* (n 80) paras 20–2 and 25–6. [113] Ibid, para 27 (emphasis in original).

[114] Ibid, paras 69–70.

particular nature of the gambling sector' where the presence of harsh competition between the different operators might increase consumers' expenditure on gaming and the risks of addiction.[115] Given that Member States are free to organize themselves internally as they see fit, the Court concluded that the choice of means to pursue the public interest is 'solely a matter for the constitutional system of each State'.[116] Germany was indeed at liberty to consider that 'it is for the *Länder* rather than the Federal authorities to adopt certain legislative measures'.[117] Regarding competence *delegation* Member States can decide freely how to organize themselves internally and the resulting polycentricity is accepted by EU law. This stance is reminiscent of cases such as *Omega* and *Josemans* where the Court was equally willing to accord a significant degree of discretion to the domestic pursuit of a public interest.[118] As a consequence a public interest need not be felt homogeneously throughout a national territory for it to justify a restriction of a fundamental freedom by an SNA. Taking the SNA rather than the Member State as the relevant regulatory framework assimilates both sets of actors, for it allows SNAs to freely regulate in their territory to the same degree as Member States can. This upholds a significant precondition for a polycentric system in that Member States can freely organize themselves as they see fit.

The question for preliminary ruling had, however, directly and explicitly referred to an aspect of domestic institutional organization that compelled the Court to abandon the principle of national institutional autonomy. After having confirmed SNAs' ability to act autonomously under the public interest criterion, the ECJ continued to reflect on the limited and localized application of the Schleswig-Holstein law. It highlighted that the regional legislation at issue with limited *ratione temporis* and *ratione loci* and could therefore not be said to seriously affect 'the appropriateness of the restrictions on games of chance applicable in all the other *Länder* to achieve the legitimate public interest objectives that they pursue'.[119] While this reasoning appears to indicate that the availability of the public interest derogation might be called into question where the divergences between different parts of the same Member States are more pronounced materially or temporarily. The outcome of the Court's reasoning is, however, unequivocal that it tolerates fragmentation within Member States in the same manner as fragmentation between Member States. Whereas it was already previously well established that the Court tolerates regulatory fragmentation on games of chances between the

[115] Ibid, para 31. [116] Ibid, para 33. [117] Ibid, para 33.

[118] Even though no public interest question was at stake here, also cases such as *Horvath* can be interpreted along these lines.

[119] *Digibet* (n 80) para 36 (emphasis in original).

various Member States, *Digibet* declares the same to be true in relation to Member States internally.[120] It thus confirms EU law's assimilation between Member States and SNAs regarding the respect of their respective regulatory autonomies. This concurred with the referring domestic court's belief that 'differences between the *Länder* … should not be distinguished from any diverging laws which may exist between large and small Member States and which must be accepted in EU law'.[121] Such tolerance of regulatory fragmentation then leads to polycentricity and underlines the assimilation between Member States and SNAs, the Court holding that fragmentation between SNAs should be considered from the same perspective as that between various Member States.

*Digibet* is significant for an additional reason given that it constitutes to date the only case on which the Court has explicitly pronounced itself on the application of the first sentence of Article 4(2) TEU to subnational regulatory autonomies. It is worth recalling that the relation between this provision of primary law and SNAs is ambiguous given that it, on the one hand, requires EU law to respect national identities inclusive of local and regional self-government, yet, on the other, proclaims the principle of Member State equality which appears to mandate that decentralization can only be accounted for where it poses no threat to such equality. The Court held that 'the division of competences between the *Länder* cannot be called into question, since it benefits from the protection conferred by Article 4(2) TEU'.[122] Article 4(2) TEU, although as previously seen not itself enshrining a conception of SNAs as insiders, nonetheless highlights the temporal dimension of SNAs' increasing connection to and interaction with the EU given that it now explicitly refers to their existence. Article 4(2) TEU accordingly comes in support of the Court's statement that subnational competences benefit from an analogous degree of protection under EU law as those of the Member States, underlining their assimilated status as insiders. While this section has thus far observed SNAs' insider status in various judicial decisions, the polycentric nature of the European legal order can also be illustrated with respect to numerous recent initiatives and declarations of EU institutions that underline the connection between SNAs and the EU. The fact that these initiatives are all relatively recent supports our conclusion that over time the features of the insider narrative find increased expression in EU law due to functional spillover. Below an additional recent initiative is highlighted which illustrates that EU institutions can be significant drivers of polycentricity and porosity.

[120] Ibid, para 39. [121] Ibid, para 17. [122] Ibid, para 34 (emphasis in original).

## 3. The Covenant of Mayors

Through the initiation of the Covenant of Mayors, a transnational alliance of mayors, the European Commission has actively encouraged polycentricity and porosity in the EU.[123] The initiative further highlights SNAs' role as loyal allies of the European institutions in the achievement of supranational policy priorities. The Covenant of Mayors is a transnational network of cities the objective of which consists in reducing carbon dioxide emissions.[124] The Covenant currently counts around 7,200 signatories, that is to say European local governments that voluntarily subscribe to the Covenant's regime.[125] Upon signature of the covenant, the participating local governments may indeed be required to develop a baseline emissions inventory and establish a Sustainable Energy Action Plan that lists their various climate change mitigation and adaptation policies in order to achieve the target of at least 20 per cent reduction in emissions.[126] The Covenant's polycentric nature is indeed evident, having been described as a 'pioneering project that combines forces between public and private organizations, operating at a local, regional, national or transnational level'.[127] It may also be seen as a reflection of the very nature of climate change, in itself a phenomenon of polycentric causes and consequences that cannot be addressed with isolated tactics.

The Covenant is administered by the Covenant of Mayors Office, which was established and funded by the European Commission in 2008 after consultation with the Committee of the Regions and numerous cities.[128] The Commission is accordingly actively supporting the involvement of subnational authorities as policymakers in this domain of environmental policy, furthering polycentricity. It moreover supports local governments in their development of their respective initiatives through the provision of guidance documents, the availability of a helpdesk and additional instruments.[129] Porosity is apparent in this polycentric structure given that completed local

[123] For an overview of this instrument, see Veerle Heyvaert, 'What's in a Name? The Covenant of Mayors as Transnational Environmental Regulation' (2013) 22(1) Review of European, Comparative and International Environmental Law 78 (hereafter Heyvaert, 'The Covenant of Mayors').

[124] The Covenant of Mayors' website is at: http://www.covenantofmayors.eu/index_en.html.

[125] Ibid.

[126] See: http://www.covenantofmayors.eu/actions/sustainable-energy-action-plans_en.html.

[127] Heyvaert, 'The Covenant of Mayors' (n 123) 78. See also Kristine Kern and Harriet Bulkeley, 'Cities, Europeanization and Multi-level Governance: Governing Climate Change through Transnational Municipal Networks' (2009) 47 Journal of Common Market Studies 309, 329.

[128] Heyvaert, 'The Covenant of Mayors' (n 123) 81; Pedro Ballestros Torres and Roman Doubrava, 'The Covenant of Mayors: Cities Leading the Fight against Climate Change' in Maryke Van Staden and Francesco Musco (eds), *Local Governments and Climate Change* (Springer 2010) 91.

[129] Heyvaert, 'The Covenant of Mayors' (n 123) 81.

policies are made available online, allowing local governments to learn from other local governments' experiences.[130] The resulting exchange has moreover been said to 'foster the conclusion of cooperative ventures between participants'.[131] The Commission thus actively fosters the involvement of SNAs and their mutual intertwining in order to achieve supranational climate objectives.

The Covenant of Mayors has been said to have a regulatory nature given that it 'seeks to influence behaviour deliberately and persistently' and does so in a sufficiently authoritative manner to meet the threshold of regulation.[132] Through its support of the Covenant the Commission accordingly actively supports local governments in their functional regulatory function in the context of climate change—supporting a regulator that may be perceived to rival its own competence in these areas. Yet, as is characteristic of polycentric regimes, the Covenant does not simply encourage local autonomy in pursuing said objectives but rather encourages the connection and accordingly also mutual influence between the said actors. Heyvaert indeed highlighted that 'the participating towns and cities are partly self-regulating entities, but their organization and execution is co-governed by the European Commission'.[133] Rather than simply encouraging subnational autonomy in this domain, the Commission has had a decisive influence on the development of the terms of the Covenant as well as its institutional infrastructure which 'manages negotiations, liaises between members internally, between members and external funding and technical support bodies, and supervises compliance'.[134] The Commission is thus not encouraging local climate change regulation but rather a transnational network of climate change principles that is informed by local experiences. This is a crucial distinction for in the current set-up the Commission continues to exercise control over local governments.

The European Commission has accordingly voluntarily created a new regulatory body creating norms and in doing so amplify the polycentric nature of the European legal space and the role of SNAs therein—acknowledging the role of SNAs as loyal partners of the Union in the achievement of these policy objectives. Looking at the Covenant's text it is indeed plain that the involvement of SNAs is considered to present benefits that cannot be achieved through unilateral action. The Covenant for instance considers that 'as multilevel governance is an effective tool to enhance the efficacy of actions to be taken against climate change'.[135] Polycentricity is evident not merely through the Commission's encouragement and support of subnational climate change

130 Ibid, 81. 131 Ibid, 81. 132 Ibid, 85. 133 Ibid, 85.
134 Ibid, 85.
135 The Covenant of Mayors: http://www.covenantofmayors.eu/index_en.html, Recital 4.

policies but moreover in the fact that as part of the Covenant structure local governments also support numerous Commission policies, including the decision to implement and fund a structure of technical and promotional support as well as its role to assume the coordination of the EU Conference of Mayors for a Sustainable Energy Europe.[136] The Covenant in addition makes explicit reference to the Commission's intention to further porosity through the facilitation of the 'exchange of information among the participating territorial units, the provision of guidelines and benchmark examples that support the role of local governments in the field of climate protection'.[137] The Covenant of Mayors hence highlights that polycentric regulatory challenges are addressed by polycentric solutions that harness the benefits of multi-actorship. The recent Pact of Amsterdam as well as the Committee of the Regions' Charter on Multi-Level Governance further embrace polycentricity in encouraging multi-sided networking between various actors of public authority in the Union in order to attain common goals.

## 4. The Pact of Amsterdam and the Committee of the Regions' Charter on Multi-Level Governance

Two notable policy declarations have been passed by EU institutions in recent years that each highlights the polycentric nature of the European Union. In 2014 the Committee of the Regions adopted the Charter for Multi-Level Governance and subsequently opened it for signature to all cities and regions in the various Member States.[138] The Charter essentially calls on public authorities at all levels to rely on and promote multi-level governance. This non-legally binding instrument formalizes polycentricity in recognizing the interdependence between the various levels of public authority in the Union and encourages these levels to connect and engage in multi-actorship.[139] Its general theme consists in the promotion of cooperation and the creation of networks between various actors in the EU.[140] This is interesting from the perspective of the insider narrative as local and regional authorities are perceived as vital actors in the Union whose interaction with other scales brings benefits for the polity as a whole. It is indeed the promotion of interconnection that constitutes the most striking aspect of the declaration.

[136] Ibid, 3. [137] Ibid, 3.

[138] Committee of the Regions, Resolution of the Committee of the Regions on the Charter for Multilevel Governance in Europe (2014), http://cor.europa.eu/en/activities/governance/Pages/charter-for-multiLevel-governance.aspx (hereafter Committee of the Regions, 'Charter for Multilevel Governance').

[139] Ibid, preamble. [140] Ibid, titles 2.2 and 2.5.

Rather than claiming increased autonomy SNAs are seeking more interconnection with other actors, which reinforces the introductory chapter's conclusion that in the contemporary supranational legal order connection is seen as more desirable and profitable than formal autonomy. The EU thus formalizes its relation to subnational authorities, a significant shift from earlier stages of European integration that were dominated by formal bi-centricity. The Charter indeed stresses the connection between polycentricity and the progress European integration has made but also the nature of contemporary governance challenges.

The Charter for Multi-Level Governance is not, however, the only formal declaration that witnesses this spirit. The Pact of Amsterdam was agreed on 30 May 2016 under the auspices of the then Dutch Presidency of the Council and establishes an 'Urban Agenda' for the EU.[141] Recognizing that the EU is one of the most urbanized areas in the world it anticipates that the development of urban areas will be determinative for the EU and its citizens.[142] Urban areas are moreover identified as key players in the pursuit of the Europe 2020 strategy and as the level closest to citizens.[143] In light of the above the informal Council meeting that agreed to the Pact of Amsterdam concluded that the involvement of urban authorities is a mandatory prerequisite in order to 'realise the full potential of the European Union and deliver on its strategic objectives' such as better regulation, funding, and knowledge.[144] It is for instance recognized that EU legislation is largely implemented in urban areas and bears direct implications for urban authorities. As a consequence EU regulation should henceforth anticipate these factors.[145] The Pact of Amsterdam moreover seeks to facilitate urban authorities' access to EU funding and create an urban policy knowledge base that assists urban authorities' evolution.[146] Crucially, the Urban Agenda is the first official policy document that explicitly labels the European Union as having a 'polycentric structure'.[147] The spirit of polycentricity, central to the insider narrative, is moreover apparent throughout the text of the Pact, which additionally recognizes that urban areas are pivotal actors in the 'further development of the European Union'.[148] This illustrates the presence of geographical spillover, as Member States but also other territorial units have become necessary allies in the furthering of

[141] Urban Agenda for the EU, 'Pact of Amsterdam' Agreed at the Informal Meeting of EU Ministers Responsible for Urban Matters on 30 May 2016 in Amsterdam, The Netherlands, http://ec.europa.eu/regional_policy/sources/policy/themes/urban-development/agenda/pact-of-amsterdam.pdf (hereafter 'Pact of Amsterdam').

[142] Ibid, 2. [143] Ibid. [144] Ibid, 3. [145] Ibid. [146] Ibid.

[147] Ibid, 4 (stating that the 'Urban Agenda for the EU acknowledges the polycentric structure of Europe').

[148] Ibid, 4.

European integration. The Urban Agenda moreover strives to establish 'more effective integrated and coordinated approach to EU policies and legislation with a potential impact on Urban Areas' and to involve SNAs in the design of supranational policies.[149] In line with the Committee of the Region's Charter for Multi-level Governance the Urban Agenda exemplifies the spirit of interconnection that is characteristic of SNAs' insider status. Rather calling for more autonomy for SNAs these documents seek to promote interconnection between subnational authorities and other levels of public authority to harness the benefits inherent in polycentricity and porosity. The subsequent section briefly underlines that polycentricity additionally bears the potential to influence democratic decision-making.

## 5. The European Citizens' Initiative

The European Citizens' Initiative (ECI), created by the Treaty of Lisbon, is the first element of direct democracy at supranational level.[150] Its potential to increase the Unions' democratic credentials has given many commentators reason to hope.[151] Regulation 211/2011, which sets out the practicalities of the ECI, came into force in 2012 and we have been able to since observe a clear interest on behalf of European citizens to make use of this instrument.[152] The importance of institutional mediation in the admissibility of such initiatives has, however, been pointed out.[153] Organ indeed criticized the manner and degree of institutional control that the European Commission exercises over the ECI through its application and interpretation of the admissibility criteria.[154] Regulation 211/2011 indeed establishes a four-part admissibility test to be employed by the Commission, which determines: (i) whether the organizing committee of the ECI is appropriately established;[155] (ii) that it doesn't 'manifestly fall outside the framework of the Commission's powers to submit a proposal for a legal act of the Union for the purpose of implementing

[149] Ibid, 5. [150] Article 11(4) TEU.

[151] See by way of example Alex Warleigh, 'On the Path to Legitimacy? The EU Citizens Initiative Right from a Critical Deliberativist Perspective' in Carlo Ruzza and Vincent Della Sala (eds), *Governance and Civil Society in the European Union* (Manchester University Press 2007) 55.

[152] Regulation (EU) No 211/2011 of the European Parliament and of the Council of 16 February 2011 on the Citizens' Initiative OJ L65/1 (hereafter 'Regulation 211/2011'). For an overview of the European Citizens' Initiatives that have been introduced to date, see: http://ec.europa.eu/citizens-initiative/public/welcome.

[153] James Organ, 'Decommissioning Direct Democracy? A Critical Analysis of Commission Decision-Making on the Legal Admissibility of European Citizens Initiative Proposals' (2014) 10 European Constitutional Law Review 422 (hereafter Organ, 'Decommissioning Direct Democracy').

[154] Ibid, 426. [155] Regulation 211/2011 (n 152) Article 4(2) (a).

the Treaties;[156] (iii) that the proposed initiative is not 'manifestly abusive, frivolous or vexatious';[157] nor (iv) manifestly contrary to the values of the Union as enshrined in Article 2 TEU.[158] The second of these conditions has been interpreted most strictly by the European Commission, which precluded some European Citizens' Initiatives from being considered.[159]

From the perspective of subnational authorities and their citizens the potential of the ECI as an avenue to directly influence EU policy-making is most noticeable, although it remains pure speculation at this stage. Considering the conditions of admissibility of the ECI, one million signatures from citizens of at least one-quarter of the Member States, one could imagine the mechanism being relied on by individual SNAs or networks of SNAs to directly pressure the Commission in its function as the supranational initiator of legislation to act in the absence of any formal avenues to do so. Whereas cities are devoid of any direct formal access to the Commission to convince it to initiate legislation (which, as seen in Chapter 2, hasn't prevented them from informal lobbying in this context) the ECI provides a potential avenue for SNAs to rely on a formal component of the EU legislative process to influence EU law-making. Large agglomerations or regions wishing to pursue a given objective at supranational level could be imagined to explore this option by incentivizing their residents to sign such a petition. Similarly networks of cities and regions could pursue the same aim. Indeed, why shouldn't one of these large networks, for instance those concerned with climate change (e.g. the Covenant of Mayors) rely on their expansive networks and access to citizens through the subnational authorities they group to advertise a related ECI. Only time will tell whether this is an option that is being relied on but the potential therefore seems clear, and it would be surprising if SNAs weren't interested in harnessing this indirect avenue to direct interaction with the EU. It is again worthwhile to reflect about the temporal dimension inherent to the emergence of this avenue for SNAs to influence EU policy. In this instance democracy itself embodies polycentricity and porosity and reveals its potential for adaptation. Indeed, it is clear that if citizens disagree with a certain policy, such as the use of herbicides in the context of the EU's agricultural strategy, action must be taken at supranational rather than subnational or national level for such action to bear fruit.[160] Democratic pressure to this effect at subnational level would be futile yet it might come to bear effects at the supranational scale. This section has thus highlighted that polycentricity can

[156] Ibid, Article 4(2) (b). [157] Ibid, Article 4(2) (c). [158] Ibid, Article 4(2) (d).

[159] Organ, Decommissioning Direct Democracy (n 153).

[160] See in this context the 'Ban Glyphosate' ECI that is currently open for signature: http://ec.europa.eu/citizens-initiative/public/initiatives/open/details/2017/000002.

be observed in many domains of EU law. The subsequent section examines the concept of porosity, already introduced more extensively in Chapter 3, to outline how it plays out throughout various domains of EU law.

## C. Porosity

Porosity has already been introduced as a concept framing the interconnection and intertwining of the norms of different levels of public authority in the contemporary European Union. The denomination flags up that the various scales of public authority that polycentricity captures are permeable rather than self-contained. Porosity enables policies to leak from one level to another, leading to a dynamic and creative process of cross-fertilization. This, as already underlined by *Omega*, explains that subnational norms have the potential to influence EU law's substantive development. In this process, experimentation and mutual learning take place. Porosity thus describes the dynamics that arise as a consequence of the interaction of international, EU, national, and subnational norms. This section introduces this central component of the insider narrative by looking to various domains of EU substantive law as well as supranational policies seeking to harness the benefits of porosity. This section introduces cases such as *Casagrande* and *Regione Sardegna* and examines numerous EU initiatives that seek to boost subnational cooperation to illustrate how porosity has become unavoidable in the EU, and how the Union is moreover actively relying on its consequences to realize its objectives.

### 1. *Casagrande*

As a consequence of European integration Member States and SNAs might no longer be in a position to freely exercise their autonomous competences. This equally applies to retained competences under Article 6 TFEU, such as education.[161] A judgment dating back to the early stages of European integration, *Casagrande* illustrates the relation between subnational education competence and EU law.[162] Donato Casagrande, an Italian national born to Italian parents in Bavaria, attended secondary school in Munich, where his father was employed. Under Bavarian legislation on educational

[161] Peter-Christian Müller-Graff, 'The German Länder: Involvement in EC/EU Law and Policy-Making' in Ulf Bernitz and Stephen Weatherill (eds), *The Role of Regions and Sub-National Actors in Europe* (Hart 2005) 107 (hereafter Müller-Graff, 'The German Länder').

[162] Case 9/74 *Donato Casagrande v Landeshauptstadt München* [1974] EU:C:1974:74 (hereafter *Casagrande*).

grants, a child attending secondary school without sufficient financial means was entitled to an educational grant. Munich, however, rejected his application given that the regional legislative framework in question provided that only German nationals, stateless persons, and aliens permanently residing in Bavaria that had the right to asylum were entitled to the grant. Casagrande's case was clearly governed by a polycentric regulatory patchwork and the question of the interaction between the supranational and subnational norms was key to its resolution.

The ECJ had to determine the compatibility between the Bavarian law with the free movement of workers. EU secondary law at the time merely provided a right for the children of migrant workers to be admitted to educational courses in the host State but not to receive individual grants.[163] The regulation at issue, however, also required Member States to encourage 'all efforts to enable such children to attend these courses under the best possible conditions'.[164] The very objective behind these provisions was that freedom of movement should not be restricted by the inability of the worker's family to integrate into the host country.[165] Such integration, the Court held, presupposed that the children of foreign workers be entitled to benefits provided in the host country subject to the same conditions as nationals.[166]

*Casagrande* is best known as the case that gave rise to the doctrine of implied powers. The question that emerged was whether the EU had stepped beyond its own competences in issuing secondary legislation that indirectly related to educational matters. As per the Court's assessment, although 'educational and training policy is not as such included' in the spheres of supranational competence, it does not follow that the exercise of the EU's competence 'is in some way limited if it is of such a nature as to affect the measures taken in the execution of a policy such as that of education and training'.[167] It follows that the supranational objective of workers' ability to move freely within the EU cannot be impeded for the sole reason of it touching on a national competence, be it exercised by the national or subnational level.[168] Weiler described this phenomenon of jurisdictional mutation as 'absorption'.[169] The terminology reflects that national policies that conflict with EU law, even in domains outside Union competence, 'will be absorbed and subsumed by the [EU]

[163] Ibid, para 5. [164] Ibid, para 5. [165] Ibid, para 6. [166] Ibid, para 7.

[167] Ibid, para 12.

[168] See Koen Lenaerts, 'Education in the European Community After "Maastricht"' (1994) 31 Common Market Law Review 7, 11–12; Paul Windolf, 'Wer ist der Schiedsrichter in der Europäischen Union? Der Konflikt Zwischen Europäischen Gerichtshof und Bundesverfassungsgericht' (2000) 40 Kölner Zeitschrift für Soziologie und Sozialpsychologie 39, 44.

[169] Joseph Weiler, 'The Transformation of Europe' (1991) 100 Yale Law Journal 2403, 2440.

measure'.[170] This can be observed in *Casagrande* as 'the national educational policy was impinging on [EU] free-movement policy and thus must give way'.[171] The temporal dimension inherent to the emergence of the insider narrative is thus already visible in 1974. The insider narrative makes an early appearance as the Court realizes that the absorption of subnational authorities into the body of agents pursuing supranational objectives is unavoidable. The facts of *Casagrande* clarify that, under the influence of porosity, subnational measures can be 'absorbed' by EU objectives just like Member State measures. Such absorption would not be possible if they did not form part of the same regulatory space, underlining SNAs' insider status. Absorption can moreover only occur thanks to the porous borders between the subnational and supranational legal orders, which enable direct interaction between them.

Another aspect of *Casagrande* is of particular interest: namely the Court's explicit engagement with the subnational dimension. The ECJ noted that in Germany, educational policy is largely within the competence of the Länder and therefore it must be enquired 'whether [the regulation] applies not only to the conditions laid down by laws emanating from the central power but also to those arising from measures taken by the authorities of a country which forms part of a Federal State, or of other territorial entities'.[172] In its decision the Court concludes that the same conditions apply to national and subnational norms, indirectly acknowledging the German regions' competence in educational matters. The Advocate General was explicit about the assimilation between Member State and subnational norms. Referring to the Bavarian measure and Munich's decision as those of 'State organs' he admitted that he used this expression 'to denote all organs of government, whether national or local, for I do not overlook that the defendant in the present case is the city of Munich or that the statute in question is a Bavarian one'.[173] This underlines the assimilation between national and subnational measures given that it is 'irrelevant that the conditions in question are laid down by rules issued by the central power, by the authorities of a country forming part of a Federal State or of other territorial entities'.[174]

The origin of a given measure is not determinative for the assessment of its compatibility with EU law; only its effects are. The functional approach in *Casagrande* thus underlines that subnational norms form a constitutive part of the polycentric legal order, interacting directly with EU norms. This can lead to the limitation of the supranational objectives through a subnational objective and the absorption of the subnational measure into EU norms. The

[170] Ibid, 2440. [171] Ibid, 2440. [172] *Casagrande* (n 162) para 11.
[173] Ibid, Opinion of Advocate General Warner. [174] Ibid, para 15.

test applied to verify whether the regional measure unduly interferes with EU objectives is the same that applies to Member States, illustrating that in such circumstances, the latter enjoy no special status by virtue of being the masters of the Treaties. It moreover highlights the porosity of jurisdictional borders in the Union as the Court recognizes that despite the absence of formal links between the subnational and supranational legal orders subnational norms bear the potential of negatively affecting supranational objectives. It is indeed imperative to note that the mutual interaction between subnational and supranational norms not merely leads to positive results from the perspective of EU law; it moreover bears the risk of subnational norms negatively affecting supranational objectives. This can moreover be observed in the example of the *Regione Sardegna* case.

## 2. *Regione Sardegna*

*Regione Sardegna* illustrates the porosity between the subnational and supranational legal spheres in outlining how their substantive norms mutually influence one another.[175]

The case arose out of a domestic dispute between the Italian government and the insular region of Sardinia. Sardinian law imposed a tax on undertakings that operated pleasure boats or airplanes and had their tax domicile outside of the island. The President of the Italian Council of Ministers challenged the measure before the Italian constitutional court, arguing, inter alia, that it violated EU law, both in respect of the free movement of services and the prohibition on State aid.[176] The domestic jurisdiction issued its first ever reference for preliminary ruling.[177] This showcases how the Italian State relies on porosity and polycentricty in EU law to reinforce its position towards its own SNA.[178] The referring court enquired, inter alia, whether Article 56 TFEU, 'must be interpreted as precluding tax legislation, adopted by a regional authority, … where that tax is imposed only on undertakings which have their tax domicile outside the territory of the region'.[179]

[175] Case C-169/08 *Presidente del Consiglio dei Minsitri v Regione Sardegna* [2009] EU:C:2009:709 (hereafter *Regione Sardegna*).

[176] Article 56 and 107(1) TFEU respectively.

[177] *Regione Sardegna* (n 175), Opinion of Advocate General Kokott in paras 1 and 21.

[178] Ibid, Opinion of Advocate General Kokott in para 22 ('[t]he present case is a particularly good illustration of the fact that, also in proceedings before national constitutional courts, questions of [EU] law may arise that are decisive for the outcome of the constitutional dispute in question').

[179] Ibid, para 19.

The ECJ found that the subnational policy fell within the scope of Article 56 TFEU.[180] It recalled that 'a national tax measure restricting that freedom may constitute a prohibited measure, whether it was adopted by the State itself or by a local authority'.[181] Under the insider narrative the effects of a subnational measure are indeed assimilated to that of a national measure. Advocate General Kokott agreed that it 'is irrelevant whether the tax measure in question was adopted by a local authority or by the State itself'.[182] The insider subnational measure can indeed have the same limiting effect on supranational objectives as that of a State. This is particularly so given that the application of the doctrine of purely internal situations was ruled out in light of the measure's potential to 'affect the cross-border provision of services' for example between Sardinia and Corsica.[183] As a consequence, the regional fiscal regime made 'the provision of services between Member States more difficult than that within one Member State or a part of it'.[184] Referring to *Carbonati Apuani*, the Court noted that while the tax 'is applicable only in a particular part of a Member State' it applied to aircraft and boats irrespective of their origin.[185] In such circumstances, the tax's regional character 'does not mean by definition that it cannot impinge on the freedom to provide services'.[186] The Sardinian tax was considered to limit the freedom to provide services, for it made the provision of the service more costly for those liable to pay the tax and consequently created an advantage for operators established on the island.[187] Sardinia's various attempts to save its protectionist policy, claiming that it could be justified by environmental objectives, the protection of public health, and the coherence of the tax system, were doomed to fail.[188] In respect of the latter, the Court took the regional, not the national, tax system as its point of reference, highlighting the assimilation between both entities as in both scenarios the relevant reference framework is that of the regulating authority.[189] This provides SNAs with the same opportunities to exercise their autonomous competences as Member States. *Regione Sardegna* confirms that subnational fiscal measures are aggregate building blocks of the European legal order just as the Member States. By virtue of EU norms and subnational norms interacting in the same legal space, and the porous nature of their respective borders, regional norms can endanger the internal market imperative, which is why the Court scrutinizes them subject to the same standards as those of the Member States. Beyond case law expressions of porosity can moreover be pinpointed in supranational policy initiatives, including the

[180] Ibid, para 20. [181] Ibid, para 29. [182] Ibid, para 49.
[183] *Regione Sardegna* (n 175) AG opinion paras 54–5. [184] Ibid, paras 54–5.
[185] Ibid, para 30. [186] Ibid, para 30. [187] *Regione Sardegna* (n 175) paras 31–2.
[188] Ibid, paras 35–7 and 40–6. [189] Ibid, paras 47–8.

Commission's encouragement of cross-border cooperation between actors at different scales. Porosity thus not only bears risks for the achievement of supranational objectives but can moreover contribute to this aim.

## 3. Cross-border cooperation in the polycentric union

Beyond the Court's case law, porosity can be perceived in many other domains of EU law, including initiatives to further cross-border cooperation. This section highlights some initiatives based on the assumption that cross-border networking between various levels of public authority is beneficial for the European Union's development and its objectives highlighting the presence of spillover in the achievement of supranational objectives. Since the late 1980s the European Commission has allocated substantial funds to promote cross-border cooperation between neighbouring border regions and assist them in the development of regional policies, such as the INTERREG initiative[190] or the PHARE and TACIS programmes for the States of Central and Eastern Europe.[191] Polycentricity is moreover a characterizing feature of the EU innovation policy, which emphasizes that 'all actors and all regions' must be involved in the innovation cycle, each focusing on its own strengths in line with the notion of smart specialization, which is introduced in further detail below.[192] It is indeed considered that 'strategies aimed at fostering cross-sectoral or cross-border cooperation have proven to be successful in generating ideas for new innovative applications and integrated solutions'.[193] Clusters that enhance knowledge creation and diffusion and assist the innovation and production processes are explicitly encouraged.[194] It is accordingly fair to observe that in the Union 'the importance of the level of connectedness of regions has increased dramatically during the last two decades'.[195] The Commission values polycentricity in underlining that SNAs are needed, as the 'nation-state is not best equipped for dealing with many of the challenges and opportunities of the twenty-first century',[196] highlighting

[190] Ibid, 88. [191] Ibid, 88.

[192] Communication from the Commission to the European Parliament, *Europe 2020 Flagship Initiative Innovation Union* SEC (2010) 1161, 8.

[193] European Union Smart Specialisation Platform, Guide to Research and Innovation Strategies for Smart Specialisation, (RIS 3) [2012] 15.

[194] Martin Henning, Jerker Moodysson, and Magnus Nilsson, *Innovation and Regional Transformation. From Clusters to New Combinations* (Region Skane, printed by Elanders 2010) 26–7.

[195] Philip McCann and Raquel Ortega-Argilés, 'Smart Specialisation, Regional Growth and Applications to EU Cohesion Policy' (2011) Economic Geography Working Paper 2011: Faculty of Spatial Sciences, University of Groningen: http://wbc-inconet/attach/s3_mccann_ortegapdf, 10.

[196] European Commission FOREN Network, 'A Practical Guide to Regional Foresight' (2001) 10.

the role polycentric governance challenges have played in the development of the polycentric legal order and that the emergence of the insider narrative is closely linked to the nature of contemporary governance challenges. Porosity is considered to spur innovation and it has been argued that the Innovation Union 'requires sustained effort, close cooperation and effective implementation at all levels (EU, national, regional)'.[197] The Commission actively harnesses such interconnection, for instance, when it comes to sustainability.[198] The EU's Strategy for Smart, Sustainable and Inclusive Growth stresses that all national, regional, and local authorities should implement the partnership, closely associating parliaments, as well as social partners and representatives of civil society, contributing to the elaboration of national reform programmes as well as to its implementation.[199] EU institutions accordingly consider polycentricity and porosity to be enabling factors of multiple supranational policy priorities. Due to concerns of space not all initiatives that encourage polycentric networking and seek to rely on the benefits of porosity can be highlighted at this stage. Rather an overview of two selected examples is provided below, namely the 'Regions of Knowledge' scheme as well as the European Grouping of Territorial Cooperation. Both initiatives underscore the link between the nature of polycentric contemporary governance challenges and the polycentric policies adopted to address them. While the polycentric relations that have emerged diverge significantly from classical bicentricity, this does not entail that they are at odds with the spirit of European integration, as they can indeed be perceived as a variant of the ever-wider and deeper cooperation between actors that was targeted from the beginnings and which has enabled and is being enabled by porosity.

## 4. The Regions of Knowledge Initiative

In the context of the EU Innovation Union agenda, SNAs are recognized as regulators, the action of which create effects within the internal market. SNAs are insiders of the Innovation Union that commits the EU to increase

[197] Paul Benneworth and Adrie Dassen, 'Strengthening Global–Local Connectivity in Regional Innovation Strategies: Implications for Regional Innovation Policy' (2011) OECD Regional Development Working Papers 2011/1 9, 28.

[198] In the context of the Structural and Cohesion Funds, see The Council Communication from the Commission to the European Parliament, the European Economic and Social Committee and the Committee of the Regions, *Regional Policy Contributing to Sustainable Growth in Europe 2020 SEC* (2011) 92 final 12.

[199] Communication from the European Commission, *Europe 2020. A Strategy for Smart, Sustainable and Inclusive Growth* (Com (2010) 2020 Final 2010) 29.

investment in research to 3 per cent of its GDP by 2020.[200] The Regions of Knowledge scheme ran from 2007–13 in order to strengthen and develop research and innovation excellence in EU regions.[201] A key objective consisted in facilitating 'transnational cooperation of clusters, and on supporting the emergence of European networks on the global stage'.[202] In the context of the Regions of Knowledge the 'importance of the regions as key players for the enhancement of innovation in Europe' has been stressed.[203] With a budget of €126 million, the initiative sought to bolster 'the research potential of European regions, in particular by encouraging and supporting the development, across Europe, of regional 'research-driven clusters' associating universities, research centres, enterprises and regional authorities'.[204] This reflects that SNAs are 'increasingly recognised as important players in the EU's research and development landscape'.[205] Examples of subnational cooperation that were financed by the program included the Insular Regions Knowledge Tracker, a project between insular regions establishing foresight methods.[206] The programme has coordinated efforts and fostered mutual learning experiences—illustrative of porosity—among Crete (Greece), Madeira (Portugal), the Canary Islands (Spain), and Sicily (Italy), the Balearic Islands (Spain), Corsica (France), Sardinia (Italy), the Azores (Portugal), and the Highlands (United Kingdom).[207] This illustrates that the EU not only values subnational innovation but also the collaboration of SNAs across national borders. A further success story financed by the Regions of Knowledge Initiative is the Dutch Food Valley, a combined centre of agro-scientific research, a food cluster, and an association of agro science start-ups, which is located in the Eastern Netherlands.[208]

Communication and cooperation between SNAs, which is rendered possible through porosity, was a central aspect that the Regions of Knowledge programme attempted to promote.[209] A 2011 review of the programme

[200] For an overview of the Innovation Union, see: http://ec.europa.eu/research/innovation-union/index_en.cfm.

[201] For a comprehensive assessment, see European Commission, Final Evaluation of the Regions of Knowledge 2007–2013 (FP7) Programme, April 2014: https://ec.europa.eu/research/regions/pdf/publications/regions_of_knowledge-final%20evaluation_report.pdf.

[202] Ibid, 3.

[203] European Commission, *Assessment of the Impact of the Regions of Knowledge Programme* (2011) 1.

[204] José Gutiérrez-Fons and Koen Lenaerts, 'The Constitutional Allocation of Powers and General Principles of EU Law' (2010) 47 Common Market Law Review 1629, Annex 1.

[205] Ibid.

[206] The website of the project is available under: http://www.intrack.org.

[207] Ibid. [208] Ibid.

[209] European Commission, *Regional Aspects in the 7th Framework Programme. Expert Advisory Group on 'Regions of Knowledge'—2012/2013* (2011) 5.

indeed confirmed its success in improving intra-regional communication,[210] as SNAs became 'increasingly aware of the enormous importance of regional interaction in research and innovation for their sustainable economic and social development'.[211] The EU has stressed the value of the polycentric exchange of know-how and experience, for instance through secondments of research staff between regional research centres. Despite having been discontinued, the Regions of Knowledge Initiative has been evaluated as having been successful in particular in facilitating networking activities within the establishment of research-driven clusters, fostering transnational collaboration between triple helix actors, and the exchange of knowledge and 'best practices' have been highlighted as valuable outcomes.[212] This brief overview indicates that in the context of research-driven specialization, SNAs are insiders collaborating directly with the EU institutions. Such polycentric collaboration between various actors that seeks to harness the benefits porosity presents for innovation are valued by EU law as they facilitate the targeting of contemporary governance challenges that require innovative solutions.

## 5. The European Grouping of Territorial Cooperation

The European Grouping of Territorial Cooperation (EGTC) is a new governance tool established to allow for cross-national territorial cooperation on matters of supranational interest that has proven much more popular than the tripartite contracts mentioned above in light of the number of ventures that have been formed.[213] Porosity plays out in this respect to the extent that the SNAs collaborating through an EGTC agree on binding objectives and norms irrespective of their geographical location. EGTCs were initiated

[210] European Commission, *Assessment of the Impact of the 'Regions of Knowledge Programme'* (2011) 8, available online: http://ec.europa.eu/research/evaluations/pdf/archive/other_reports_studies_and_documents/assessment_of_the_impact_of_the_regions_of_knowledge_programme.pdf.

[211] European Commission, Regional Aspects in the 7th Framework Programme. Expert Advisory Group on 'Regions of Knowledge' (2011): https://ec.europa.eu/research/fp7/pdf/advisory-groups/eag_regions_2011.pdf 4.

[212] European Commission, Mobilising Regions for Jobs and Growth. Regions of Knowledge and Research Potential (2014) 62: https://ec.europa.eu/research/regions/pdf/publications/rec-13-056_rok_03.pdf.

[213] This new legal and governance tool was set up by Regulation (EC) No 1082/2006 of the European Parliament and of the Council of 5 July 2006 on a European grouping of territorial cooperation (EGTC) OJ L 210/19 (hereafter 'The EGTC Regulation 2006'). On EGTCs generally see Elisabetta Nadalutti, 'Does the "European Grouping of Territorial Co-operation" Promote Multi-level Governance within the European Union'? (2013) 51 Journal of Common Market Studies 756; Estelle Evrard, 'The European Grouping of Territorial Cooperation (EGTC): Towards a Supraregional Scale of Governance in the Greater Region SaarLorLux?' (2016) 21 Geopolitics 513.

under the pressure of certain regions located in cross-border areas whose cooperation was previously based on ad hoc civil law agreements.[214] In contrast, the EGTC Regulation allows them to pursue cross-border cooperation on the basis of an EU law tool and for a potentially indefinite duration.[215] EGTCs moreover have legal personality, which, for instance, endows them with budgetary autonomy.[216] The mechanism was primarily developed to administer projects co-financed by EU structural funds but can be used more widely to further territorial cooperation in the absence of EU funding.[217] Currently sixty-three EGTCs have been formed.[218] It is worth noting that EGTCs are one of the rare areas where the Committee of the Regions plays a more active role given that, in accordance with Article 307 TFEU, it shall be consulted by the Parliament, Council, or Commission that concern cross-border cooperation. In the context of the EGTC the Committee of the Regions adopts political opinions, monitors the implementation of EGTC legislation at national level, keeps track of the EGTC's evolution, and produces studies and organizes networking events for those involved in the administration of these instruments.[219] A particularly noteworthy initiative in this respect is the 'EGTC Platform' that integrates the representatives of all existing EGTC in order to allow them to exchange experiences, again underlining how the Union is aware and seeks to harness the benefits presented by polycentricity and porosity.[220] The Alzette-Belval EGTC was created in 2013 to facilitate cooperation between local actors in the Franco-Luxembourgish border region.[221] Whereas the twelve border towns in question have worked together since the 1990s they decided to conclude an EGTC to facilitate their cooperation.[222] Another current example of an EGTC is the European Urban Knowledge Network, a partnership between Cyprus, Belgium, the Czech Republic, France, Germany, Hungary, Luxembourg, The Netherlands, and Romania, and Spain as an

[214] Gianluca Spinaci and Gracia Vara-Arribas, 'The European Grouping of Territorial Cooperation (EGTC): New Spaces and Contracts' EIPASCOPE 2009/2 (hereafter Spinaci and Vara-Arribas, 'The European Grouping of Territorial Cooperation').

[215] The EGTC Regulation 2006 (n 213).

[216] See ibid, Article 1(3) and Recital 9 (providing that the EGTC should have the 'capacity to act on behalf of its members, and notably the regional and local authorities of which it is composed').

[217] Spinaci and Vara-Arribas, 'The European Grouping of Territorial Cooperation' (n 214).

[218] On 1 July 2016, 63 EGTCs were in existence according to the Committee of the Regions' online registry: https://portal.cor.europa.eu/egtc/CoRActivities/Pages/egtc-list.aspx.

[219] An overview of the Committee of the Region's activities can be found under: https://portal.cor.europa.eu/egtc/about/Pages/platform.aspx.

[220] See: https://portal.cor.europa.eu/egtc/about/Pages/platform.aspx.

[221] https://portal.cor.europa.eu/egtc/CoRActivities/Pages/GECT-ALZETTE-BELVAL.aspx.

[222] Ibid.

observer, which deals with strategic urban issues. It provides knowledge support to its members 'via demand-driven Policy Labs targeting national issues in a wider European context and offers support to national knowledge institutes dealing with urban policy, research and practice'.[223] It is again worth noting that porosity serves as a key component of this initiative as the network aims at providing knowledge support via policy labs as well as an interactive website that, for instance, contains an e-library with extensive case studies.[224] Just like the previous Regions of Knowledge mechanism, EGTCs strive to increase intertwining between various levels of public authority in the Union. The fact that they have been initiated by the Union itself is illustrative of the supranational level's awareness that porosity and polycentricity facilitate the achievement of supranational objectives such as innovation and cross-border cooperation. The next section reflects on another characteristic of the insider narrative, namely the role of local and regional authorities as allies in the realization of supranational goals, which equally underlines the functional importance of SNAs for the supranational agenda.

## D. Subnational Authorities as Allies in the Achievement of Supranational Objectives

In Chapter 3 we have observed that primary legislation envisages the fulfilment of supranational objectives to fall on the Member States and the European Union. As masters of the Treaties, the States are obliged to see to the fulfilment of the obligations agreed to at Union level. Whereas no such formal obligation rests on local and regional authorities this section will highlight numerous instances that illustrate that SNAs have become functionally vital actors in the achievement of such objectives in line with the idea of geographical spillover. Subnational authorities indeed oftentimes fulfil the same role as Member States in the achievement of supranational objectives, underlining the polycentric fulfilment of the aims inherent to European integration. This will be readily observed in a number of cases; *Carbonati Apuani, Josemans, Walloon Waste*, and *Fratelli Costanzo* as well as the tripartite contracts instrument. We start with an analysis of *Carbonati*

[223] See: https://portal.cor.europa.eu/egtc/CoRActivities/Pages/European-Urban-Knowledge-Network-(EUKN).aspx.

[224] Ibid.

*Apuani*, which makes the emergence of subnational authorities' insider status explicit.

## 1. *Carbonati Apuani*

SNAs often hold fiscal competence that enables them to express policy choices, for instance in determining tax levels, and use fiscal revenue for redistributive purposes. Fiscal autonomy allows SNAs to address local needs and preferences. Under the Tieboutian logic it is considered normatively desirable for SNAs to be fiscally independent to allow citizens to match their own preferences by 'voting with their feet'.[225] SNAs can moreover choose to rely on attractive tax rates as a strategy to attract economic operators.[226] Even where an SNA has extensive fiscal autonomy as a matter of domestic law it must be weary of supranational requirements in its exercise thereof. This can be observed in the example of the *Carbonati Apuani* case, which reveals that as a consequence of SNAs' duty of loyalty towards the Union they are restricted in their policy autonomy.

In *Carbonati Apuani*, also referred to as the *Carrara Marble* case, the ECJ refused to save a municipal tax measure from the application of EU law by declaring it to fall under the doctrine of purely internal situations.[227] Italian legislation had empowered the Carrara municipal council to tax the marble excavated within, and transported from, its territory. The municipal tax was applicable only to marble transported out of the local territory, not the marble used within its territory.[228] The ECJ had to determine whether a tax 'levied solely in one municipality of a Member State and imposed on one class of goods' constitutes a charge having equivalent effect to a customs duty contrary to Article 30 TFEU.[229]

The municipality and the Italian government emphasized that the tax applied without distinction to marble exported to other parts of Italy and other Member States and should as such not fall within the ambit of Article 30 TFEU. [230] The 'chargeable event', it was claimed, did not consist in crossing inter-State borders but rather that of the municipality.[231] This argument sought to position Carrara as an outsider of EU law, claiming that the fiscal

[225] Charles Tiebout, 'A Pure Theory of Local Expenditures' (1956) 64 Journal of Political Economy 416.

[226] As seen later such a policy choice, however, bears the risk of being caught by the prohibition on State aid under Article 107 TFEU.

[227] Case C-72/03 *Carbonati Apuani* [2004] EU:C:2004:506 (hereafter *Carbonati Apuani*).

[228] Ibid, paras 3–6. [229] Ibid, para 15. [230] Ibid, para 16.

[231] Ibid, para 18.

effects did not extent to the internal market but remained confined to Italy. The ECJ disagreed. It held that *any* pecuniary charge 'imposed unilaterally on domestic or foreign goods by reason of the fact that they cross a frontier, and which is not a customs duty in the strict sense' constitutes a charge having equivalent effect.[232] This conclusion might surprise in light of the textual formulation of Article 30 TFEU, which prohibits such charges between Member States only:

> [c]ustoms duties on imports and exports and charges having equivalent effect shall be prohibited between Member States. This prohibition shall also apply to customs duties of a fiscal nature.

Article 30 TFEU indeed does not consider SNAs to be sites of fiscal competence of relevance to the EU. The ECJ does. Aware of the provision's text, the Court explained that any pecuniary charge imposed on goods by reason of the fact that they cross a border 'constitutes an obstacle to the movement of such goods'.[233] Subnational taxes have the same potential as national taxes to negatively impact the market project. As such, the ECJ went on to argue, Article 30 TFEU must be read as requiring that free movement be 'ensured within the union generally, not in trade between Member States alone, but more broadly throughout the territory of the customs union'.[234] If the Treaties only make express reference to States, the Court explained, 'that is because the framers of the Treaty took it for granted that there were no charges exhibiting the features of a customs duty in existence within the Member States'.[235]

The above statement is pivotally important in situating the insider narrative in the temporal evolution of EU law. Initially, the Court admits, the EU was concerned with States only, yet, over time, it became plain that the objectives of European integration, in this case the realization of an internal market not only free of national but any territorial borders to trade, could only be realized with the cooperation of SNAs. As a consequence, SNAs and their norm-generating capacity must be acknowledged in its relevance to the supranational project. *Carbonati Apuani* underscores that, despite the framers' inability to foresee conflict between subnational and supranational norms, such conflicts nonetheless arise. We have indeed observed that the temporal dimension is vital to make sense of the co-existence between the outsider and insider narratives as it is only through the development of

[232] Ibid, para 20.

[233] Ibid, para 22, citing Joined Cases 2/69 and 3/69 *Brachfeld and Chougol* [1969] EU:C:1969:30, para 14; Joined Cases C-363/93, C-407/93 to C-411/93 *Lancry and Others* [1994] EU:C:1994:315, para 25.

[234] *Carbonati Apuani* (n 227) para 22.

[235] Ibid.

European integration that SNAs' functional insider status has been unveiled. Where the Court is faced with such a situation it evaluates subnational norms in the same manner as national norms. While this may appear to conflict with Article 30 TFEU, the equation of the national and the subnational finds support in Article 26(2) TFEU, which defines the internal market as an 'area without internal frontiers' not distinguishing between frontiers of a national or subnational nature.[236] This leads the Court to conclude that 'the absence of charges—whether between States or within a State—exhibiting the features of a customs duty is a precondition essential to the realization of a customs union in which the free movement of goods is ensured'.[237]

The ruling in *Carbonati Apuani* wasn't the first recognition of the polycentric nature of fiscal policies in the EU. *Legros,*[238] *Lancry,*[239] and *Simitzi,*[240] which concerned some of the EU's outermost regions, established that a charge imposed on a good when crossing a territorial boundary in a Member State amounts to a charge having an equivalent effect to a customs duty.[241] Just like those measures, the Carrara tax, albeit of minimal impact on the internal market, might 'create an impediment to trade in the form of customs duty, unilaterally imposed by a competent public authority of a Member State'.[242] Indeed, for the purposes of classifying a tax as a charge having an effect equivalent to a customs duty, 'the size of the territorial administrative authority which levied the tax is therefore immaterial, in so far as that tax constitutes an obstacle to trade in the internal market'.[243] The assimilation of subnational and national policies highlights SNAs' insider status as well as the porosity of jurisdictional borders given that a municipality's tax measure is considered as a threat to the realization of the internal market. As a consequence, SNAs behave loyally towards the EU and frame their policies in manners that assist the achievement of supranational aims. Other cases illustrate that sometimes SNAs contribute to the achievement of such objectives without necessarily intending to do so and that the alliance between the subnational measure and a supranational objective can save the SNA from a finding of incompatibility.

[236] Ibid, paras 23–4. [237] Ibid, para 24.

[238] Case C-163/90 *Legros and Others* [1992] EU:C:1992:326.

[239] Cases C-407/93 to C-411/93 *Lancry and Others* EU:C:1994:315.

[240] Case C-486/93 *Simitzi* [1995] EU:C:1995:281.

[241] For an overview of EU law and the EU's outermost regions, see Dimitri Kochenov, *EU law of the Overseas: Outermost Regions, Associated Overseas Countries and Territories, Territories Sui Generis* (Kluwer 2011).

[242] *Carbonati Apuani* (n 227) para 28. [243] Ibid.

## 2. *Josemans*

In *Josemans* local regulatory competence was found to contribute to the achievement of supranational objectives. [244] A local authority was indeed portrayed as an insider capable of promoting objectives through polycentricity in light of the Court's association of subnational with supranational objectives. The case arose out of a local regulation on the sale of cannabis. Maastricht had introduced a narcotics policy via municipal regulation that stood in opposition to national policy. Under a 1976 statute, the Netherlands operated a policy of tolerance regarding the sale and consumption of cannabis in coffee shops.[245] Maastricht's municipal council had chosen to derogate from this policy in light of problems associated with drug tourism. Situated in close proximity to Belgium and Germany, Maastricht attracted many visitors who cannot lawfully buy and consume cannabis at home. Considering the number of foreign visitors to be excessive, the city decided that coffee shops should solely admit and serve Dutch residents.[246] The factual background of the case underlines that porosity also occurs domestically as after Maastricht's decision a number of policy changes took place in the Netherlands, which were triggered by the SNA's initial stance.[247] While these evolutions are not directly related to *Josemans*, they illustrate that municipal action can trigger national policy changes through porosity. The local idea of the necessity of revising the policy of tolerance creates discussion and political pressure, which ultimately triggers legal change at the national level.

Mr Josemans, the owner of a coffee shop in Maastricht, argued that the municipal measure restricted his freedom to provide goods and services to individuals residing abroad. This ECJ refused to validate that argument considering that Article 56 TFEU does not apply to coffee shops that sell the soft drug. It recalled that 'all' Member States (ignoring the Netherlands' more nuanced position) as well as various international agreements consider cannabis to be a dangerous narcotic[248] and that the combat of drug trafficking and addiction are supranational objectives.[249] Given the nature of cannabis, a

[244] Case C-137/09 *Marc Michel Josemans v Burgemeester van Maastricht* [2010] EU:C:2010:774 (hereafter *Josemans*). For a case comment, see Luke Haasbeek, 'Soft Drugs under Scrutiny: How "Easy Going" Is the Court?' (2011) 38 Legal Issues of Economic Integration 389.

[245] 1976 Law on opium (Opiumwet 1976) and *Josemans* (n 244) para 15. Coffee shops are institutions in which consumers can buy and consume cannabis in the same manner as food and non-alcoholic beverages.

[246] *Josemans* (n 244) paras 18–19 and 57.

[247] Molly Moore, 'Changing Patterns in Social Fabric Test Netherlands' Liberal Identity', *The Washington Post*, 23 June 2007.

[248] *Josemans* (n 244) paras 36–7.

[249] Ibid, paras 3–11 and paras 26–9 of the AG opinion.

coffee-shop proprietor cannot rely on the economic freedoms or the principle of non-discrimination 'in so far as concerns the marketing of cannabis, to object to municipal rules such as those at issue in the main proceedings'.[250] This finding was unsurprising in light of the Court's earlier case law that had already established that trade in narcotics falls outside the scope of EU law.[251]

The Court then proceeded to evaluate whether the local measure was constitutive of discrimination on the basis of nationality. It is well established that, in principle, distinctions based on residence violate this principle of equal treatment.[252] Having established that drug trade does not fall within the ambit of EU law, the Court merely had to assess this question with regard to the marketing of non-alcoholic beverages and food in coffee shops.[253] Seventy per cent of all Maastricht coffee shop visitors do not reside in the Netherlands and the local measure was undeniably directed at them.[254] The Court, however, considered that combating drug tourism and the accompanying public nuisance 'concerns both the maintenance of public order and the protection of the health of citizens, at the level of the Member States and also of the European Union' which are considered to be legitimate interests that justify restrictions on obligations imposed under EU law.[255] Finding the measure proportionate, Maastricht's policy was declared compatible with Union law.[256] The protection of EU public order is accordingly carried out in a polycentric fashion with Maastricht as a subnational insider contributing to its success.

Protecting *its own* public order was doubtlessly a motivating factor behind Maastricht's cannabis policy. The Court immediately equated this with the protection of *European* public order. Advocate General Bot underlined that the measure supports the combat against 'drug tourism and the criminal activities which accompany it'.[257] Maastricht's regulation, he argued further, expressed the municipality's 'duty to contribute to the maintenance of European public order'.[258] Article 71(5) Schengen Implementing Convention obliges the Member States to contribute to the maintenance of public order in the context of narcotics trafficking and consumption.[259] Despite this obligation only

[250] Ibid, para 42.

[251] Case C-289/86 *Vereniging Happy Family Rustenburgerstraat* [1988] EU:C:1988:360; Case C-158/98 *Coffeeshop 'Siberië'* [1999] EU:C:1999:334.

[252] *Josemans* (n 244) paras 58–9. [253] Ibid, para 56. [254] Ibid, para 63.

[255] Ibid, paras 65–6. [256] Ibid, para 75. [257] Ibid, para 6–7.

[258] Ibid, para 8.

[259] Article 71(5) of the Convention implementing the Schengen Agreement of 14 June 1985 between the Governments of the States of the Benelux Economic Union, the Federal Republic of Germany, and the French Republic on the gradual abolition of checks at their common borders OJ L239/19 ('[t]he Contracting Parties shall do their utmost to prevent and combat the negative effects arising from the illicit demand for narcotic drugs and psychotropic substances of whatever

formally binding Member States the Court considered the subnational measure to contribute directly to the European public order to bind SNAs that collaborate directly with the EU to achieve public order objectives in the polycentric Union. This underlines the direct relation between the EU and the municipality as well as the fact that, as immediate partners of the EU in the protection of European public order, SNAs are insiders.

*Josemans* moreover constitutes an intriguing manifestation of porosity as the subnational and the EU measures connect, notwithstanding the Netherland's policy of tolerance. Nicola argued that in assimilating Maastricht's policy with the supranational objective, the Court 'transformed a contested local interest, namely the fight against drug tourism, into a European goal of preventing and eliminating the trafficking of drugs in the Union'.[260] One may indeed wonder whether Maastricht really had these overarching goals in mind when formulating its policy. The Court's technique here is very similar to that observed in *Omega*. It connected the local public policy with wider, overarching aims of the European legal order and presented the local action as a specific manifestation of that wider aim. One may criticize this approach for intervening 'profoundly in state-local matters'[261] but it also highlights porosity in the European legal order. Porosity occurs through the local measure's contribution to the supranational goal and also in the Luxembourg Court's ability to influence domestic discussions. *Josemans* is moreover a model case to observe the insider narrative's assimilation of national and subnational norms. Undoubtedly faced with a municipal decision the Court referred to it, as it almost always does, as that of the Member State due to the principle of non-interference in domestic affairs. It for instance considered that '*Member States* cannot be denied the possibility of pursuing the objective of combating drug tourism and the accompanying public nuisance'.[262] This led Nicola to argue that the ECJ 'confused for a statewide policy was in reality an open struggle among cities with conflicting agendas towards the sale of soft drugs'.[263] Yet the Court was in no way unaware of the local origin of the measure, it simply referred to it as that of the Member State as it generally considers any measure issued on a domestic scale to be that of the State. Rather than denying SNAs' regulatory autonomy this stance is precisely why SNAs and Member States are assimilated and can, as a matter of EU law, exercise their competences in

type, including cannabis. Each Contracting Party shall be responsible for the measures adopted to this end').

[260] Fernanda Nicola, 'Invisible Cities in Europe' 35 Fordham International Law Journal (2012) 1282, 1321 (hereafter Nicola, 'Invisible Cities').

[261] Ibid, 1321. [262] *Josemans* (n 244) para 82 (emphasis added).

[263] Nicola, 'Invisible Cities' (n 260) 1321.

an analogous manner. *Josemans* has thus highlighted that supranational law considers subnational authorities to be loyal partners in the achievement of its objectives. The case also highlights that the subnational measure's effect rather than intention are determinative in this respect. The *Walloon Waste* case presents us with an additional facet of subnational authorities' contributory role to supranational objectives.

### 3. *Walloon Waste*

*Walloon Waste* concerned a conflict between the free movement imperative and a regional environmental protection measure. Wallonia had legislated to prohibit the storage, tipping, and dumping of hazardous and non-hazardous waste from other Member States or other Belgian regions in its territory.[264] The Commission argued that Belgium had failed to comply with its obligations under EU secondary law as well as the free movement of goods.[265] Reading *Walloon Waste*, it first appears that the regional measure is recognized as a policy addressing regional concerns, conflicting with EU law. A second look, however, reveals that the Court's judgment may be motivated by the regional measure's contribution to the objectives contained in the directive on hazardous waste and also general waste as regards the principle of disposal close to source. According to this view EU and subnational goals are aligned.

Advocate General Jacobs considered the regional law to be of equivalent effect to a quantitative restriction.[266] He argued that if a measure restricts imports from other Member States, it must be qualified as a measure of equivalent effect, it being irrelevant whether it 'also restricts trade as between the regions of the Member State concerned'.[267] He even considered that the ban on waste imports from other regions is capable 'of reinforcing the ban on imports from other Member States, given that it might prevent the treatment of waste from other Member States in the Flanders or Brussels regions, followed by final disposal in Wallonia'. [268] Rather than situating SNAs outside the EU legal order and its internal market, Advocate General Jacobs considered that by virtue of their insider status, they are in a position to adversely affect EU objectives. In the exercise of their autonomous

[264] Case C-2/90 *Commission v Belgium* [1992] EU:C:1992:310 (hereafter *Walloon Waste*).

[265] Council Directive 75/442/EEC on waste [1975] OJ 1975 L194 and Council Directive 84/631/EEC on the supervision and control within the European Community of the transfrontier shipment of hazardous waste [1984] OJ L 326.

[266] Opinion Advocate General Jacobs of 10 January 1991 in *Walloon Waste* [1991] EU:C:1991:344, para 17 (two opinions were issued in this case).

[267] Ibid. [268] Ibid.

competences, SNAs cannot rely on the argument that they also discriminate against goods of their neighbouring regions to evade the application of the free movement rules.[269]

The Court disagreed with its Advocate General. It concluded that the regulation met the imperative requirements of environmental protection and the protection of health.[270] The ECJ's framework of reference in *Walloon Waste* was the subnational scale, highlighting the assimilation between national and subnational norms given that Member State measures are assessed against a national background. The Court recognized that Wallonia was subject to an 'abnormal large-scale inflow of waste from other regions' and that 'there was a real danger to the environment, having regard to the limited capacity of that region'.[271] The measure was accordingly 'well founded'.[272] Such recognition could have been anchored in environmental protection, the principle of self-sufficiency in regards to waste, or whether it is acknowledged as an independent exercise of regulatory discretion.[273] The regional measure rather seems to have been tolerated because it pursued an autonomous aim, recognized under EU law, namely environmental protection, notwithstanding the fact that this protective goal limited EU internal market aims. On the other hand, the regional measure could have been considered to contribute to a common supranational aim, the disposal of waste close to its source. Article 5(2) of the 1975 Waste Framework Directive already enshrined this principle at the time of *Walloon Waste*.[274] The Court indeed explicitly recognized that according to the former Article 130r(2) of the Treaty, 'it is for each region, municipality or other local authority' to ensure that its own waste is collected, treated and disposed of 'as close as possible to the place where it is produced, in order to limit as far as possible the transport of waste'.[275] This recognizes that waste treatment and environmental protection are networked policy challenges that manifest in a polycentric manner and are consequently best addressed in a polycentric fashion. According to this alternative reading, SNAs emerge as insiders of EU aims that help to achieve supranational objectives in a polycentric fashion. The *Fratelli Costanzo* case formalizes SNAs' contribution to supranational aims in subjecting them to the duty of loyal cooperation.

[269] The doctrine of purely internal situations constitutes an exception to this rule.

[270] *Wallloon Waste* (n 264) para 29. [271] Ibid, para 31. [272] Ibid, para 32.

[273] I discuss this further in Michèle Finck, 'Above and Below the Surface: The Status of Sub-National Authorities in EU Climate Change Regulation' (2014) 26 Journal of Environmental Law 443.

[274] Council Directive 72/442/EEC on Waste, OJL194/39 (1975).

[275] *Wallloon Waste* (n 264) para 34.

## 4. SNAs' duty of loyalty towards the EU

This section outlines an additional aspect of supranational law that portrays SNAs as insiders: their duty to behave loyally towards the EU when faced with a conflict between a domestic norm and a norm of EU law. The Court has established that in the exercise of their autonomous competences, SNAs are, just like Member States, bound to comply with this obligation. At first sight local and regional authorities do not appear to be bound to behave loyally towards the Union as the thereto-related Treaty obligation, enshrined in Article 4(3) TEU, merely binds Member States.[276] In accordance with Article 4(3) TEU, Member States must take appropriate measures to fulfil obligations arising under the Treaties or resulting from acts of the EU institutions and must facilitate the achievement of EU objectives. The provision imposes a positive obligation on Member States to contribute to the success of the European project. This derives logically from their status as masters of the Treaties. It may appear just as logical to exempt SNAs from any duty to behave loyally towards the Union. Nonetheless, in 1989 the ECJ established that SNAs are bound to act loyally towards the EU. *Fratelli Costanzo* concerned a dispute between a private company and the city of Milan regarding an award of public work contracts.[277] In preparation of the 1990 FIFA World Cup, Milan had issued a call for tenders to undertake alterations to its football stadium. Costanzo was excluded from the call and put forward that its exclusion was based on a national legislation incompatible with EU secondary law. In *Becker* and *Marshall* the Court had already established that where the provisions of a directive appear, as far as their subject matter is concerned, to be unconditional and sufficiently precise, an individual may rely on them against 'the State' in domestic proceedings if the State fails to implement the directive after the end of the implementation period.[278] The referring court enquired whether 'administrative authorities, including municipal authorities, are under the same obligation as a national court' to apply the directive, and in particular also 'to refrain from applying provisions of national law which conflict with them'.[279]

[276] It provides that '[p]ursuant to the principle of sincere cooperation, the Union and the Member States shall, in full mutual respect, assist each other in carrying out tasks which flow from the Treaties'.

[277] Case C-103/88 *Fratelli Costanzo v Comune di Milano* [1989] EU:C:1989:256 (hereafter *Fratelli Costanzo*).

[278] Ibid, para 29. See also Case C-8/81 *Becker v Finanzamt Münster-Innenstadt* [1982] EU:C:1982:7; Case C-152/84 *Marshall v Southampton and South-West Hampshire Area Health Authority* [1986] EU:C:1986:84.

[279] *Fratelli Costanzo* (n 277) para 28.

The Court noted in *Fratelli Costanzo* that there would be a contradiction in allowing individuals to rely on a directive against administrative authorities but to 'hold at the same time that those authorities are under no obligation to apply the provisions of the directive and refrain from applying provisions of national law which conflict with them'.[280] Accordingly, when the conditions under which individuals may rely on directives in domestic proceedings are fulfilled and the transposition period has expired, 'all organs of the administration, including decentralised authorities such as municipalities, are obliged to apply those provisions'.[281] This frames SNAs as integral components of the polycentric EU legal order subject to direct obligations towards the EU: to apply the provisions of an EU directive. SNAs are insiders because they are the public authority giving effect to EU law, underlining porosity. *Fratelli Costanzo* hence creates an obligation falling on SNAs to set aside an obligation of national law if consistent interpretation proves impossible.[282] In *Pfeiffer* the Court had found that a national court's duty of consistent interpretation is 'inherent in the system of the Treaty'.[283] As agents of the State, national courts must comply with the said obligation to ensure that the Treaties are respected. Where consistent application does not allow solving a conflict of norms, the duty to disapply domestic law emerges as a consequence of supremacy and binds not only Courts but also subnational authorities, highlighting the unavoidable governance spillovers when it comes to the achievement of supranational goals. This highlights that there is a direct obligation lying on subnational authorities to behave loyally towards the EU. SNAs import supranational norms into the domestic legal order where the Member State fails to fulfil its role as importer, showing that the polycentric structure can benefit the achievement of the EU's substantive goals. This underscores the benefits supranational law draws from its polycentric enforcement through a multiplication of enforcement agents.

*Fratelli Costanzo* indeed goes further than merely subjecting SNAs to the duty of loyal cooperation, as the ECJ insisted that local and regional authorities disapply internal law which conflicts with EU law, and this even without securing a court order.[284] Verhoeven considers this to be paradoxical, as 'European law is generally not concerned with the internal state structure of

[280] Ibid, para 31. [281] Ibid, para 31.

[282] Ibid, para 31. See also Case C-224/97 Ciola [1999] EU:C:1999:212; Case C-198/01 *Consorzio Industrie Fiammiferi* [2003] EU:C:2003:430.

[283] Joined cases C-397/01 to C-403/01 *Pfeiffer* [2004] EU:C:2004:584, para 114.

[284] Stephen Weatherill, 'The Challenge of the Regional Dimension in the European Union' in Stephen Weatherill and Ulf Bernitz (eds), *The Role of Regions and Sub-National Actors in Europe* (Hart Publishing 2005) 5.

the Member States'.[285] The *Fratelli Costanzo* solution may be better explained by the objectives it fulfils. The functional obligation can be seen to safeguard the protection of individual rights that emerge under a directive, but also the efficacy of the European legal order as it sees to the application of a given norm where the Member State has failed adequately apply it, and this without the timely and costly recourse to a domestic court. This underlines that a polycentric structure is of benefit to the Union and the achievement of its objectives.

The exact contours of the *Fratelli Costanzo* obligation, however, remain somewhat hazy. Subsequent case law confirmed that where an administrative authority observes a conflict between a national and a EU norm, it must interpret the national norm in light of EU law, or set aside the incompatible national norm and apply the directly effective provision of EU law instead.[286] Nonetheless, the future of the *Fratelli Costanzo* doctrine seems uncertain as it has never been reaffirmed as explicitly as in 1989. In a case involving an administrative body, not an SNA, the Grand Chamber applied the doctrine in *Petersen* only to identify that there is a duty for national courts to apply national law.[287] In *Fuß*, the Court confirmed that municipalities must directly apply a directive instead of conflicting national law.[288] In this case, the Court explicitly invoked Article 4(3) TEU to hold that 'all authorities of the Member State' must achieve the result envisaged by the European directive.[289] Where national authorities are unable to interpret and apply national law in compliance with the requirements of EU law 'it is for the national courts and administrative bodies to apply EU law in its entirety and to protect rights which the latter confers on individuals, disapplying, if necessary, any contrary provision of domestic law'.[290] This was also affirmed in *Gaviero*.[291] In *Amia*, it was further confirmed that if the relevant provisions of a directive have direct effect, 'they are binding on all the authorities of the Member States, that is to say, not merely the national courts but also all administrative bodies, including decentralised authorities, and those authorities are required to apply them'.[292] Noticeably, however, the Court then applied *Fratelli Costanzo*

[285] Maartje Verhoeven, 'The "Costanzo Obligation" and the Principle of National Institutional Autonomy: Supervision as a Bridge to Close the Gap?' (2010) 3 Review of European Administrative Law 23, 23 (hereafter Verhoeven, 'The Costanzo Obligation').

[286] Case C-224/97 *Ciola* [1999] EU:C:1999:212; Case C-198/01 *Consorzio Industrie Fiammiferi* [2003] EU:C:2003:430.

[287] Case C-341/08 *Petersen* [2010] EU:C:2010:4, paras 80–1.

[288] Case C-429/09 *Fuß* [2010] EU:C:2010:717.

[289] *Fratelli Costanzo* (n 277) para 38–9.

[290] Ibid, para 40.

[291] Case C-444/09 *Rosa María Gavieiro* [2010] EU:C:2010:819, para 73.

[292] Case C-97/11 *Amia* [2012] EU:C:2012:306, para 38.

only to state that the provisions of such directives may be directly relied on in front of a domestic court.[293]

*Fratelli Costanzo* can be seen as a variant of the principle 'according to which the whole of the Member State is responsible for breaches of EU law by any of its parts or emanations'.[294] This principle, Bengoxtea argued, 'was turned over and formulated as a positive obligation' as also SNAs 'were expected and obliged to observe [EU] law'.[295] We can identify an interesting paradox that highlights the coexistence between the outsider and insider narratives in EU law. Indeed, the combination of national institutional autonomy—according to which only States bear direct responsibility under EU law—and the *Fratelli Costanzo* obligation results in the fact that on the one hand, the EU 'has a relationship with its Member States, and respects the internal state structure. On the other, obligations such as the *Costanzo* obligation are not addressed to the Member States themselves, but to the administrative authorities within these states'.[296]

It remains somewhat uncertain in which scenarios and to which extent the Union's judiciary is willing to apply *Fratelli Costanzo*. The judgment is nonetheless pivotal for it affirms, first, that EU law imposes direct obligations on SNAs to ensure the success of EU objectives. In this domain we indeed perceive SNAs' role as insider allies of the European legal order. Second, SNAs are insiders as they actively participate in EU integration and the thereto-connected harmonization of laws and must give effect to harmonizing measures. In the polycentric EU, SNAs are direct allies of the EU as they fulfil the Member State's obligation where the latter falls short of doing so. Porosity is at play to the extent that the subnational measure is capable of having the same direct impact on the supranational legal order as State actions, and Member States as well as SNAs are assimilated as agents charged with enforcing EU law. The case also allows us to pinpoint the insider narrative's temporal dimension given that it is evident that the need for such a principle only becomes evident once the Court has developed the doctrines of direct effect and consistent interpretation.

The Court has more recently imposed variants of the *Fratelli Costanzo* obligation on SNAs in related contexts. *Carmen Media Group* concerned a refusal by Schleswig-Holstein to grant a licence to market sports bets via the Internet.[297] The dispute concerned the same regional law that was at stake in

[293] *Fratelli Costanzo* (n 277) paras 40–1.

[294] Joxerramon Bengoetxea, 'Autonomous Constitutional Regions in a Federal Europe' in Elke Cloots, Geert de Baere, and Stefan Sottiaux (eds), *Federalism in the European Union* (Hart 2012) 239 (hereafter Bengoetxea, 'Autonomous Constitutional Regions').

[295] Ibid, 237.

[296] Verhoeven, 'The Costanzo Obligation' (n 285) 61.

[297] Case C-46/08 *Carmen Media Group* [2010] EU:C:2010:505.

*Digibet*, introduced further below, and the refusal was anchored in the fact that the Land held a public monopoly over receiving bets on sporting competitions.[298] In this context, the question emerged whether Article 56 TFEU must be interpreted as precluding 'the establishment, by a regional entity, of a public monopoly on the organisation of bets on sporting competitions and lotteries' and whether the answer to that question may be affected by the fact that the regulation of other games of chance falls at least partly within the competence of the federal State'.[299] The Court held that,

> whilst EU law does not preclude an internal allocation of competences whereby certain games of chance are a matter for the Länder and others for the federal authority, the fact remains that, in such a case, the authorities of the *Land* concerned and the federal authorities are jointly required to fulfil the obligation on the Federal Republic of Germany not to infringe Article 49 EC. It follows that, in the full measure to which compliance with that obligation requires it, those various authorities are bound, for that purpose, to coordinate the exercise of their respective competences.[300]

*Carmen Media Group* thus confirms that just like Member States, SNAs are bound to ensure the *effet utile* of EU law. Despite the uncertainty surrounding the precise obligation inherent in *Fratelli Costanzo*, SNAs' status as insiders that have to ensure that the obligations that arise under EU law are complied with seems well established.

That spirit of loyalty can also be pinpointed in other contexts. *Bero* for example illustrates another variant of the related responsibility.[301] It concerned the situation of a woman who 'is probably a Syrian national' who had her application for asylum denied and was ordered to be kept in detention for the purpose of her removal under the Returns Directive.[302] In Germany, the Länder are charged with carrying out detention measures for the purpose of removal and Hesse placed her in an ordinary prison, rather than a 'specialised detention facility' as required under Article 16(1) of the Returns Directive.[303] In contrast to other German states, Hesse had no specialized detention facilities within the meaning of the directive. The ECJ had to pronounce itself on the compatibility of that practice with the Returns Directive.[304] The Grand Chamber established that in a federal structure not every state is required to set up specialized detention facilities but that it must nonetheless be ensured that 'the competent authorities of a federated state that does not have such facilities can provide accommodation for third-country nationals pending

[298] *Fratelli Costanzo* (n 277) para 25. [299] Ibid, para 53. [300] Ibid, para 70.

[301] Joined Cases C-473/13 and C-514/13 *Bero* EU:C:2014:2095 (hereafter *Bero*). I am grateful to Cathryn Costello for bringing this case to my attention.

[302] Ibid, para 9. [303] Ibid, para 10. [304] Ibid, para 24.

removal in specialized detention facilities located *in other federated states*'.[305] While *Carmen Media Group* established that States and SNAs are required to loyally cooperate for the purposes of implementing EU law; *Bero* signals that such cooperation is mandatory between various SNAs within the same State as one State must allow access to its detention facilities to another, despite the possibility that from a purely domestic perspective this may give rise to financial conflicts. Where this is the case, loyalty must prevail over domestic inter-level conflicts as a matter of supranational law. This evidences that in the polycentric EU connections between all levels have become a functional necessity to achieving supranational goals.

The above case law has highlighted that subnational authorities serve as loyal insiders of the European legal order. Their loyalty has indeed become a functional necessity to preventing SNAs from threatening the achievement of supranational aims through conflicting policies but also requiring them to proactively contribute to these aims in a constructive manner. Local and regional authorities' role as partners of the EU in the fulfilment of supranational goals is furthermore illustrated by the instrument of tripartite contracts.

## 5. Tripartite contracts

Tripartite contracts are a polycentric policy instrument that allows the European Union to enlist Member States, but also local and regional authorities, to realize supranational objectives.[306] Such contracts are concluded between the Union, the Member State, and a regional or local authority with a view to achieve common objectives. The idea of contractual tools between these various levels was first put on the table in the European Commission's 2001 White Paper on Governance in order to involve subnational authorities in the achievements of targets set at supranational level.[307] The Commission's Communication on tripartite contracts is explicit about their underlying objective, highlighting that they serve to recognize 'the growing role of regional and local authorities in the design and above all the execution of [EU] policies' which, it is argued, 'must nevertheless be given fuller recognition'.[308]

[305] Ibid, para 31 (my emphasis).

[306] See generally European Commission, 'A framework for target-based tripartite contracts and agreements between the Community, the States and regional and local authorities' COM (2002) 709 final (hereafter European Commission, 'A Framework for Tripartite Contracts').

[307] European Commission, 'A White Paper' COM (2001) 428 final.

[308] European Commission 'A Framework for Tripartite Contracts' (n 306).

Tripartite contracts encourage SNAs 'to play a growing role in the framing and implementation' of EU policies, while the EU ensures that SNAs enjoy more flexibility in the means provided for legislative implementation, especially that with a strong territorial impact, 'provided the level playing field at the heart of the internal market can be maintained'.[309] SNAs are at once implementers of common norms and agents with independent localized interests. The contracts have indeed been said to lead to 'a more direct, active and horizontal partnership between levels of government within the European Union'.[310] While such contracts further recognize the autonomy of subnational levels in the implementation of supranational objectives it should not be lost from sight that the close contractual relationship also allows EU institutions to keep a close eye on SNAs' actions in order to ensure the homogenous application of supranational objectives—highlighting an additional interest of the EU institutions in polycentric governance structures and the growing connection and intertwining of the actors' respective interests.

The first, and to date last, tripartite agreement was signed in 2004 between the Commission, Italy, and Lombardy in the context of sustainable mobility.[311] The contract concerned the putting into place of 'an innovative, open and efficient governance of the mobility sector' as at the time, mobility in Lombardy had 'significant shortcomings with regard to its effectiveness, transparency, openness and coherence'.[312] Lombardy itself had initiated the contract's conclusion in order to innovate with regard to its mobility sector.[313] Indeed, '[a]ny one of the future contracting parties may take the initiative to establish such tripartite relations' showing that SNAs are not subordinated parties in this triangular relation.[314] The region indeed assumed an active role in seeking EU support to further the policy objective. While Member States are involved in this process, the relation between the SNA and the EU is nonetheless of a direct nature, as they communicate directly. Such direct contact has been said to constitute 'solid evidence that state governments have lost control of the relations between European agencies and sub-national actors'.[315] While tripartite agreements do not actively encourage

[309] Ibid.

[310] Martino Mazzoleni, 'The First Tripartite Agreement in the EU. An Actor-Centred Analysis of an Experimental Multi-Level Interaction' (2006) 16 Regional and Federal Studies 263, 263 (hereafter Mazzoleni, 'The First Tripartite Agreement').

[311] Ibid, 263. [312] Ibid, 270. [313] Ibid, 264.

[314] European Commission, 'A Framework for Tripartite Contracts' (n 306).

[315] Mazzoleni, 'The First Tripartite Agreement' (n 310) 275.

decentralization as such, they help regions seeking to innovate and regulate autonomously, within the limits set by EU law. The Lombardy-Italy-EU tripartite contract, however, appears to be the only tripartite contract that has been concluded to date.[316] Panara has noted that further applications for such tripartite relations have been submitted by Birmingham, Lille, and Pescara but none of them appears to have been accepted by the Commission, although the reasons therefore are unclear.[317] Vara Arribas has attributed the instruments' lack of success to the lack of EU funding to support it.[318] Panara considers this to not have diminished the emblematic character of the instrument 'as it shows that the EU ascribes to the sub-national authorities the status of contractual partners on an equal footing with other tiers of government and the ability to negotiate contracts and agreements with the Commission'.[319] In practical terms, however, tripartite contracts have had a much more limited success in stimulating polycentricity and porosity than other EU policy instruments, including the European Groupings of Territorial Cooperation, which has already been examined above.

This section has highlighted that case law and innovative policies furthering polycentric cooperation in the EU portray subnational authorities as insiders regarding supranational policies. The subsequent section further reflects on the polycentric nature of the EU legal order in emphasizing that SNAs are functionally aligned with the Member States.

## E. The Assimilation of Member States and SNAs

The present section highlights various domains of supranational law where subnational authorities are functionally assimilated to the Member States despite their starkly divergent formal status (which was subject to analysis in the preceding chapter). This underlines that, whereas the outsider narrative rests on a formal paradigm, the insider narrative is grounded in a functional analysis of EU law. This section examines these points in looking towards case law as well as the Commission's smart specialization agenda. We start our analysis with the *Flemish Care Insurance* case.

[316] Carlo Panara, *The Sub-national Dimension of the EU: A Legal Study of Multilevel Governance* (Springer 2015) 50 (hereafter Panara, *The Sub-national Dimension*).

[317] Ibid, 49–50.

[318] Gracia Vara Arribas and Delphine Bourdin, *Tripartite Arrangements: An Effective Tool for Multilevel Governance?* (EIPA Publications 2005) 23.

[319] Panara, *The Sub-national Dimension* (n 316) 50.

### 1. *Flemish Care Insurance*

The *Flemish Care Insurance* case concerned a decree of the Flemish Parliament setting up a care insurance scheme in Belgium's Dutch-speaking region and the bilingual region of Brussels-Capital.[320] The scheme conferred entitlement, up to a given amount, for an insurance fund to cover certain costs incurred in case of a state of dependence for health reasons. Residents of Belgium's Walloon Region were excluded from its benefits, even if they were employed in Flanders or Brussels. Individuals residing in another Member State could, however, rely on the insurance provided that they were employed in the Dutch-speaking or bilingual region. According to Advocate General Sharpston, the case raised the question:

> whether [EU] law prevents an *autonomous entity of a Member State* from making the grant of social security benefits conditional on residence in the territory of the autonomous entity concerned or in the territory of another Member State, thereby excluding persons working in the autonomous entity in question who are resident in another part of the national territory. Still more broadly, what is the *impact of [EU] law on the federal or decentralised structure of a Member State* and on what is deemed to be a 'purely internal situation' outside the scope of [EU] law?[321]

These introductory statements recognize the direct relation between subnational and supranational norms. Polycentricity and porosity are visible to the extent that dynamics arising in EU law affect subnational autonomies and vice versa. The doctrine of purely internal situations, the application of which in *Flemish Care Insurance* was subject to debate, is, however, based on the opposite presumption, which led the Advocate General to criticize its rationale.[322] The above statement is noteworthy, not only for addressing the status of subnational regulatory autonomies under EU law, but also because it utters a vision of the European Union according to which the latter cannot be fully integrated if SNAs can shield themselves from the application of EU law. Such isolation, which can be interpreted as SNAs remaining at the

[320] Case C-212/06 *Government of the French Community and Walloon Government v Flemish Government* [2008] EU:C:2008:178 (hereafter *Flemish Care Insurance*). For a comment, see: David Martin, 'Comments on Gouvernement de la Communauté française and Gouvernement wallon (Case C-212/06 of 1 April 2008) and Eind (Case C-291/05 of 11 December 2007)' (2008) 10 European Journal of Migration and Law 365; Camille Dautricourt, 'La jurisprudence de la Cour de justice et du Tribunal de première instance. Chronique des arrêts. Gouvernement de la Communauté française et Gouvernement wallon contre Gouvernement flamand' (2008) 3 Revue du droit de l'Union européenne 603; Herwig Verschueren, 'La régionalisation de la sécurité sociale en Belgique à la lumière de l'arrêt de la Cour de justice européenne portant sur l'assurance-soins flamande' (2008) Revue belge de sécurité sociale 173.

[321] *Flemish Care Insurance* (n 320) AG opinion, paras 2–3 (emphasis added).

[322] On this, see further Chapter 3.

outside of the internal market enterprise and thus EU law, can, in the eyes of the Advocate General no longer be accepted in the contemporary EU. While SNAs might, through the doctrine of purely internal situations, be *de jure* outsiders of EU law, they are de facto insiders. The Advocate General acknowledged this insider status in pointing out that subnational measures have the same effects on the internal market as national norms. This hints at the temporal relation between the outsider and insider narratives as the latter is gradually conquering areas formerly governed by the former as EU integration develops. SNAs are insiders given that the entities between which barriers to the free movement need to be abolished 'are not necessarily always the Member States, but the entities that have the *relevant regulatory authority* (be these Member States or decentralised authorities within a single Member State)'.[323] In light of the parallels between national and subnational norms, the latter should not benefit from an exemption under EU law that Member States cannot invoke. As insiders, SNAs may not take actions that limit any of the four freedoms. Otherwise, the Advocate General continued,

> [t]he beneficial effects of dismantling barriers to freedom of movement between Member States can easily be undermined if decentralised authorities of Member States have the relevant competences and are free to establish such barriers between themselves. In the light of trends towards regional devolution in several Member States, this may be a serious issue. However beneficial devolution may be from the perspective of subsidiarity and democratic accountability, it must not come at the cost of (de facto) endangering the area of freedom of movement or the *effet utile* of [EU] law.[324]

This is key given that SNAs are not necessarily insiders because it serves them and their autonomy but *Flemish Care Insurance* rather illustrates that they are also insiders because it is in the EU's interest, which accordingly seeks to control what they do. By virtue of porosity and SNAs' insider status, subnational norms can create effects that may undermine EU objectives and integration. This insider status should be recognized through the abolition of the doctrine of purely internal situations, as otherwise the detrimental effect of EU norms on supranational integration may go unsanctioned, whereas the effects created by Member State norms are subject to scrutiny. The Advocate General explicitly assimilated regional authorities and Member States in her analysis in stating that, since the Belgian Communities and Regions act as:

> autonomous legislators within their spheres of competence, their position is, in that respect, equivalent to that of a Member State. Were Flanders an independent

[323] *Flemish Care Insurance* (n 320) AG opinion, para 117 (emphasis in original).
[324] Ibid, para 118.

Member State of the Union, the impossibility for those living in Wallonia but working in Flanders to affiliate to the Flemish care insurance scheme would clearly fall foul of the Treaty.[325]

This amounts to a clear deviation from the outsider narrative under which Member States and SNAs have a distinctively different status. It moreover echoes the relatively large agreement in legal scholarship that, as a consequence of EU integration, the shielding of subnational norms from EU law is no longer tenable. Indeed, as European integration has progressed, the claim that supranational law need purely concern itself with barriers to trade between States is outdated.

The ECJ chose not to follow the Advocate General's bold suggestion to mark the end of the doctrine of purely internal situations.[326] The Grand Chamber concluded that the situation was only in part internal, notably as regards the exclusion of Belgian nationals who work in Flanders or Brussels and live in the French- or German-speaking regions and had never exercised their freedom to move within the EU.[327] This, the Grand Chamber conceded, was a proper purely internal situation.[328] The situation of Belgian nationals who had exercised their Treaty freedoms before returning to Belgium as well as of nationals from other Member States was to the contrary considered to fall within the ambit of EU law.[329] The likelihood that the Flemish scheme affected at least some individuals falling within the second scenario was considered to be strong so that the regional insurance scheme could not be qualified as being outside the scope of EU law.

The Court's reluctance to rely on the doctrine, which has been introduced in the preceding chapter as a manifestation of the outsider narrative, however, highlights that as EU law develops, subnational authorities' outsider status is increasingly ceding the way for them to be treated as insiders. While the doctrine hasn't been formally overruled the Court interprets the doctrine in a very narrow manner so that, irrespective of the nationality of a European

[325] Ibid, para 120.

[326] See also Thomas Vandamme, 'Case C-212/06, Government of the French Community and the Walloon Government v. Flemish Government, judgment of the Court of Justice (Grand Chamber) of 1 April 2008, nyr' (2009) 46 Common Market Law Review 287, 296.

[327] *Flemish Care Insurance* (n 320), paras 37–8.

[328] Ibid, paras 37–8 (the ECJ added: '[i]t may nevertheless be remarked that interpretation of provisions of Community law might possibly be of use to the national court, having regard too to situations classed as purely internal, in particular if the law of the Member State concerned were to require every national of that State to be allowed to enjoy the same rights as those which a national of another Member State would derive from Community law in a situation considered to be comparable by that court').

[329] *Flemish Care Insurance* (n 320) paras 34–9.

citizen and their place of residence, it suffices that they have exercised a fundamental freedom to fall within the scope of the European Treaties.[330] Finding the doctrine not to apply to the main proceedings, the Court went on to examine the conflict between the subnational policy and the EU free movement imperative. In doing so, it treated the subnational norm as if it were that of a Member State.

The non-application of the doctrine of purely internal situations entailed that the subnational measure was in the same position vis-à-vis EU law as national measure. The Grand Chamber established that the Flemish scheme restricted the free movement of workers and the freedom of establishment, as it potentially deterred those contemplating moving to certain parts of Belgium from doing so for fear of not being eligible for care insurance. One of the arguments put forward by the Flemish government was that, due to internal distributions of competences, it was unable to provide insurance for residents of Wallonia. The Court rejected that argument, reiterating that 'Member States' cannot plead provisions, practices, or situations within their domestic structure to justify a failure to comply with obligations arising under the Treaties.[331] The Advocate General recalled that Member States alone are responsible for fulfilling obligations arising under the Treaties.[332] The Flemish government put forward arguing that this interpretation of EU law 'would make it de facto impossible for Member States to adopt a federal structure'.[333] The Advocate General countered that EU law:

> has not made it impossible for other federal Member States, and/or their decentralised authorities, to exercise their competences as defined by national law. However, a Member State cannot use its decentralised structure as a cloak in order to justify a failure to comply with its obligations under [EU] law.[334]

Indeed, SNAs can exercise their competences no more or no less than Member States themselves, underlining their assimilation for the purposes of EU law. The mere existence of regulatory autonomies can thus not be advanced to justify the breach of an obligation arising under EU law. Just like national measures breaching Articles 45 and 49 TFEU, those of a subnational nature can, however, be justified. In this sense, SNAs also enjoy the same status of autonomy as Member States. It is worthy of special emphasis that the Court considered that migrant workers 'contemplating the pursuit of employment

[330] On this, see also Case 115/78 *Knoors* [1979] EU:C:1979:31, para 24; Case C-19/92 *Kraus* [1993] EU:C:1993:125, paras 17–18; Case C-419/92 *Scholz* [1994] EU:C:1994:62, para 9.

[331] *Flemish Care Insurance* (n 320) paras 57–9.

[332] *Flemish Care Insurance* (n 320) AG opinion, para 101.

[333] Ibid, para 104.

[334] Ibid, para 105.

or self-employment in one of those two regions, might be dissuaded from making use of their freedom of movement'.[335] Taking the subnational as the relevant framework of reference underscores the assimilation between national and subnational measures. The sole ground of justification put forward was that 'the Flemish Community could exercise no competence in relation to care insurance in respect of persons residing in the territory of other linguistic communities', a line of argument rejected by the CJEU.[336] The Court established that the existence of a domestic decentralization arrangement cannot per se justify a failure to comply with the Treaties.

In light of this finding, Verschueren interpreted *Flemish Care Insurance* as establishing that 'the principle of the free movement of persons within the European internal market takes precedence over the internal constitutional organization of a Member State'.[337] It is true that Member States' internal organization, per se, cannot, except for the possible application of Article 4(2) TEU, be invoked to excuse violations of a free movement imperative. This does not, however, limit the regulatory autonomies of SNAs any more than those of States. Verschueren predicted that 'the mandatory application of EU internal market law to relationships between a Member State's subnational entities would render meaningless the federal structure of that Member State'.[338] For the purposes of my analysis, it is, however, this very fact which explains that SNAs are insiders, not outsiders. The Court determines that SNAs are subject to the free movement rules, and that they may not claim the existence of their regulatory autonomies, as such, to be exempted from obligations arising under EU law. The *Aragonesa* case is another classical internal market case, this time relating to the free movement of goods, which equally underscores the functional assimilation between Member States and SNAs.

## 2. *Aragonesa*

*Aragonesa* arose out of a dispute between a company operating advertising hoardings and Catalonia.[339] The region had imposed administrative fines on the company after the latter's infringement of Catalan legislation which prohibited the advertisement of strong alcoholic beverages in the media, streets,

[335] Ibid, para 48. [336] Ibid, para 57–8.

[337] Herwig Verschueren, 'The Impact of EU Law on the Devolution of Social Powers in the Member States' in Elke Cloots, Geert de Baere, and Stefan Sottiaux (ed), *Federalism in the European Union* (Hart Publishing 2012) 275.

[338] Ibid, 284.

[339] Joined Cases C-1/90 and C-176/90 *Aragonesa de Publicidad Exterior SA v Departamento de Sanidad y Seguridad Social de la Generalitat de Cataluña* [1991] EU:C:1991:327 (hereafter *Aragonesa*).

highways, cinemas, and public transport.[340] The company put forward the argument that the regional law infringed Article 34 TFEU in limiting the marketing opportunities for beverages from other Member States. As such the regional measure's compatibility with EU law had to be examined. The question that arose was whether, and if so in which manner, EU law limits SNAs' capacity to initiate measures aimed at the protection of the health of their citizens. The Court's response underscores that local and regional authorities have the same leeway in this respect as the Member States themselves.

The Court emphasized that all domestic authorities, including SNAs, are bound to comply with EU law.[341] It follows that measures with a 'limited territorial scope' cannot 'escape being characterized as discriminatory or protective' if they affect the sale of products from other parts of the national territory or from other Member States.[342] As insiders to the EU legal order, subnational measures have the same potential to hinder trade as those of the States, again underlining that porosity not merely enables SNAs to contribute to the achievement of supranational objectives but also to have a limiting effect on them.[343] In the interest of achieving the supranational free movement goals their regulatory autonomy must be subject to the same restrictions as those of the Member States.[344]

The Catalan legislation was held to be constitutive of a measure having an equivalent effect to a quantitative restriction under Article 34 TFEU but capable of justification as it sought to protect public health, a goal explicitly recognized by Article 36 TFEU.[345] In the absence of harmonization, public authorities retain the capacity to define the appropriate degree of public health protection and the manner in which such protection is to be achieved, provided that the principle of proportionality is respected.[346] *Aragonesa* establishes that the same is true for SNAs. The 'national measure' could not be criticized for being 'disproportionate to its stated objective' given its limited impact on trade. It merely concerned beverages with strong alcoholic content and only targeted advertisements in specific locations, such as those frequented by motorists and young persons.[347] In addition, the measure was not discriminatory or protective in character.[348] The fact that Catalonia produced more alcoholic beverages that fall below the threshold of alcohol

[340] *Aragonesa* (n 339) para 3. Law No 20/85 enacted on 25 July 1985 by the Parliament of the Autonomous Community of Catalonia on prevention and assistance with regard to substances likely to lead to dependency (DOG No 572, of 7 August 1985, p. 465). The prohibition applied to any drink having an alcoholic strength superior to 23 degrees.

[341] *Aragonesa* (n 339), para 8. [342] Ibid, para 24. [343] Ibid, para 11.

[344] Ibid, paras 22–3. [345] Ibid, paras 11–13. [346] Ibid, para 16.

[347] Ibid, paras 17–18. [348] Ibid, paras 24–5.

content that triggers the application of the law was not in itself sufficient to constitute arbitrary discrimination or a disguised restriction on trade.[349] This reasoning underlines that where an SNA issues a regulation, the subnational territory constitutes the relevant threshold for the examination of that regulation. Whereas subnational authorities are subject to the same restrictions as a matter of EU law, they can equally benefit on the same derogations as the Member States themselves. A brief analysis of *Anton Las* allows us to observe the assimilation between the insider Member States and subnational authorities on hand of a case concerning the protection of subnational linguistic identity. Assimilation is accordingly functionally relevant as it is necessary to secure adherence to EU objectives.

### 3. *Anton Las*

In *Anton Las* the Court was called upon to assess the compatibility of a Flemish law with workers' free movement rights.[350] The regional legislation required all employers established in Flanders to draft employment contracts in Dutch, one of Belgium's three official languages, and the standard language in Flanders.[351] Such legal requirements could evidently dissuade foreign employers and employees from joining the Flemish labour market, yet reflected Belgium's linguistic and national identity, which EU law is bound to respect in accordance with Articles 3(3) and Article 4(2) TEU.[352]

From the perspective of EU law, the pertinent question was whether a regional law protecting linguistic identity that reflects the national identity of a Member State can be reconciled with the free movement imperative.[353] The ECJ acknowledged that different objectives were enshrined in the Flemish legislation, including the protection of a national language and of employees as well as the effective supervision by national authorities were EU objectives.[354] It also indicated that EU law in principle accepts that the protection of a language common to merely part of a Member State can

[349] Article 45 TFEU. *Aragonesa* (n 339), para 25.

[350] Case C-202/11 *Anton Las v PSA Antwerp NV* [2013] EU:C:2013:239 (hereafter *Anton Las*). For a comment, see Elke Cloots, 'Case C-202/11, Anton Las v. Psa Antwerp NV, Judgment of the Court of Justice (Grand Chamber) of 16 April 2013' (2014) 51 Common Market Law Review 623 (hereafter Cloots, 'Anton Las').

[351] Article 4 of the Belgian Constitution divides Belgium into four language areas: the Dutch language area, the French language area, the bilingual (French and Dutch) language area of Brussels-Capital, and the German language area.

[352] *Anton Las* (n 350) para 22.

[353] For a closer examination of this dilemma, see Cloots, 'Anton Las' (n 350).

[354] *Anton Las* (n 350) paras 24–8.

justify restrictions upon the fundamental freedoms.[355] This had previously merely been recognized with regard to languages spoken throughout an entire State.[356] In holding that an SNA can regulate to protect its linguistic identity, the Court confirmed that from the perspective of EU law, SNAs and Member States are assimilated. The subnational measure is examined against the subnational framework, Dutch being the standard language in Flanders. Just like Member States, SNAs can limit the free movement of workers to further autonomous objectives. Member States enjoy no special status by virtue of being masters of the Treaties in this respect. However, both infra-State bodies and States can only exercise their regulatory autonomies provided that they do so within the limits prescribed by EU law. According to Advocate General Jääskinnen, the '[p]rotection of an official language, whether national or regional, is an objective of general interest which the Court has accepted as a legitimate justification for adopting a policy for the protection and promotion of a language'.[357]

However, in order for a subnational exercise of regulatory authority to be compatible with EU law, the measure taken must be 'duly justified by legitimate objectives and by the use of means which are both appropriate and proportionate to their attainment'.[358] In casu, the Flemish law was considered disproportionate to the aims it sought to achieve. As parties to cross-border employment do not necessarily have knowledge of Flemish, the Court concluded that the legal requirement that such contracts be concluded in Dutch may prevent workers from consenting to the contract in an informed manner.[359] The Flemish law consequently went beyond what was strictly necessary to achieve its declared aim.[360] Flanders is treated as if it were a Member State in this respect, allowing it to operate the same policy choices as a matter of EU law as Member States. SNAs' role as allies in the achievement of supranational objectives that fulfil a role analogous to those of the Member States can in addition be perceived on hand of the smart specialization agenda, which highlights that functional importance of subnational authorities in the internal market project.

[355] *Anton Las* (n 350) para 26. ('According to the fourth subparagraph of Article 3(3) TEU and Article 22 of the Charter of Fundamental Rights of the European Union, the Union must respect its rich cultural and linguistic diversity. In accordance with Article 4(2) TEU, the Union must also respect the national identity of its Member States, which includes protection of the official language or languages of those States' (see, to that effect, C-391/09 *Runevic-Vardyn and Wardyn* [2011] EU:C:2011:291).)

[356] See by way of example *Runevic-Vardyn and Wardyn* [2011] EU:C:2011:291.

[357] *Anton Las* (n 350) AG opinion, para 55.

[358] *Anton Las* (n 350) para 23.

[359] Ibid, para 32.

[360] Ibid, paras 33–4.

## 4. The smart specialization agenda

The smart specialization agenda in essence requires subnational authorities to identify their respective comparative advantage and subsequently develop that sector to the detriment of others.[361] The rationale is that 'by concentrating knowledge resources and linking them to a limited number of priority economic activities, countries can become—and remain—competitive in the global economy'.[362] The agenda demonstrates, on the one hand, that local and regional authorities are crucial economic actors, and, on the other, that the success of the internal market is contingent on the success of subnational economies. Subnational and supranational economic objectives and strategies have become largely aligned, as the smart specialization agenda requires SNAs to pursue economic aims that are vital to the internal market's success. This portrays the internal market as a polycentric construction with porous borders where the action of one scale influences the project's overall success, reminding us of Fuller's spider's web in which a pull on one strand distributes tensions into the entire web.

The EU has turned smart specialization into a pivotal component of the Europe 2020 growth strategy.[363] It has been referred to as 'a crucial part of Europe's response to the economic crisis'[364] as the Commission anticipates that the strategy will lead to 'economic growth and prosperity, by enabling regions to focus on their strengths'.[365] Boosting subnational economies emerges as an imperative for the overall success of the internal market. It is no coincidence that SNAs are the addressees of this economic blueprint. The Commission not only considers that they are in an adequate position to fulfil the targeted objectives but goes as far as to say that the 'national level is ineffective when it comes to stimulating new regional poles of activity'.[366]

[361] For an overview, see Assembly of European Regions, Smart Specialisation Website, online at http://aer-www.ameos.net/knowledge-centre/thematic-expertise-thematic-issues/economy-research-innovation/smart-specialisation.html.

[362] EU Smart Specialisation Platform, *Guide to Research and Innovation Strategies for Smart Specialisation* (RIS 3) [2012] 12.

[363] Communication from the European Commission, Europe 2020, A Strategy for Smart, Sustainable and Inclusive Growth, Com (2010) Final.

[364] Research EU Focus, A Competitive Europe. Research Regionally Develop Globally (March 2009) 8.

[365] European Commission, Smart Specialisation Strategies—Focusing on Regional Strengths in Innovation Activities (2014), available online: http://ec.europa.eu/growth/tools-databases/newsroom/cf/itemdetail.cfm?item_id=7901&lang=en.

[366] European Commission FOREN Network, 'A Practical Guide to Regional Foresight' (2011) 11, available online: http://foresight.jrc.ec.europa.eu/documents/eur20128en.pdf.

The OECD supports this idea as the globalization of economic processes does not imply that the 'differentiation between localities is disappearing'.[367] Smart specialization is not a top-down policy as it involves 'businesses, research centres and universities working together to identify a region's most promising areas of specialisation, but also the weaknesses that hamper innovation'.[368] SNAs do not operate in isolation when they restructure their economies but rather in consultation with the State and the EU, making it a polycentric process. The online 'Smart Specialisation Platform' assists this process as it allows for the exchange of information between all scales, underlining that porosity also plays out in policy-making as the EU encourages policies being taken at different scales and in different Member States, and influencing another.[369] The Commission indeed considers that smart specialization 'needs to exploit regional diversity, stimulate cooperation across national and regional borders and open up new opportunities, by avoiding fragmentation and ensuring that knowledge flows more freely across the EU'.[370] The smart specialization agenda accordingly stresses the polycentric nature of the internal market's success underlining that supranational policies are insufficient to achieve the targeted objectives and that the contribution of subnational authorities is needed.

## F. Subnational Authorities as Internal Market Participants

The internal market has long been the backbone of European integration. Article 3(3) TEU mandates that the EU establish an internal market which, as per Article 26 TFEU, shall comprise 'an area without internal frontiers in which the free movement of goods, persons, services and capital is ensured'. Before the Lisbon reforms, economic integration was in strict constitutional terms a means to an end rather than an end in itself, illustrating the close connection between internal market law and European integration.[371] The

[367] OECD, Cities and Regions in the New Learning Economy (2001) 7, report available online at: http://www.oecd-ilibrary.org/education/cities-and-regions-in-the-new-learning-economy_9789264189713-en.

[368] Communication from the Commission to the European Parliament, the Council, the Economics and Social Committee and the Committee of the Regions, Regional Policy Contributing to Smart Growth in Europe 2020, Com (2010) 553 final (hereafter Regional Policy Contributing to Smart Growth in Europe 2020), 7.

[369] http://s3platform.jrc.ec.europa.eu/home.

[370] Regional Policy Contributing to Smart Growth in Europe 2020 (n 368) 7.

[371] See Article 2 EEC '[i]t shall be the aim of the Community, by establishing a Common Market and progressively approximating the economic policies of Member States, to promote throughout

internal market's constitutional centrality cannot be denied as, according to the ECJ, freedom of movement is 'one of the foundations of the system'.[372] The Court has even gone as far as to argue that the completion of the internal market is 'the fundamental aim of the Treaty'.[373] The internal market's centrality to the Union's constitutional development has indeed led some to observe that the Union has an 'economic constitution'.[374] In light of its significance to the wider project of European integration, internal market law permits us to reflect upon the nature of the European legal order more widely, and indeed provides opportunities for the Court to do the same. Relevant interrogations include, for instance, the issue of common regulatory standards and their implications for different levels of public authority's autonomies. Pursuant to Kingston, subnational autonomies 'perhaps pose the greatest challenge' where they conflict with internal market law.[375] Indeed, how does one respect 'the Article 4(2) TEU principle in light of the ECJ's consistent jurisprudence that the specificities of national law cannot lead to differences in the application of rules that lie at the core of the EU Treaties?'[376] This section engages with SNAs' capacity as internal market participants and the corresponding lessons for their status in supranational law. Local and regional authorities are insiders when it comes to the internal market, not merely in their regulatory capacity but also that of market participants.

## 1. Public procurement law

European public procurement law regulates public authorities' purchasing of goods and services to eliminate discrimination based on nationality by opening calls for tender to any economic operator in the EU.[377] Its rationale consists in the elimination of restrictions that exclude or limit the possibility for operators established in one Member State to participate as contractors or

the Community a harmonious development of economic activities, a continuous and balanced expansion, an increased stability, an accelerated raising of the standard of living and closer relations between its Member States'.

[372] Case C-194/94 *CIA Security International v Signalson & Securitel* [1996] EU:C:1996:172, para 40.

[373] Joined Cases C-403/08 and C-429/08 *FA Premier League v Media Protection Services Ltd* [2011] EU:C:2011:631, para 115.

[374] Miguel Maduro, *We The Court, The European Court of Justice and the European Economic Constitution* (Hart Publishing 1998).

[375] Suzanne Kingston, 'The European Court of Justice and the Devolution of Taxation Powers' in Elke Cloots, Geert de Baere, and Stefan Sottiaux (eds), *Federalism in the European Union* (Hart Publishing 2012) 250 (hereafter Kingston, 'The European Court of Justice), 250–1.

[376] Ibid, 250–1.

[377] On the principle of non-discrimination generally see Article 21 TEU.

sub-contractors in contracts awarded by another State, or legal persons governed by public law in this State.[378] The purchasing of virtually all goods and services by public actors is subject to these rules.[379] Public procurement regulation is an important building block of the internal market and is mainly governed by the two 'Procurement Directives'.[380] The significance of these rules for any SNA cannot be overstated as they must be respected whenever a public authority contracts for goods or services, which forms part and parcel of many SNAs' day-to-day operations. This section evaluates two procurement cases, *Rüffert* and *Mobistar Belgium*, to illustrate EU law's respect of SNAs as autonomous levels of governance in its polycentric structure, assimilating them to the Member States.

### a. *Rüffert*

*Rüffert* forms part of the *Viking* saga that raised momentous questions for labour relations in the Union.[381] It concerned legislation of Lower Saxony pursuant to which public building contracts awards exceeding a given financial threshold could only be awarded to contractors rewarding workers with at least the same level of pay as workers employed in Lower Saxony. This was determined by a collective agreement through a *Tarifstreueklausel* to prevent the undercutting of wages. Many other German Länder had enacted provisions to the same effect.[382] In 2003, following a public invitation to tender, Lower Saxony awarded a contract for the construction of a prison to a German company that subcontracted to a Polish undertaking, providing that the *Tarifstreueklausel* be respected. The Polish undertaking was employing workers hired in Poland and entitled to less than half the remuneration required by the *Tarifstreueklausel*. As a consequence, the German company

[378] Peter Trepte, *Public Procurement in the EU: A Practitioner's Guide* (Oxford University Press 2007) 28.

[379] With the notable exception of military equipment.

[380] See Directive 2004/18/EC of the European Parliament and of the Council of 31 March 2004 on the coordination of procedures for the award of public works contracts, public supply contracts and public service contracts [2004] OJ L 351/44; and Directive 2004/17/EC of the European Parliament and of the Council of 31 March 2004 coordinating the procurement procedures of entities operating in the water, energy, transport and postal services sectors [2004] OJ L 134.

[381] Case C-346/06 *Rüffert* [2008] EU:C:2008:189 (hereafter *Rüffert*). See also Cases C-438/05 *Viking* [2007] EU:C:2007:772; C-341/05 *Laval* [2007] EU:C:2007:809. For a comprehensive analysis of the public procurement issues involved in *Rüffert*, see Christopher McCrudden, 'The Rüffert Case and Public Procurement' in Marise Cremona (ed), *Market Integration and Public Services in the European Union* (Oxford University Press 2011); Claire Kilpatrick, 'Internal Market Architecture and the Accomodation of Labour Rights: As Good as It Gets?' (2011) EUI Working Paper, Law 2011/04 (hereafter Kilpatrick, 'Accomodation of Labour Rights').

[382] See Jakob Steiff and Tobias Andre, 'Konsequenzen aus dem EuGH-Urteil zur Tariftreue' (2008) 9 Neue Zeitschrift für Baurecht und Vergaberecht 364.

and Lower Saxony terminated the contract. Rüffert, the liquidator of the German undertaking, claimed that the requirement to comply with such collective agreements breached the freedom to provide services. The ECJ had to determine whether Article 56 TFEU precludes 'an authority of a Member State' from adopting legislation that requires contracting authorities to designate as contractors only those that agree to respect the domestic level of wages.[383] The Posted Workers Directive (PWD) comes into play, which provides that, whatever the law applicable to the employment relationship, the undertaking posting workers to another State must ensure that they benefit from the host State's conditions of employment as laid down in law, regulations, and administrative provisions, or collective agreements and arbitration awards that have been declared 'universally applicable'.[384] Agreements that have been declared universally applicable have been defined as those that must be observed by all undertakings in the relevant geographical area and profession or industry.[385] The relevant question then of course was whether the regional law at issue could be considered *universally* applicable despite applying to merely part of the national territory.

The Advocate General opinion on *Rüffert* is an unambiguous expression of the insider narrative. Advocate General Bot noted that most German collective agreements are of a limited territorial scope and, as a consequence, usually not declared universally applicable.[386] Article 3(7) of the directive was interpreted to allow for enhanced protection provided by the regional legislation.[387] In respect of Article 56 TFEU the Advocate General stressed that a measure can be justified if it attempts, in a proportionate manner, to protect workers and prevent social dumping.[388] In this determination he explicitly engaged with the subnational dimension, recognizing that Lower Saxony 'does not have competence to declare a collective agreement to be universally applicable'.[389] The Land therefore 'sought to give mandatory force in a field within its competence, namely public procurement, to the collective agreement applicable at the place where the services are performed'.[390] In taking the subnational as opposed to the national framework as the relevant background, the Advocate General attempts to protect the SNA's regulatory competences from being rendered meaningless through the application of EU law in taking into account its inability to declare agreements universally

[383] *Rüffert* (n 381) para 17.

[384] Article 3(1) of Directive 96/71/EC concerning the posting of workers in the framework of the provision of services [1996] OJ L 18/1/431 (hereafter 'the Posted Workers Directive').

[385] Ibid, Article 8.

[386] *Rüffert* (n 381) Opinion of Advocate General Bot, paras 24–8.

[387] Ibid, para 94.

[388] Ibid, para 119.

[389] Ibid, para 129.

[390] Ibid, para 129.

applicable. Lower Saxony was indeed not unable to declare collective agreements universally applicable as a matter of EU, but rather of German law. This stresses SNAs' insider position, as EU law does not distinguish between States and SNAs, allowing both to impose universally applicable constraints on contractual relationships. Under Advocate General Bot's approach local and regional authorities are associated to the insider Member States and enjoy the same protection of their competences as a matter of EU law. The Court, however, chose a different approach, holding that since the regional standard was not universally applicable it was incompatible with the PWD.[391] As per Kilpatrick:

> [t]he collective agreement in question was not universally applicable, as the power to make collective agreements universally applicable is not available to Länder. Ominously for the division of powers between different levels of public authority, the Court found that where a Member State had the power to make collective agreements universally applicable, as in Germany, no collective standards other than those in universally applicable collective agreements could be applied.[392]

In Germany, the federal level alone is able to declare collective agreements universally applicable and as a consequence any subnational legislation is automatically incompatible with Article 56 TFEU and the PWD. While the Advocate General sought to prevent such an outcome, the effect of the Court's ruling is that SNAs can no longer regulate social and labour policy.[393] Both the insider and the outsider narratives can be pinpointed in *Rüffert*, exemplifying their coexistence in EU law. Whereas the Court itself sticks with a classic State-centred interpretation of EU law, the Advocate General pushes for an assimilation of SNAs and the Member State, as the directive itself does. Article 3(8) of the PWD indeed refers to the 'geographical area concerned' as the relevant framework of assessment regarding the universally applicable criterion. SNAs undoubtedly can, as a matter of EU law, recognize collective agreements as universally applicable. Merely in the absence of such agreements that are universally applicable in the *geographical area concerned* does the PWD require States to base themselves on collective agreements that are concluded 'at national level and which are applied throughout national territory'.[394] This secondary law framework accordingly explicitly allows SNAs to have an insider status—if the necessary domestic arrangements are in place,

[391] Ibid, paras 27–9. [392] Kilpatrick, 'Accommodation of Labour Rights' (n 381) 14.

[393] See further Thomas Blanke, 'Die Entscheidungen des EuGH in den Fällen Viking, Laval und Rueffert—Domestizierung des Streikrechts und europaweite Nivellierung der industriellen Beziehungen' (2008) 18 Oldenburger Studien zur Europäisierung und zur transnationalen Regulierung: http://www.cetro.uni-oldenburg.de/download/Nr._18_jm.pdf.

[394] Article 8 of the Posted Workers Directive (n 394) (my own emphasis).

which wasn't the case in Germany. A similar assimilation of Member States and SNAs can also be observed in *Coditel Brabant*.

### b. Coditel Brabant

*Coditel Brabant* concerned the application of EU public procurement law to municipal television networks.[395] The dispute involved a private company, Coditel Brabant, the municipality of Uccle, and the Belgian region of Brussels-Capital, as well as an inter-municipal cooperative managing municipal television networks. In accordance with Belgian law, inter-municipal cooperatives may form associations with specific objects in the municipal interest that are devoid of a commercial character. Between 1969 and 1999 Uccle had authorized Coditel Brabant to operate its cable television network. In 1999 the municipality decided to itself purchase the network and launched a call for tenders to find a concessionaire or sell it. Various operators, including Coditel, submitted tenders and/or purchasing bids. Considering Coditel's bid too low Uccle decided to join Brutélé, an inter-municipal cooperative society. Coditel challenged the decision, arguing that, by the municipality omitting to compare the advantages of the inter-municipal network with its own offer, it had infringed the principle of non-discrimination and the obligation of transparency under EU law.[396]

The referring court considered that Uccle's affiliation to the cooperative constituted a public service concession rather than a public service contract, in which case the public procurement framework doesn't apply. *Telaustria and Telefonadress* had, however, established that non-discrimination on grounds of nationality implies an obligation of transparency also for public service concessions.[397] This would have resulted in an obligation on behalf of Uccle to examine whether the award of the concession to economic operators other than Brutélé would have been a more attractive course of action. The Belgian Conseil d'Etat enquired whether these requirements should be set aside in light of *Teckal*, which established that these constraints do not apply where the concession-granting public authority exercises control over the concessionaire and where the concessionaire carries out the essential part of its activities in that authority (the 'in house exception').[398] The ECJ had to determine whether Uccle's affiliation to an inter-municipal cooperative amounted to a concession, governed by EU procurement law, or whether it constituted

[395] Case C-324/07 *Coditel Brabant* [2008] EU:C:2008:621 (hereafter *Coditel Brabant*).

[396] Ibid, para 19.

[397] Case C-324/98 *Telaustria and Telefonadress* [2000] EU:C:2000:669.

[398] Case C-107/98 *Teckal* [1999] EU:C:1999:562.

a situation that can be equated with in-house performance and is therefore exempt from public procurement law.

The Court classified the membership as a public service concession not falling within the scope of the public procurement directives.[399] Nonetheless, it went on to establish, this did not relieve national authorities from complying with the respect for equal treatment and non-discrimination and the concomitant obligation of transparency.[400] Pursuant to *Telaustria and Telefonadress* the obligation of transparency requires the concession-granting authority to ensure 'a degree of advertising sufficient to enable the service concession to be opened up to competition and the impartiality of the procurement procedures to be reviewed'.[401] If control exercised over the concessionaire by the concession-granting public authority is similar to that which the authority exercises over its own departments and if, at the same time, that entity carries out the essential part of its activities with the controlling authority or authorities, then the concession partly escapes the application of these principles.[402] This was found to be the case in relation to Uccle's control over Brutélé.[403] The public procurement rules accordingly did not apply so that Uccle's decision to join the cooperative was not precluded by EU law.

The Court's finding implies that Uccle could exercise its right to self-government without being constrained by EU law. The Advocate General dedicated an entire section of her analysis to the 'value of inter-municipal cooperation', illustrating that EU law gains benefits from the cooperation of various actors in the polycentric Union, including experimentation and adaptation enabled through porosity.[404] She recalled that while public procurement is 'one of the most influential policy instruments of the Member States and institutions of the EU in the process of European integration', it should not be used 'indiscriminately; rather its purpose must be brought into harmony with the values of other policy areas'.[405] Would an agreement such as the one at hand be subject to public procurement law, 'inter-municipal cooperation would in future be rendered virtually impossible. For it is an important feature of genuine cooperation that decisions are made as equals and that one of the partners in the cooperative does not dominate.'[406] In the eyes of the Advocate General, subnational autonomy amounts to a public policy consideration to be taken into account by EU law and balanced against competing considerations. The *Teckal* criterion, she went on to state, should not be construed so narrowly to attach disproportionate weight to

[399] *Coditel Brabant* (n 395) paras 24–5. [400] Ibid, para 25. [401] Ibid, para 25.
[402] Ibid, para 26. [403] Ibid, para 27. [404] Ibid, AG opinion, paras 80–7.
[405] Ibid, AG opinion, para 81. [406] Ibid, para 82.

competition objectives and interfere heavily with 'municipalities' right to self-government and with it in the competences of the Member States'.[407] This right to municipal self-government, the Advocate General argued, is reflected in national constitutional imperatives as well as the Council of Europe's European Charter on Local Self-Government signed by all Member States and ratified by most of them.[408] She further drew attention to the Committee of the Regions, the existence of which testifies to 'a certain recognition of self-government alongside the possibility of providing institutionalised machinery for bringing to bear regional and municipal perspectives'.[409] The Lisbon Treaty was moreover considered to stress 'the role of regional and local self-government for the relevant national identity to which heed is to be paid'.[410] This led the Advocate General to conclude that:

> [m]unicipalities have themselves to decide whether they wish to carry out their general-interest tasks with their own administrative, technical and other means, without being compelled to have recourse to external establishments that do not form part of their own departments, or whether they wish to carry them out with the assistance of an establishment legally distinct from them in their capacity as public entity awarding the contract or concession.[411]

*Coditel Brabant* affirms SNAs' right to self-government, which includes the right to freely determine how public goods and services are to be provided. It is true that SNAs' right to self-government must be balanced against EU objectives, just as is the case for Member States. The explicit acknowledgement of SNAs' right to self-government, however, underlines that they have a right to self-government equal to that of States. This assimilation of SNAs to the States underlines their insider status in the insider narrative. An overview of public procurement law has indeed revealed that SNAs must behave loyally towards the EU in their quality as market participants, respecting the related prescriptions as formulated by procurement law. The EU in turn benefits from SNAs behaviour, as the non-discrimination objectives that underlie this domain of the law could not be achieved without their assistance. The subsequent section locates the insider narrative in the area of State aid law.

## 2. State aid law

The State aid law judgments examined below are those cases the subnational dimension of which has been documented most extensively.[412] In their

[407] Ibid, para 84. [408] Ibid, para 85. [409] Ibid, para 85.
[410] Ibid, para 85. [411] Ibid, para 86.
[412] For comments on these cases, see inter alia: Andreas Bartosch, 'With Greetings from the Azores' (2006) 5 European State Aid Law Quarterly 667; Saturnina Moreno González, 'Regional Fiscal

policy-making capacity SNAs must pay heed to State aid law given the risk that their measures conflict with these supranational prescriptions.[413] Despite State aid law's importance for SNAs uncertainty, long prevailed as to how its prescriptions apply to decentralized territories, in particular those in Member States with asymmetric devolution. This changed in 2006 when the Grand Chamber decided *Azores*.[414] It established that if an SNA is 'sufficiently autonomous' its status of autonomy is to be taken into account in determining whether a measure amounts to State aid.[415] *Azores* remains the Court's most explicit engagement with SNAs and was even interpreted as 'the most important legal development of the regional question up to that point by any of the EU institutions'.[416] The Court nonetheless went less far in recognizing SNAs as insiders than in many other cases, which is attributed to State aid law being one of the rare exclusive competences of the Union.[417]

To grasp the impact of *Azores* we start with a brief excursion into State aid law. Article 107(1) TFEU sets out a general prohibition to allocate State aid. In order for State intervention to constitute aid, it must (i) be granted by the State or through State resources;[418] (ii) confer an advantage on the recipient;[419] (iii) be selective in nature;[420] (iv) and have an effect on intra-Union trade and distort competition in the internal market.[421] This prohibition seeks to prevent Member States from providing financial assistance to economic operators to further domestic policy objectives. Selectivity plays on many levels. A measure can be selective in favouring a certain sector or

Autonomy from a State Aid Perspective: The ECJ's Judgment in Portugal v. Commission' (2007) 47 European Taxation 328; Julie Bousin and Jorge Piernas, 'Developments in the Notion of Selectivity' (2008) 7 European State Aid Law Quarterly 634 (hereafter Bousin and Piernas, 'Developments in the Notion of Selectivity'); Andrea Biondi, 'The Rationale of State Aid Control: A Return to Orthodoxy' (2010) 12 Cambridge Yearbook of European Legal Studies 35 (hereafter Biondi, 'The Rationale of State Aid Control'); Koen Lenaerts and Nathan Cambien, 'Regions and the European Courts: Giving Shape to the Regional Dimension of Member States' (2010) 35 European Law Review 609.

[413] For an example, see Müller-Graff, 'The German Länder' (n 161) 107 ('[t]he control of state aids in the case of local public banks (*Sparkassen*) may cause conflicts with competences in local government law') (emphasis in original).

[414] Case C-88/03 *Portugal v Commission* [2006] EU:C:2006:511 (hereafter *Azores*). For a comment, see Jan Winter, 'Case C-88/03 Portuguese Republic v. Commission' (2008) 45 Common Market Law Review 183 (hereafter Winter, *Azores*).

[415] Ibid. [416] Bengoetxea, 'Autonomous Constitutional Regions' (n 294) 239.

[417] Article 3(1)(b) TFEU.

[418] This criteria means that the measure must be imputable to the State. On this, see by way of example Case C-482/99 *France v Commission* ('*Stardust Marine*') [2002] EU:C:2002:294, para 51.

[419] Opinion of Advocate General Jacobs in Case C-256/97 *DMT* [1999] EU:C:1999:332, para 29.

[420] Case C-143/99 *Adria-Wien Pipeline* [2001] EU:C:2001:598.

[421] Case C-148/04 *Unicredito Italiano* [2005] EU:C:2005:774, para 55.

certain goods, but also by virtue of its geographic dimension.[422] It was for a long time uncertain how geographic selectivity should be applied to regional tax schemes that are by definition geographically selective as they solely apply to a subnational territory. Before *Azores*, the Court had never defined the circumstances in which regionally specific tax measures are selective. This was in part due to the relative absence of asymmetrically devolved taxation schemes.[423] In Member States with symmetrical fiscal decentralization, such as Germany, there is no national tax rate in comparison to which the regional tax rate can be considered. In these circumstances a subnational measure is not per se geographically selective. This is different in Member States such as Portugal that define a national tax rate, but some regions, such as the Azores islands, set independent rates.

The Court had only ruled a few times on the relation between the selectivity criterion and SNAs before 2006. In 1987, it affirmed in *Germany v Commission* that aid granted by North Rhine-Westphalia constituted 'aid granted by the Member State or through State resources' provided that the conditions of Article 107(1) TFEU are satisfied.[424] This was later confirmed in a case concerning Wallonia.[425] Whereas these cases were not concerned with selectivity, they equated regional measures with those of the State, in line with the monolithic nature of statehood under the outsider narrative. In *Territorio Histórica de Álava*, the General Court had moreover established that regional measures fall within the ambit of Article 107(1) TFEU 'in the same way as measures taken by the federal or central authority'.[426] In 2000 the Court was faced with the same legal question as that in *Azores*. In *Juntas Generales de Guipúzcoa,* the compatibility of provincial legislation adopted by three Territories belonging to the Spanish Autonomous Community of the Basque Country was at stake.[427] Advocate General Saggio took the view that devolution did not constitute 'any specificity' of these Territories.[428] The measures were found to bring about an advantage, 'which companies

[422] Case T-308/00 *Salzgitter v Commission* [2004] EU:T:2013:30, para 38.

[423] Kingston, 'The European Court of Justice (n 375) 252. See also para 43 of the opinion in *Azores* (n 414).

[424] Case C-248/84 *Germany v Commission* [1987] EU:C:1987:437, para 17.

[425] Joined Cases 62/87 and 72/87 *Exécutif regional wallon and SA Glaverbel v Commission* [1988] EU:C:1988:132.

[426] Joined Cases T-127/99, T-129/99 and T-148/99 *Disputación Foral de Álava and Others v Commission* [2002] EU:T:2002:59.

[427] Joined Cases C-400/97, C-401/97 and C-402/97 *Juntas Generales de Guipúzcoa and Diputación Foral de Guipúzcoa* [2000] EU:C:2000:87.

[428] *Azores* (n 414) AG opinion, para 38. This statement has been described as 'cynical' by Kingston, 'The European Court of Justice' (n 375) 253.

intending to carry out similar economic operations in other areas in the same State cannot enjoy'.[429] He concluded that:

> [t]he fact that the measures at issue were adopted by regional authorities with exclusive competence under national law is, as observed by the Commission, merely a matter of form, which is not sufficient to justify the preferential treatment reserved to companies which fall within the scope of the provincial laws. If this were not the case, the State could easily avoid the application, in part of its own territory, of provisions of [EU] law on State aid simply by making changes to the internal allocation of competence on certain matters, thus raising the 'general' nature, for that territory, of the measure in question.[430]

The Court never ruled on *Juntas Generales de Guipúzcoa* as the reference for preliminary ruling was withdrawn. Prior to *Azores*, the Commission's practice continued to reflect Advocate General Saggio's concern for the efficiency of the State aid prohibition. When assessing the selectivity of a subnational measure, the Commission used the national level as a benchmark, but only if there was one: that is to say, solely in instances of asymmetrical structures.[431] Alongside Advocate General Saggio the Commission considered a measure's subnational dimension as a mere matter of form.[432] As a consequence, the Commission declared the fiscal policies of the Basque Country incompatible with Article 107(1) TFEU.[433] The Commission's practice had established that advantages only available to operators in a limited geographical area were automatically in breach of the State aid prohibition.[434] In systems of asymmetrical devolution subnational fiscal competences were as a consequence rendered meaningless through the application of EU law.[435] The Union's highest court had, however, never validated the Commission's interpretation of regional selectivity. When it finally had the opportunity to do so in *Azores* it established that a regional tax regime is *not* per se selective. Rather, if an SNA is 'sufficiently autonomous', selectivity should be assessed against a regional rather than a national background:

[429] *Azores* (n 414) AG opinion, para 35. [430] Ibid, para 37.

[431] This was supported by both case law of the Court (see for example Case C-73/03 *Spain v Commission* [2004] EU:C:2004:711, para 28) and soft law of the Commission such as the Commission notice on the application of the state aid rules to measures relating to direct business taxation [1998] OJ C 384 (para 17).

[432] This position has found support in academic writing, see Biondi, 'The Rationale of State Aid Control' (n 412) 50.

[433] See for example Decision 93/337, OJ L134/25 (1993); Decision 2000/795, OJ L318/36 (2000) and Decision 99/718, OJ L292/1 (1999).

[434] See also Case 248/84 *Commission v Germany* [1987] EU:C:1987:437.

[435] *Azores* (n 414) AG opinion, para 60.

It is possible that an infra-State body enjoys a legal and factual status which makes it sufficiently autonomous in relation to the central government of a Member State, with the result that, by the measures it adopts, it is that body and not the central government which plays a fundamental role in the definition of the political and economic environment in which undertakings operate. In such a case it is the area in which the infra-State body responsible for the measure exercises its powers, and not the country as a whole, that constitutes the relevant context for the assessment of whether a measure adopted by such a body favours certain undertakings in comparison with others in a comparable legal and factual situation, having regard to the objective pursued by the measure or the legal system concerned.[436]

*Azores* unequivocally acknowledged that SNAs may have competence to determine tax rates under domestic provisions. This is in line with the recognition of SNAs as independent generators of norms under the insider narrative. Strikingly, however, the mere existence of subnational autonomy is not decisive; rather there must be a sufficient degree of autonomy, as assessed by EU law. Rather than being automatically assimilated to Member States, SNAs are only acknowledged where their autonomy is sufficiently pronounced. Out of a concern that States modify their internal structures to avoid the State aid regime, the Court developed a test to determine whether an SNA should be recognized as an independent fiscal regulator. In this regard the (i) institutional, (ii) procedural, and (iii) economic/financial autonomy of the SNA are taken into consideration.[437]

### a. *Azores and the 'sufficiently autonomous' test*

The first criterion, 'institutional autonomy', refers to an SNA's capacity to formulate its own fiscal policies independently of the State. *Azores* established that this requires that a region's political and administrative status be constitutionally separate from that of the State.[438] *UGT-Rioja* for instance qualified the Basque Country to be institutionally autonomous from Spain.[439] Second, 'procedural autonomy' mandates that the central government cannot influence regional policies.[440] No autonomy can be established if the SNA must obtain prior authorization from the central authority to pursue a given policy.[441] *Unión General de Trabajadores de la Rioja* clarified that the SNA should be under no obligation to account for national interests when formulating

[436] *Azores* (n 414) para 58.

[437] Whereas the AG referred to 'true autonomy' in this respect, the Court, at paras 64–6 in *Azores* (n 414), favoured the terminology of 'sufficiently' autonomous.

[438] *Azores* (n 414) para 67.

[439] Joined Cases C-428/06 to C-434/06 *Unión General de Trabajadores de La Rioja* [2008] EU:C:2008:488 (hereafter *UGT Rioja*).

[440] *Azores* (n 414) para 47.

[441] Ibid, para 67.

its policies.[442] Finally, 'economic' or 'financial autonomy' is the most difficult criterion to satisfy. The SNA must illustrate that it bears financial responsibility for its fiscal policies, which cannot be offset by financial transfers from other SNAs or the State. Economic independence presupposes that 'the infra-State body . . . assumes the political and financial consequences of such a measure'.[443] The Azores islands were found not to be sufficiently autonomous under this criterion of the test.

The *Azores* test has been subsequently confirmed and refined. *Unión General de Trabajadores de la Rioja* concerned fiscal legislation passed by some of the Basque Country's Autonomous Territories that applied a lower corporation tax and a more favourable regime of tax deductions as elsewhere in Spain. The Luxembourg court reiterated that 'a measure conferring an advantage in only one part of the national territory is not selective on that ground alone'.[444] Rather, the 'sufficiently autonomous test' is applied to ascertain whether the SNA 'plays a fundamental role in the definition of the political and economic environment in which the undertakings operate'.[445] The difficulty in this case resided in the fact that it was unclear which SNA was to be taken into consideration to determine selectivity.[446] The Autonomous Community of the Basque Country is made up of three provinces—Álava, Vizcaya, and Guipúzcoa—the boundaries of which coincide with those of the historical territories, 'bodies which enjoy rights of ancient origin called "fueros", entitling them to levy and collect tax'.[447] The Historical Territories are, however, solely competent for matters of taxation, while the Autonomous Community has competence in other matters of an economic nature.[448] This, the Court found, precluded the Historical Territories from being considered 'sufficiently autonomous' as they did not 'assume responsibility for the political and financial consequences of a tax reduction measure'.[449] The Court, however, went on to state that the sharing of competence between the Historical Territories and the Autonomous Community 'necessitates close collaboration between the different bodies'.[450] As such reference should be made to both communities to determine whether there is sufficient autonomy.[451] A different conclusion would indeed have made it impossible for a body competent to levy taxes to do so. The Basque institutions' institutional autonomy was not particularly contentious. Regarding procedural autonomy, the Court considered that as long as the State cannot veto a subnational tax measure, this criterion is fulfilled.[452] Economic and financial autonomy, however, does not require

[442] *Azores* (n 414) AG opinion, paras 85–97. [443] *Azores* (n 414) paras 67–8.
[444] Ibid, paras 46–8 and 50. [445] Ibid, para 55. [446] Ibid, para 65.
[447] Ibid, para 66. [448] Ibid, paras 66–7. [449] Ibid, para 67.
[450] Ibid, para 70. [451] Ibid, para 75. [452] Ibid, para 109.

that the 'financial consequences of a reduction of the national tax rate for undertakings in the region must not be offset by aid or subsidies from other regions or central government'.[453] Holding that the mere existence of financial transfers is insufficient to negate economic autonomy, the Court considered the Basque measure was not geographically selective. The test applied in *Unión General de Trabajadores de la Rioja* has been said to be somewhat less strict than that defined in *Azores*, which may be due to different standards of judicial review. While the latter concerned a reference for preliminary ruling, the former was a direct action for annulment of a Commission decision.[454] *Azores* has also been applied in *Regione Sardegna* and *Gibraltar*.[455] In *Gibraltar* the Court had to determine whether a territory within the meaning of Article 355(3) TFEU that does not 'form part of the territory of a Member State' can be used as a reference framework for the application of Article 107 TFEU.[456] The question was whether 'the United Kingdom and Gibraltar formed a unit, or whether it should be accepted that Gibraltar was the appropriate reference framework'.[457] The General Court answered this in the affirmative and the ECJ did not overturn its finding.[458] In *Regione Sardegna* the Court applied *Azores* to find a Sardinian fiscal scheme not to be geographically selective.[459] This did not, however, prevent the tax from being materially selective as it did not apply to all operators of boats or aircraft stopping over in Sardinia.[460]

The *Azores* decision recognizes the supranational legal order's polycentric structure in that subnational authorities are recognized as autonomous regulators the policies of which can, due to porosity, influence EU market objectives. At the same time the Court is ready to assimilate SNAs to Member States in this domain, but merely where an SNA is sufficiently autonomous. Advocate General Kokott considered that determining the regional scale as the relevant framework of analysis flows from the Union's duty to 'respect the national identities of its Member States'.[461] This duty must be reconciled with

[453] Ibid, para 123.

[454] José Luís da Cruz Vilaca, 'Material and Geographic Selectivity in State Aid—Recent Developments' (2009) 8 European State Aid Law Quarterly 450 (hereafter Vilaca, 'Material and Geographic Selectivity in State Aid').

[455] Case T-211/04 *Government of Gibraltar v Commission* [2008] EU:T:2008:595; Joined Cases C-106/09 P and C-107/09 P, *European Commission, Kingdom of Spain v Government of Gibraltar and United Kingdom* [2011] EU:C:2011:732. For comments, see John Temple Lang, 'The Gibraltar State Aid and Taxation Judgment—A 'Methodological Revolution'?' (2012) 11 European State Aid Law Quarterly 805; Pierpaolo Rossi-Maccanico, 'Gibraltar: Beyond the Pillars of Hercules of Selectivity' (2012) 11 European State Aid Law Quarterly 423.

[456] *Azores* (n 414) AG opinion, para 2. [457] Ibid, para 54.

[458] The CJEU did not have to pronounce on this matter after finding that the regional measure was in fact materially selective.

[459] *Azores* (n 414) para 59. [460] Ibid, paras 60–4.

[461] *Azores* (n 414) AG opinion, para 54.

the established rule that States 'cannot plead provisions, practices or situations prevailing in its domestic legal order, including those resulting from the constitutional organisation of that State' to justify a failure to comply with EU law.[462] The *Azores* test was considered by the Advocate General to strike a 'reasonable balance' between these two concerns.[463] Subsequent to *Azores* the Court no longer automatically counts the Member State as the appropriate reference framework when assessing regional selectivity. Rather, it is now possible 'that for tax rules adopted by a local or regional authority its territory alone forms the reference framework if that authority is sufficiently autonomous'.[464]

There has been a large amount of scholarly commentary on *Azores*. Bousin and Piernas welcomed the case as 'an even more respectful approach vis-à-vis the internal constitutional arrangements within a Member State'.[465] According to Vilaca, however, 'it is doubtful whether the concept of "sufficient autonomy" can be deemed a useful tool to ascertain in every case the "selectivity" of a regional tax measure'.[466] Due to the test's uncertain contours and its application on a case-by-case basis as well as apparently different standards depending on the nature of judicial review involved, it seems to lack in legal certainty. Some judge *Azores* to go too far in recognizing subnational autonomies, fearing that in combination with 'the current trend towards greater decentralization or federalization in the Member States (Belgium?) it is likely to lead to a further erosion of the effectiveness' of State aid law.[467] Biondi also criticized the Court for having abandoned 'its classic effects-based approach in favour of a complicated constitutional test'.[468] State aid control, he went on to state, should not be mixed with alien concerns such as the respect of 'constitutional diversities and the allocation of competence in different national systems'.[469] Bengoextea on the other hand observed that a 'new awareness of regional diversity is emerging' and that supranational institutions are henceforth obliged to account for the State's constitutional identity even in the context of State aid law.[470] Bengoextea furthermore considers that if EU law were to treat a decentralized Member State as a unitary State, Article 4(2) TEU would be infringed.[471] This is interesting as it implies that Article 4(2) TEU has modified supranational law's

462 Ibid, para 55. 463 Ibid, para 56.
464 *UGT Rioja* (n 439) AG opinion, para 43.
465 Bousin and Piernas, 'Developments in the Notion of Selectivity' (n 412) 651.
466 Vilaca, 'Material and Geographic Selectivity in State Aid' (n 454) 449.
467 Winter, *Azores* (n 414) 195.
468 Biondi, 'The Rationale of State aid Control' (n 412) 49. 469 Ibid, 50.
470 Bengoetxea, 'Autonomous Constitutional Regions' (n 294) 241, 242.
471 Ibid, 242.

ability to automatically treat a Member State as a monolithic entity, which may explain why more expressions of the insider narrative emerge over time. The recognition of SNAs as insiders nonetheless seems more limited in State aid law than in the other domains examined in this chapter. This, it is argued, is due to the special nature of State aid law, which constitutes one of the few areas of exclusive EU competence.[472]

We must finally wonder whether *Azores* solely applies to regional or also to local authorities given that it has so far only been applied to the former. Advocate General Kokott referred generically to local and regional authorities when describing the test.[473] Winter agrees that it is difficult to see why *Azores* would apply to regions only, but warns that it is necessary to interpret the sufficiently autonomous test 'in a very strict way'.[474] The smaller an SNA, 'the more likely it is that their aid policies are undifferentiated and devoid of material specificity'.[475] Especially small SNAs are feared to 'promise financial support to any type of company that will undertake operations boosting the local economy.[476] It is unclear how this rationale plays out differently with regard to localities than it does in relation to regions or (small) Member States. The Court's case law itself indicates that no distinction should be operated between local and regional governments. In *Azores*, the Court simply referred to 'an infra-State body'[477] and the Advocate General invariably referred to 'local authorities' to designate any level of public authority situated below the central State.[478] Further, in *Unión General de Trabajadores de la Rioja*, the Court considered that *Azores* concerned 'the situation in which a regional or local authority adopts, in the exercise of sufficiently autonomous powers in relation to the central power'.[479] In theory, it thus seems possible for local measures to be subject to the *Azores* test—in line with all other expressions of the insider narrative where no distinction is operated between local and regional SNAs. In practice, it nonetheless appears unlikely that any locality could ever fulfil the sufficiently autonomous test.

[472] In Case C-288/11 P *Mitteldeutsche Flughafen* (2012) EU:C:2012:821 the Court of Justice confirmed that the subsidiarity principle does not apply in the field of State aid, in which the Commission has exclusive competence. In this regard it is interesting to note that, according to Maduro, State aid law is one of the areas 'which fits well with the majoritarian approach' as 'cases have been decided from a majoritarian point of view, taking the European Union as the relevant political community'. Miguel Poiares Maduro, *We, The Court. The European Court of Justice and the European Economic Constitution* (Hart Publishing 1998) 76.

[473] *UGT Rioja* (n 439) AG opinion, para 43.

[474] Winter, *Azores* (n 414) 196.

[475] Ibid, 196.

[476] Ibid, 196.

[477] *Azores* (n 414), para 58.

[478] *Azores* (n 414) AG opinion, paras 52, 55.

[479] *Azores* (n 414) para 49.

### *b. Azores and SNAs as insiders*

At first sight, *Azores* may appear to be the most wide-ranging recognition of SNAs in EU law. It explicitly recognizes their regulatory autonomies, rejecting any theory of blindness, and develops a framework within which they are taken into account. For such recognition to occur, the Court, however, developed a number of—rather stringent—conditions, weakening SNAs' insider position. *Azores* is as a matter of fact strikingly different from other areas of EU law for three reasons.

First, the Court did not automatically and unconditionally equate the subnational measure with that of a Member State, a technique observed elsewhere under the insider narrative. To the contrary, it developed a test pursuant to which SNAs are treated differently from Member States, thus precluding any automatic assimilation between SNAs and Member States. This does not, however, mean that we should frame *Azores* as an expression of the outsider narrative. Polycentricity is acknowledged as it is accepted that SNAs fashion tax regimes, and so is porosity for these measures are seen to impact on internal market objectives. At the same time, however, the assimilation between Member State and SNA norms is absent from the judgment so that *Azores* displays hybrid features, with elements of both the insider and the outsider model.

Further, while *Azores* was interpreted as an expression of EU law's duty to respect national identities, we must question whether that is really the case. Article 4(2) TEU rather seems to imply that EU law recognizes Member States' choices regarding their own internal structures rather than requiring that such choices fit into pre-determined moulds fashioned by EU law. Such a stance rather appears to interfere with domestic institutional choices in requiring national measures to comply with an EU law standard rather than accepting the Member State's autonomy. Indeed only the regulatory autonomies of SNAs that match the *Azores* criteria are respected rather than those regulatory autonomies that are recognized by the Member States.

Third, *Azores* devised a special status for regions with a pronounced degree of autonomy. As such, it creates three categories of subnational authorities. First, SNAs that form part of a system of symmetrical devolution whose tax systems are examined in against the same benchmarks as those of a State in light of the absence of a national tax regime serving as a reference framework. Second, SNAs that form part of asymmetrical fiscal regimes and are deemed 'sufficiently autonomous'. Their fiscal policies are examined using the same standard as those of the Member States. Third, SNAs forming part of asymmetrical devolutionary regimes that, despite having fiscal competences on a domestic scale, are not considered sufficiently autonomous. It follows that where there is symmetric decentralization[480] EU law simply validates domestic institutional choices and treats a subnational tax regime as that of the Member State (full expression of the insider narrative). Where there is asymmetric devolution, the Court judges Member States' choices regarding domestic structure (partial expression of the insider narrative) against criteria developed by EU law. The rationale for such discrepancy is unclear and no parallel tests can be observed in other areas of EU law.[481] This can only be attributed to the fact that the EU has exclusive competence in respect of State aid law, which leaves less room for domestic autonomies, at central and subnational level. The above-described fragmentation presents a striking contrast to the general stance according to which any Member State measure—whether federal or central, big or small—is treated in the same manner by EU law in accordance with the paradigms of sovereign equality and national identity enshrined in Article 4(2) TEU. Under the *Azores* test, the same is not, however, true for SNAs. While polycentricity and porosity are recognized under State aid law, SNAs are not automatically assimilated to the Member States.

A survey of the status of subnational authorities under the law of State aid has revealed a complex picture that highlights a desire to recognize subnational autonomies in this context but equally underscores that such an attempt is burdened by the special nature of State aid control as one of the few exclusive EU competences. Despite this additional burden in recognizing SNAs, this domain has also confirmed the overall conclusion the present chapter offers, namely that local and regional authorities have in many ways become insiders of the European legal order. We have observed that in numerous domains subnational authorities relate directly to the European Union and that their respective relationship is in many ways analogous to that between Member States and the Union itself. This functional account of SNAs in EU law stands in contrast to the formal account that has been documented in the previous chapter. Finally, we move to our conclusion, which offers some reflections on the coexistence of the outsider and insider narratives.

[480] As is the case in Germany for instance.

[481] *Azores* (n 414) AG opinion, paras 50–4.

# 5
# Conclusion

This research project has highlighted that the role and status of local and regional authorities in EU law can be seen through two distinct lenses—one formal and one functional. Examining the supranational legal order from a formal legal perspective, subnational authorities can be seen to have no formal legal status as a matter of EU law so that any relation between SNAs and the EU, if at all, occurs through the intermediary of the Member State. The book has adopted the terminology of the 'outsider' to denote that whereas the Member States are integral components of the European legal order, SNAs are not. If, however, our perspective is of a functional nature, a rather different image of SNAs' status and role in the contemporary Union emerges. We have seen that local and regional authorities in many contexts act as direct allies of the European Union in the realization of supranational objectives; that they are key market participants; that they are in a position to contribute to supranational law's substantive development; and that a relation of loyalty has emerged between SNAs and the Union. The fact that subnational authorities are central EU actors the role of which can in many ways be equated with that of the Member States has been labelled by the terminology of the 'insider'.

The complex relationship between SNAs and the EU could be conceptualized in a number of different manners and the present study certainly raises no claim to exhaustiveness in this respect. The outsider and insider narratives rather provide a snapshot of a highly complex interactive dynamic with all their contradictions and tensions. The relationship between both sets of actors could be tested relying on a whole range of additional variables, which will be for future research to tackle. The adoption of the outsider/insider dichotomy has, however, had the merit of not merely projecting two different and in many manners opposed narratives of SNAs, but also of the supranational legal order in itself. We have seen that the formal lens captures the European legal order as a bi-centric structure shaped by the interactions of the institutions of the EU and its Member States. Formally, EU law is respective of the monolithic nature of statehood and thus unable to directly recognize SNAs, so that the formal interactions between SNAs and the EU

Subnational Authorities in EU Law. First Edition. Michèle Finck.  Published 2017 by Oxford University Press.

diverge significantly. Acknowledging SNAs as insiders, however, allows us to take note of an additional variant of the European legal order, the structure of which is polycentric, shaped by the interaction of multiple levels of public authority, including SNAs. We have observed that the borders delimiting the various levels of public authority are porous, allowing the norms of these various levels to interact and mutually influence one another. From this functional standpoint, Member States and local authorities are aligned as they in many respects fulfil identical objectives.

The preceding chapters have thus revealed a multifaceted relationship between subnational authorities and European integration. It is worth recalling that the interconnection between subnational authorities and the European Union under the insider narrative generates different dynamics. Interconnection can be seen as a tool of empowerment. We have observed that the supranational can empower the subnational, as in *Josemans*, where the local authority was able to further its own policy goals that conflicted with domestic prescriptions in relying on Union law.[1] Similarly the possibility for SNAs to lobby and influence EU policy-making has empowered them to exercise influence beyond national borders. Conversely, the subnational can also be seen to empower the supranational. In acting as allies of the Union, such as when they implement EU secondary legislation or serve as partners in policy initiatives such as smart specialization, SNAs lend support to the EU and its legitimacy.[2] Seen from this angle interconnection appears as a cooperative feature of mutual support. The constraining feature of polycentricity should not, however, be ignored. Through interconnection actors are also capable of exercising control over one another. We have been able to observe that the Commission's creation of the Covenant of Mayors has not only empowered SNAs to collectively shape the European climate change mitigation and adaptation strategies but that this initiative moreover permits the Commission to control SNAs' actions in this respect. The smart specialization regime moreover allows the Commission to influence subnational economic governance just as the Pact of Amsterdam can be read not only as a tool facilitating the integration of SNAs into the supranational political process, but also as formalizing an obligation falling on SNAs to behave in EU-friendly manners. This constraining aspect of the interconnection between the subnational and supranational is not, however, unidimensional. Local and regional authorities similarly have the capacity to watch over EU action. This can readily be seen in the various free movement cases examined earlier such as *Aragonesa*

[1] Case C-137/09 *Josemans* [2010] EU:C:2010:774.
[2] On this, see further Chapter 4.

and *Walloon Waste* in which SNAs have been able to obtain derogations from the free movement regime in order to pursue their own objectives, and thus indirectly to control the contours of supranational economic policy.[3]

Returning to Fuller's image of the spider's web, we see that pulls on one end of the polycentric supranational legal order give rise to tensions in other locations so that no actor in the EU can invoke isolation and autonomy. This book has thus far told the story of the interaction between the subnational and the supranational through the lens of the outsider and insider narratives. The project has highlighted that the insider and outsider narratives portray diametrically opposed visions of the European legal order, one based on legal formality and the other on functional necessity. While the research project has sought to examine its research question as exhaustively as possible, many open questions remain, which can only be addressed by future research. These final pages will nonetheless attempt to address one such question, namely that of the causes and consequences of the coexistence of the insider and outsider narratives. Below the surface of these two narratives we can indeed identify an additional 'metanarrative' that relates to the coexistence of the insider and outsider accounts.

The coexistence of the outsider and insider narratives underscores the discrepancy between the law in the books and the law in action. Any (text) book on European Union law will study supranational legal integration from the lens of the Member States and the EU just as the Court of Justice of the European Union will portray any domestic authority or legal norm as that of the Member State itself. Bi-centric conceptualizations of the Union's legal complexity are of course anchored in the bi-centric structure of the Treaties themselves. While the law in the books falls short of giving any meaningful role to SNAs, the law in action utters a completely different narrative. While general principles of EU law are customarily presented as being generated through the communication of supranational law and national (constitutional) principles, *Omega* has illustrated that subnational authorities can influence the said process as well.[4] In the said situation formal legalistic principles point in one direction whereas reality points in another, and we are still uneasy when it comes to finding words to describe the latter, which is why the research project has introduced its own terminology of 'insider' and 'outsider', 'polycentricty' and 'porosity'.

[3] Joined Cases C-1/90 and C-176/90 *Aragonesa de Publicidad Exterior SA v Departamento de Sanidad y Seguridad Social de la Generalitat de Cataluña* [1991] EU:C:1991:327 and Case C-2/90 *Commission v Belgium* [1992] EU:C:1992:310.

[4] Case C-36/02 *Omega Spielhallen-und Automatenaufstellungs-GmbH v Oberbürgermeisterin der Bundeststadt Bonn* [2004] EU:C:2004:614.

Law is inevitably obliged to operate abstractions and simplifications of the always more complex reality that underlies it. Yet in this case we can understand the disconnect between legal abstraction and complex reality also as hinting at the temporal evolution of the EU and its legal order. The formal principles and terminology relied on to study the Union remain anchored in its public international law inspired beginnings.[5] As time progressed so has European integration and the lens of the subnational allows us to register that neofunctionalism's promises of functional but also geographical spillover have been realized. While the law on the books remains moulded by explicit and formal processes of law-making, including Treaty revision, and the progress of European integration remains contingent on the political will and bargaining underlying the said processes, the insider narrative reveals that below such formality a distinct, and importantly independent, process of integration unfolds. SNAs' insider status underlines that underneath the surface of that formal and explicit process, an organic process of functional overlap continues to unfold.

The integration of subnational actors and their norms into the fabric of Union law has unfolded in the absence of any explicit directions to this effect, which is why we can label it as an organic and autonomous process. Stagnation in political will to deepen the process of integration has not prevented the geographical deepening of integration to transform the formerly outsider SNAs into insiders. This proves correct assumptions that spillover from existing integration has a dynamic effect on actors not explicitly targeted by the integration process. The centrality of polycentricity and interconnection and the weakening of formal paradigms of independence and autonomy hint at a currently occurring paradigm shift. While the outsider narrative has never been formally questioned a parallel account has emerged that carries different and even opposite assumptions regarding the nature of public authority. The coexistence of the formal and the functional and the uneasy tension between the law in the books and the law in action can certainly be observed when it comes to subnational authorities in their relation to the law of the Union. While devoid of any formal legal status as a matter of EU law, SNAs have become functionally vital actors in the realization of central supranational policies, as highlighted by the numerous policy instruments examined in Chapter 4 and as recently given explicit recognition via the Pact of Amsterdam. The uneasy relation between the conflicting paradigms of independence and interdependence can, however, be observed more broadly.

[5] On the commonalities and differences between early Union law and public international law, see Pierre Pescatore, *Le Droit de l'Intégration* (Bruylant 2005).

Writing this conclusion in the aftermath of the June 2016 British referendum on membership of the European Union, we must indeed be aware that despite the organic nature of functional, and as this book has highlighted, also geographical, spillover in the EU, democratic sentiment may stand in stark contrast with such interconnection. The United Kingdom has certainly not been on the outside of the emergence of a polycentric Union, yet decided in a seismic vote to sever its ties to the spider's net and regain 'autonomy'[6] and 'take back control'.[7]

While the newer paradigm of interconnection is clearly alive and kicking, older paradigms are far from gone and we must thus identify avenues that allow for their reconciliation, despite the apparent difficulty in reconciling these often diametrically opposed notions. The early days of the post-Brexit referendum world appear to confirm that regaining isolation is very difficult, and maybe impossible, to realize. This leads us to realize that while interconnection has progressed to an extent from which there is no coming back, older paradigms of independence and autonomy are still with us. The only reasonable solution hence appears to strive for a cherishing of interconnection that goes hand in hand with a cherishing of autonomy and diversity.

Right now 'United in Diversity' should be more than a mere slogan. Public authorities at all scales have come to realize that connection to others is key to the realization of common, but also independent, objectives. Scholarship on subnational autonomies can be helpful in that undertaking. It is from this perspective reassuring that while the study of the impact of European integration on subnational autonomies has long been an under-documented subject of European legal studies this is now evolving.[8] In light of demographic and socio-economic change, especially cities are becoming increasingly important governance actors and have conversely sparked increased academic attention over the past few years.[9] The benefits of interconnection are indeed manifold and powerful, from the avoidance of armed conflict (as in an age of

[6] The then leader of the United Kingdom Independence Party, Nigel Farage, labeled 23 June as the UK's 'independence day', see: http://www.bbc.com/news/uk-politics-eu-referendum-36613238.

[7] 'Take back control' was the slogan used by the leave campaign in the run-up to the Brexit referendum of 23 June 2016.

[8] This, of course, doesn't mean that it has not been examined from the domestic perspective. In Germany, for instance, the consequences of European integration on local self-administration have been examined already in the 1980s, such as for instance in Peter Mombaur and Hans von Lennep, 'Die deutsche kommunale Selbstverwaltung und das Europarecht' (1988) Die Öffentliche Verwaltung.

[9] See, for instance, Helmut Philipp Aust, *Das Recht der globalen Stadt* (Mohr Siebeck 2017) and Josephone van Zeben, 'Local Governments as Subjects and Objects of EU Law', in Elaine Fahey and Samo Bardutzky (eds), *Framing the Subjects and Objects of Contemporary EU Law* (Edward Elgar 2017).

interconnected markets and infrastructure harming others would often entail harming oneself) to hopefully a kinder world of increased mutual understanding, communication, and solidarity. The European Union in 2017, however, also tells us that interconnection must be handled well. From the perspective of SNAs we must be careful to avoid potential drawbacks (both real and perceived) of the vanishing of subnational identities and autonomies, especially since the preservation thereof is not irreconcilable with European integration. Rather, as subnational authorities are becoming insiders of the European legal order, it is worth reflecting about how their own identities are being protected and valued. Article 4(2) TEU can be read as a step towards this goal but such recognition has limited reach where it is hidden away in dry treaties and must also find other modes of expression. The Union should continue to highlight that the EU institutions not only cherish subnational authorities for their capacity to act as allies in the achievement of common supranational objectives but equally as territorial entities with distinct identities, that the European project is deeply committed to a common project and identity but equally to the preservation and valuation of distinct identities, and that its strength lies precisely in the acceptance of such diversity within the frame of common values and principles.

# *Bibliography*

## BOOKS AND ACADEMIC JOURNALS

Abando J, 'Early Warning and Regional Parliaments: In Search of a New Model. Suggestions from the Basque Experience' (2013) 5 Perspectives on Federalism 74

Ackermann T, 'Case C-36/02, *Omega Spielhallen- und Automatenaufstellungs-GmbH v. Oberbürgermeisterin der Bundesstadt Bonn*, Judgment of the Court of Justice (First Chamber) of 14 October 2004, nyr' (2005) 42 Common Market Law Review 1107

Albi A and Ziller J (eds), *The European Constitution and National Constitutions: Ratification and Beyond* (Kluwer 2007)

Alemanno A, 'À la recherche d'un juste équilibre entre libertés fondamentales et droits fondamentaux dans le cadre du marché intérieur. Quelques réflexions à propos des arràts « Schmidberger » et « Omega »' (2004) Revue du Droit de l'Union Européenne 709

Aligica P and Tarko V, 'Polycentricity: From Polanyi to Ostrom, and Beyond' (2012) 25 Governance: An International Journal of Policy, Administration, and Institutions 237

Alilonttinen P and Ruà S, 'Lisbon Treaty Ratification: Will the Aland Islands Become Finland's Greenland?' (2008) The Centre for European Policy Studies 1/2008

Anagnostaras G, 'The Allocation of Responsibility in State Liability Actions for Breaches of Community Law' (2001) 26 European Law Review 138

Arnull A and Wincott D (eds), *Accountability and Legitimacy in the European Union* (Oxford University Press 2002)

Arnull A, Barnard C, Dougan M, and Spaventa E (eds), *A Constitutional Order of States? Essays in Honour of Alan Dashwood* (Hart 2011)

Aust A, *Modern Treaty Law and Practice* (Cambridge University Press 2000)

Aust H, *Das Recht der globalen Stadt* (Mohr Siebeck 2017)

Aust H, 'Auf dem Weg zu einem Recht der globalen Stadt? "C40" und der "Konvent der Bürgermeister" im globalen Klimaschutzregime' (2013) 73 Zeitschrift für ausländisches öffentliches Recht und Völkerrecht 673

Avbelj M and Komárek J (eds), *Constitutional Pluralism in the European Union and Beyond* (Hart 2012)

Azopardi K, *Sovereignty and the Stateless Nation: Gibraltar in the Modern Legal Context* (Hart 2009)

Azoulai L (ed), *The Question of Competence in the European Union* (Oxford University Press 2014)

Azoulai L, 'Integration Through Law and Us' (2016) 14 International Journal of Constitutional Law 449

Barnard C and Scott J (eds), *The Law of the Single European Market: Unpacking the Premises* (Hart Publishing 2002)

Barnard C, *The Substantive Law of the EU* (Oxford University Press 2010)

Bengoetxea J, 'Autonomous Constitutional Regions in a Federal Europe' in Geert De Baere, Elke Cloots, and Stefan Sottiaux (eds), *Federalism in the European Union* (Hart 2012) 230

Benneworth P and Dassen A, 'Strengthening Global–Local Connectivity in Regional Innovation Strategies: Implications for Regional Innovation Policy' (2011) OECD Regional Development Working Papers 2011/1

Besselink L, *A Composite European Constitution* (Europa Law Publishing 2007)

Besselink L, 'National and Constitutional Identity Before and After Lisbon' (2010) 6 Utrecht Law Review 46

Betsill M and Bulkeley H, 'Cities and the Multilevel Governance of Global Climate Change' (2006) 12 Global Governance 141

Blank Y, 'Localism in the New Global Legal Order' (2006) 47 Harvard Journal of International Law 263

Bobek M, *Comparative Reasoning in European Supreme Courts* (Oxford University Press 2013)

Bogdanor V, *Devolution in the United Kingdom* (Oxford University Press 1999)

Bogojevíc S and Groussot X, 'Subsidiarity as a Procedural Safeguard of Federalism' in Azoulai L (ed), *The Question of Competence in the European Union* (Oxford University Press 2014) 234

Brenner N, *New State Spaces: Urban Governance and the Rescaling of Statehood* (Oxford University Press 2004)

Breyer S, 'Does Federalism Make a Difference?' [1999] Public Law 651

Bröhmer J, 'Anmerkung zum Urteil des EuGH vom 14.10.2004 in der Rechtssache C-36/02, Omega Spielhallen und Automatenaufstellungs-GmbH' (2004) 15 Zeitschrift für Europäisches Wirtschaftsrecht 755

Brown C, 'Case C-112/00, *Eugen Schmidberger, Internationale Transporte und Planzuge v. Austria*. Judgment of 12 June 2003, Full Court' (2003) 40 Common Market Law Review 1499

Bulkeley H and Kern K, 'Local Government and the Governing of Climate Change in Germany and the UK' (2006) 43 Urban Studies 2237

Bulkeley H and Broto V, 'Governing by Experiment? Global Cities and the Governing of Climate Change' (2013) 38 Transactions of the Institute of British Geographers 361

Bulkeley H, Castan Broto V, and Edwards G, *An Urban Politics of Climate Change. Experimentation and the Governing of Socio-Technical Transitions* (Routledge 2015)

Canedo M, 'L'intérêt à agir dans le recours en annulation du droit communautaire' (2000) 36 Revue Trimestrielle de Droit Européen 451

Carpano E, 'Droits fondamentaux et libertés communautaires de circulation: brèves remarques sur le développement du système communautaire de protection des droits fondamentaux' (2005) 120 Les Petites Affiches 27

Chamon M and van der Loo G, 'The Temporal Paradox of Regions in the EU Seeking Independence: Contraction and Fragmentation Versus Widening and Deepening?' (2014) 20 European Law Journal 613

Christiansen T, 'Second Thoughts on Europe's "Third Level": The European Union's Committee of the Regions' (1996) 26 Publius: The Journal of Federalism 93

Claes M, 'The Europeanization of National Constitutions in the Constitutionalization of Europe: Some Observations against the Background of the Constitutional Experience of the EU-15' (2007) 3 Croatian Yearbook of European Law and Policy 1

Claes M and de Visser M, 'Are You Networked Yet? On Dialogues in European Judicial Networks' (2012) 8 Utrecht Law Review 100

Clark G, 'Scottish Devolution and the European Union' (1999) 3 Public Law 505

Cloots E, de Baere G, and Sottiaux S (eds), *Federalism in the European Union* (Hart Publishing 2012)

Cloots E, 'Case C-202/11, Anton Las v. Psa Antwerp NV, Judgment of the Court of Justice (Grand Chamber) of 16 April 2013' (2014) 51 Common Market Law Review 623

Constantinesco V, 'La subsidiarité comme principe constitutionnel de l'intégration européenne' (1991) 46 Aussenwirtschlaft 411

Craig P and de Búrca G (eds), *The Evolution of EU law* (Oxford University Press 2001)

Craig P, 'Competence: Clarity, Conferral, Containment and Consideration' (2004) 29 European Law Review 338

Craig P, *The Lisbon Treaty: Law, Politics, and Treaty Reform* (Oxford University Press 2010)

Craig P, 'Subsidiarity: A Political and Legal Analysis' (2012) 50 Journal of Common Market Studies 72

Cremona M (ed), *Market Integration and Public Services in the European Union* (Oxford University Press 2011)

Criekemans D and Salomonson T, 'La Belgique, la Flandre et les forums multilatéraux' (2001) 10 Bulletin d'histoire politique 125

Criekemans D, 'Foreign Policy and Diplomacy of the Belgian Regions; Flanders and Wallonia' (2010) Netherlands Institute of International Relations 'Clingendael': http://www.clingendael.nl/sites/default/files/20100300_cdsp_discussion_paper_in_diplomacy_criekemans.pdf

Cygan A, 'The Parliamentarisation of EU Decision-Making? The Impact of the Treaty of Lisbon on National Parliaments' (2011) 36 European Law Review 478

Cygan A, 'The Regions Within Multi-Level Governance: Enhanced Opportunity for Improved Accountability?' (2014) 21 The Maastricht Journal of European and Comparative Law 265

Dautricourt C, 'La jurisprudence de la Cour de justice et du Tribunal de première instance. Chronique des arrêts. Gouvernement de la Communauté française et Gouvernement wallon contre Gouvernement flamand' (2008) 3 Revue du droit de l'Union européenne 603

Dawson M, *New Governance and the Transformation of European Law* (Cambridge University Press 2011)

Day O'Connor S, 'Altered States: Federalism and Devolution at the Real Turn of the Millennium' (2001) 60 Cambridge Law Journal 493

De Baere G and Roes T, 'EU Loyalty as Good Faith' (2015) 64 International and Comparative Law Quarterly 829

de Búrca G, 'Reappraising Subsidiarity's Significance After Amsterdam' (1999) Jean Monnet Working Paper 7/99: http://www.jeanmonnetprogram.org/archive/papers/99/990701.html

de Búrca G, 'Setting Constitutional Limits to EU Competence?' (2001) Faculdade de Direito da Universidade Nova de Lisboa Francisco Lucas Pires Working Paper Series on European Constitutionalism Working Paper 2001/02

de Búrca G and de Witte B, 'The Delimitation of Powers between the EU and its Member States' in Arnull A and Wincott D (eds), *Accountability and Legitimacy in the European Union* (Oxford University Press 2002) 201

de Búrca G, 'Rethinking Law in Neofunctionalist Terms' (2006) 12 Journal of European Public Policy 310

de Vries S, 'Balancing Fundamental Rights with Economic Freedoms According to the European Court of Justice' (2013) 9 Utrecht Law Review 169

de Witte B, 'Community Law and National Constitutional Values' (1991) 18 Legal Issues of Economic Integration 1

de Witte B, 'Treaty Revision in the European Union: Constitutional Change Through International Law' (2004) 35 Netherlands Yearbook of International Law 51

Della Porta D and Tarrow S, *Transnational Protest and Global Activism* (Rowman & Littlefield 2005)

Delledonne G and Martinico G, 'Handle with Care! The Regional Charters and Italian Constitutionalism's "Grey Zone"' (2009) 5 European Constitutional Law Review 218

Denza E, *British Overseas Territories Law* (Kluwer 2012)

Edward D and Bengoetxea J, 'The Status and Rights of Sub-State Entities in the Constitutional Order of the European Union' in Arnull A, Barnard C, Dougan M, and Spaventa E (eds), *A Constitutional Order of States? Essays in Honour of Alan Dashwood* (Hart 2011) 29

Enchelmaier S, 'No-one slips through the net? Latest Development, and Non-Developments, in the European Court of Justice's Jurisprudence on Art. 230(4) EC' (2005) 24 Yearbook of European Law 173

Endo K, 'Subsidiarity and Its Enemies: To What Extent is Sovereignty Contested in the Mixed Commonwealth of Europe?' (2001) EUI Working Paper RSC 2001/24

Erk J, 'Austria: A Federation without Federalism' (2004) 34 Publius: The Journal of Federalism 1

Eslava L, *Local Space, Global Life: The Everyday Operation of International Law and Development* (Cambridge University Press 2015)

Estella A, *The EU Principle of Subsidiarity and Its Critique* (Oxford University Press 2002)

Evans A, 'UK Devolution and EU Law' (2003) 28 European Law Review 475

Evans A, 'Regional Dimensions to European Governance' (2003) 52 International and Comparative Quarterly 21

Everling U, 'The Maastricht Judgment of the German Federal Constitutional Court and the Significance for the Development of the European Union' (1994) 14 Yearbook of European Law 1

Evrard E, 'The European Grouping of Territorial Cooperation (EGTC): Towards a Supraregional Scale of Governance in the Greater Region SaarLorLux?' (2016) 21 Geopolitics 513

Ferran R (ed), *Foreign Policy of Constituent Units at the Beginning of the 21st Century* (Collecció Institut d'Estudis Autonòmics 2010)

Finck M, 'Above and Below the Surface: The Status of Sub-National Authorities in EU Climate Change Regulation' (2014) 26 Journal of Environmental Law 443

Finck M, 'The Role of Localism in Constitutional Change: A Case Study' (2014) 15 The Journal of Law and Politics 53

Finck M, 'Challenging the Subnational Dimension of Subsidiarity in EU Law' (2015) 8 European Journal of Legal Studies 5

Finck M and Ranchordás S, 'Sharing and the City' (2016) 49 Vanderbilt Journal of Transnational Law 1299

Franklin J, *Bodin On Sovereignty: Four Chapters from The Six Books of the Commonwealth* (Cambridge University Press 1992)

Frenz W, 'Menschenwürde und Dienstleistungsfreiheit' (2005) 24 Neue Zeitschrift für Verwaltungsrecht 48

Frowein J, 'The Reunification of Germany' (1992) 1 American Journal of International Law 86

Frug G, 'The City as a Legal Concept' (1980) 93 Harvard Law Review 1059

Fuller L, 'The Forms and Limits of Adjudication' (1978) 92 Harvard Law Review 353

Garagarza M, 'The Spanish State Structure and EU Law: The View of the Spanish Constitutional Court' in Elke Cloots, Geert de Baere, and Stefan Sottiaux (eds), *Federalism in the European Union* (Hart Publishing 2012) 381

Gerken H, 'Federalism All the Way Down' (2010) 124 Harvard Law Review 4

Gerkrath J, 'The Figure of Constitutional Law of the "Integrated State": The Case of the Grand Duchy of Luxembourg' (2014) 10 European Constitutional Law Review 109

Gerth H and Wright C (eds), *From Max Weber: Essays in Sociology* (Oxford University Press 1946)

Gragl P, 'A Giant Leap for European Human Rights? The Final Agreement on the European Union's Accession to the European Convention on Human Rights' (2014) 51 Common Market Law Review 13

Gros B and Schmitt-Egner P, *Europas Kooperierende Regionen: Rahmenbedingungen und Praxis Transnationaler Zusammenarbeit Deutscher Grenzregionen in Europa* (Nomos 1994)

Gupta J, Betsill M, and Bulkeley H, 'Cities and the Multilevel Governance of Global Climate Change' (2006) 12 Global Governance 141

Gutiérrez-Fons J and Lenaerts K, 'The Constitutional Allocation of Powers and General Principles of EU Law' (2010) 47 Common Market Law Review 1629

Haas E, *The Uniting of Europe: Political, Social and Economic Forces 1950–7* (Stevens 1958)

Haas E, *Beyond the Nation State* (Stanford University Press 1964)

Haasbeek L, 'Soft Drugs under Scrutiny: How "Easy Going" Is the Court?' (2011) 38 Legal Issues of Economic Integration 389

Harlow C, 'Francovich and the Problem of the Disobedient State' (1996) 2 European Law Journal 199

Henning M, Moodysson J, and Nilsson M, *Innovation and Regional Transformation. From Clusters to New Combinations* (Region Skane, printed by Elanders 2010) 26

Heyvaert V, 'What's in a Name? The Covenant of Mayors as Transnational Environmental Regulation' (2013) 22(1) Review of European, Comparative and International Environmental Law 78

Hoffman-Riem W, 'Législation Expérimentale En Allemagne' in Morand C (ed), *Evaluation législative des lois expérimentales* (Presses Universitaires d'Aix Marseille 1992) 177

Hrbek R, 'The Federal Republic of Germany' in Michelmann H (ed), *Foreign Relations in Federal Countries* (McGill–Queen's University Press 2009) 142

Husa J, *The Constitution of Finland. A Contextual Analysis* (Hart 2011)

Ipsen H, 'Als Bundesstaat in der Gemeinschaft' in *Festschrift für Walter Hallstein zu seinem 65. Geburtstag* (Caemmerer 1966) 203

Jääskinen N, 'The Case of the Åland Islands—Regional Autonomy versus the European Union of States' in Stephen Weatherill and Ulf Bernitz (eds), *The Role of Regions and Sub-National Actors in Europe* (Hart 2005) 89

Jackson V, 'Constitutional Dialogue and Human Dignity: States and Transnational Constitutional Discourse' (2004) 65 Montana Law Review 15

Jacobs F, 'Citizenship of the European Union—A Legal Analysis' (2007) 13 European Law Journal 591

Jeffery C, 'Conclusions: Sub-National Authorities and European Domestic Policy' (1996) 6 Regional & Federal Studies 204

Jeffery C, 'Sub-national Mobilization and European Integration: Does it Make Any Difference?' (2000) 38 Journal of Common Market Studies 1

Jeffery C, 'Regions and the European Union: Letting them In, and Leaving them Alone' in Stephen Weatherill and Ulf Bernitz (eds), *The Role of Regions and Sub-National Actors in Europe* (Hart Publishing 2005) 33

Jennings R and Watts A, *Oppenheim's International Law* (Longman 1992)

Keating M, *The New Regionalism in Western Europe—Territorial Restructuring and Political Change* (Edward Elgar 1998)

Keating M and Hughes J (eds), *The Regional Challenge in Central and Eastern Europe* (Presses Universitaires Européennes 2003)

Khanna P, *Connectography: Mapping the Future of Global Civilization* (Random House 2016)

Kiiver P, 'The Treaty of Lisbon, the National Parliaments and the Principle of Subsidiarity' (2008) 15 Maastricht Journal of European and Comparative Law 77

Kiiver P, 'The Conduct of Subsidiarity Checks of EU Legislative Proposals by National Parliaments: Analysis, Observations and Practical Recommendations' (2012) 12 ERA Forum 535

Kilpatrick C, 'Internal Market Architecture and the Accommodation of Labour Rights: As Good as It Gets?' (2011) EUI Working Paper, Law 2011/04

Kingston S, 'The European Court of Justice and the Devolution of Taxation Powers' in Elke Cloots, Geert de Baere, and Stefan Sottiaux (eds), *Federalism in the European Union* (Hart Publishing 2012) 249

Kochenov D, *EU law of the Overseas: Outermost Regions, Associated Overseas Countries and Territories, Territories Sui Generis* (Kluwer 2011)

Kommers D, *The Constitutional Jurisprudence of the Federal Republic of Germany* (Duke University Press 1997)

Kottmann J, 'Europe and the Regions: Subnational Entity Representation at Community Level' (2001) 26 European Law Review 159

Kranenborg H and Bulterman M, 'What if rules on free movement and human rights collide? About laser games and human dignity: The Omega case' (2006) 31 European Law Review 93

Kroll D and Leuffen D, 'Enhanced Cooperation in Practice. An Analysis of Differentiated Integration in EU Secondary Law' (2014) 3 Journal of European Public Policy 353

Lenaerts K, 'Education in the European Community After "Maastricht"' (1994) 31 Common Market Law Review 7, 11–12

Lenaerts K and Cambien N, 'Regions and the European Courts: Giving Shape to the Regional Dimension of Member States' (2010) 35 European Law Review 609

Lenaerts K, 'EU Federalism in 3-D' in Cloots E, de Baere G, and Sottiaux S (eds), *Federalism in the European Union* (Hart Publishing 2012) 13

Loughlin J, 'The Regional Question, Subsidiarity, and the Future of Europe' in Stephen Weatherill and Ulf Bernitz (eds), *The Role of Regions and Sub-National Actors in Europe* (Hart 2005) 157

Louis J-V, 'The Lisbon Treaty: The Irish "no": National Parliaments and the Principle of Subsidiarity—Legal Options and Practical Limits' (2008) 4 European Constitutional Law Review 429

Lozner S, 'Diffusion of Local Regulatory Innovations: The San Francisco CEDAW Ordinance and the New York City Human Rights Initiative' (2004) 104 Columbia Law Review 768

Lyons C, Walker N, and Beaumont P (eds), *Convergence and Divergence in European Public Law* (Hart Publishing 2002)

Maduro M, *We The Court, The European Court of Justice and the European Economic Constitution* (Hart Publishing 1998)

Mandrino C, 'The Lisbon Treaty and the New Powers of Regions' (2008) 10 European Journal of Law Reform 515

Martin D, 'Comments on Gouvernement de la Communauté française and Gouvernement wallon (Case C-212/06 of 1 April 2008) and Eind (Case C-291/05 of 11 December 2007)' (2008) 10 European Journal of Migration and Law 365

Martinico G, 'Dating Cinderella: On Subsidiarity as a Political Safeguard of Federalism in the European Union' (2011) 6 European Public Law 652

Martinico G and Pierdominici L, 'Crisis, Emergency and Subnational Constitutionalism in the Italian context' (2014) 6 Perspectives on Federalism 116

Maunz T, *Deutsches Staatsrecht* (Beck 1964)

Mazzoleni M, 'The First Tripartite Agreement in the EU. An Actor-Centred Analysis of an Experimental Multi-Level Interaction' (2006) 16 Regional and Federal Studies 263

McCann P and Ortega-Argilés R, 'Smart Specialisation, Regional Growth and Applications to EU Cohesion Policy' (2011) Economic Geography Working Paper 2011: Faculty of Spatial Sciences, University of Groningen: http://wbc-inconet/attach/s3_mccann_ortegapdf

McCrudden C, 'The Rüffert Case and Public Procurement' in Cremona M (ed), *Market Integration and Public Services in the European Union* (Oxford University Press 2011) 117

Michelmann H (ed), *Foreign Relations in Federal Countries* (McGill-Queen's University Press 2009)

Mombaur P and von Lennep H, 'Die deutsche kommunale Selbstverwaltung und das Europarecht' (1988) Die Öffentliche Verwaltung

Morand C (ed), *Evaluation législative des lois expérimentales* (Presses Universitaires d'Aix Marseille 1992)

Murkens J, 'The Blunders of Brexit: Economics, Sovereignty, and the Constitution' *Law Society and Economy Working Paper Series* 14-2016 (2016)

Müller-Graff P-C, 'Die europäischen Regionen in der Verfassung der EG' (1997) 20 Integration 145

Müller-Graff P-C, in Weatherill S and Bernitz U, *The Role of Regions and Sub-National Actors in Europe* (Hart Publishing 2005) 110

Nadalutti E, 'Does the "European Grouping of Territorial Co-operation" Promote Multi-level Governance within the European Union'? (2013) 51 Journal of Common Market Studies 756

Nagelschmidt M, 'Les relations internationales des Länder allemands et l'évolution du système fédéral dans l'Union Européenne: le cas du Bade-Wurtemberg' (1999) 30 Etudes Internationales 679

Nergelius J, 'The Committee of the Regions Today and in the Future—A Critical Overview' in Stephen Weatherill and Ulf Bernitz (eds), *The Role of Regions and Sub-National Actors in Europe* (Hart 2005) 124

Nic Shuibhne N, 'Free Movement of Persons and the Wholly Internal Rule: Time to Move on?' (2002) 39 Common Market Law Review 731

Nic Shuibhne N, 'Limits Rising, Duties Ascending: The Changing Legal Shape of Union Citizenship' (2015) 52 Common Market Law Review 889

Nicola F, 'Invisible Cities in Europe' 35 Fordham International Law Journal (2012) 1282

Nieman A and Schmitter P, 'Neofunctionalism' in Antje Wiener and Thomas Diez, *European Integration Theory* (Oxford University Press 2009)

Nijman J, 'The Future of the City and the International Law of the Future' in Muller S et al. (eds), *Law of the Future and Future of the Law* (Torkel Opsahl EPublisher 2011) 213

Ohmae K, *End of the Nation State: The Rise of Regional Economies: How Regional Economics Will Soon Reshape the World* (Free Press 1995)

Organ J, 'Decommissioning Direct Democracy? A Critical Analysis of Commission Decision-Making on the Legal Admissibility of European Citizens Initiative Proposals' (2014) 10 European Constitutional Law Review 422

Ostrom E, 'Polycentric Systems for Coping with Collective Action and Global Environmental Change' (2010) 20 Global Environmental Change 550

Osofsky H, 'Is Climate Change "International"? Litigation's Diagonal Regulatory Role' (2009) 49 Virginia Journal of International Law 585

Panara C and De Becker A (eds), *The Role of the Regions in EU Governance* (Springer 2011)

Panara C, *The Sub-National Dimension of the EU* (Springer 2015)

Paquin S, 'Paradiplomatie identitaire et diplomatie en Belgique fédérale: le cas de la Flandre' (2003) 36 Canadian Journal of Political Science/Revue canadienne de science politique 621

Payre R, 'The Importance of Being Connected. City Networks and Urban Government: Lyon and Eurocities (1990–2005)' (2010) 34 International Journal of Urban and Regional Research 260

Pernice I, 'The Treaty of Lisbon: Multilevel Constitutionalism in Action' (2009) 15 Columbia Journal of European Law 349

Pescatore P, *Le Droit de l'Intégration* (Bruylant 2005)

Piris J-C, *The Lisbon Treaty: A Legal and Political Analysis* (Cambridge University Press 2010)

Poiares Maduro M, 'The Scope of European Remedies: The Case of Purely Internal Situations and Reverse Discrimination' in Novitz T, Kilpatrick C, and Skidmore P (eds), *The Future of European Remedies* (Hart Publishing 2000) 117

Polanyi M, *The Logic of Liberty* (University of Chicago Press 1951)

Pollack M, 'Creeping Competence: The Expanding Agenda of the European Community' (1994) 14 Journal of Public Policy 519

Prechal S, *Directives in EC Law* (Oxford University Press 1995)

Raich S, *Grenzüberschreitende und Interregionale Zusammenarbeit in einem "Europe der Regionen"* (Nomos 1995)

Resnik J, 'Law's Migration: American Exceptionalism, Silent Dialogues, and Federalism's Multiple Ports of Entry' (2006) 115 Yale Law Journal 1564

Rodriguez C, 'The Significance of the Local in Immigration Regulation' (2008) 106 Michigan Law Review 567

Ross A and Salvador Crespo M, 'The Effect of Devolution on the Implementation of European Community Law in Spain and the United Kingdom' (2003) 28 European Law Review 210

Rousseau J-J, *Du Contrat Social* (Flammarion 2001)

Ruzza C and Della Sala V (eds), *Governance and Civil Society in the European Union* (Manchester University Press 2007)

Sassen S (ed), *Global Networks, Linked Cities* (Routledge 2002)

Sassen S, 'The City: Today's Frontier Zone' (2014) 1 Glocalism: Journal of Culture, Politics and Innovation 1

Scheuerman W, *Liberal Democracy and the Social Acceleration of Time* (John Hopkins University Press 2004)

Schönenbroicher K, *Ordnungsbehördengesetz Nordrhein-Westfalen* (Verlag Reckinger 2011)

Schütze R, 'Dual Constitutionalism Constitutionalised: the Emergence of Exclusive Competences in the EC Legal Order' (2007) 32 European Law Review 3

Schütze R, *From Dual to Cooperative Federalism: The Changing Structure of European Law* (Oxford University Press 2009)

Schwarze J, 'Der Schutz der Grundrechte durch den EuGH' (2005) 48 Neue Juristische Wochenschrift 3457

Schweizer R and Brunner S, *Die Mitwirkung der Bundesländer an EU-Vorhaben in der Bundesrepublik Deutschland und Österreich: Ein Modell für die Mitwirkung der Kantone in der Aussenpolitik* (Stämpfli Verlag 1998)

Scott J, 'Case C-95/97 Région Wallonne v. Commission of the European Communities [1997] ECR I-1787 (ECJ) and Case T-70/97 [1997] ECR II-1513 (CFI)' (1999) 36 Common Market Law Review 227

Scott J, 'The Multi-Level Governance of Climate Change' in Craig P and de Búrca G (eds), *The Evolution of EU law* (Oxford University Press 2001) 805

Scott J and Trubek D, 'Mind The Gap: Law and New Approaches to Governance in the European Union' (2002) 8 European Law Journal 1

Seidle L, 'Local Voting Rights for Non-Nationals: Experience in Sweden, the Netherlands and Belgium' (2015) 16 Journal of International Migration & Integration 27

Sharpe L, *The Rise of Meso-Government in Europe* (Sage Publications 1993)

Shaw J, 'European Union Legal Studies in Crisis? Towards a New Dynamic' (1996) 16 Oxford Journal of Legal Studies 231

Skouris V, 'Die Zusammenarbeit zwischen BVerwG und EuGH—eine positive Bilanz' (2013) 1 Neue Zeitschrift für Verwaltungsrecht 33

Skoutaris N, 'Comparing the Subnational Constitutional Space of the European Sub-State Entities in the Area of Foreign Affairs' (2012) 4 Perspectives on Federalism 239

Skoutaris N, 'The Role of Sub-State Entities in the EU Decision-Making Process' in Elke Cloots, Geert de Baere, and Stefan Sottiaux (eds), *Federalism in the European Union* (Hart Publishing 2012) 214

Slaughter A-M, 'Judicial Globalization' (2000) 40 Virginia Journal of International Law 1103

Slaughter A-M, 'A Global Community of Courts' (2003) 44 Harvard International Law Journal 191

Smith D and Timberlake M, 'Hierarchies of Dominance Among World Cities' in Sassen S (ed), *Global Networks, Linked Cities* (Routledge 2002) 117

Spinaci G and Vara-Arribas G, 'The European Grouping of Territorial Cooperation (EGTC): New Spaces and Contracts' EIPASCOPE 2009/2

Steiff J and Andre T, 'Konsequenzen aus dem EuGH-Urteil zur Tariftreue' (2008) 9 Neue Zeitschrift für Baurecht und Vergaberecht 364

Stewart R, 'States and Cities as Actors in Global Climate Regulation: Unitary vs. Plural Architectures' (2008) 50 Arizona Law Review 681

Strazzani D, 'Harmonising Trends vs Domestic Regulatory Frameworks: Looking for the European Law on Cross-Border Cooperation' (2011) 4 European Journal of Legal Studies 151

Stubb A, *Negotiating Flexibility in the European Union: Amsterdam, Nice and Beyond* (Palgrave 2002)

Sunstein C, 'Social Norms and Social Roles' (1996) 96 Columbia Law Review 903

Tatham M, 'Devolution and EU Policy-Shaping: Bridging the Gap Between Multi-Level Governance and Liberal Intergovernmentalism' (2011) 3 European Political Science Review 53

Thies A, 'The *Locus Standi* of the Regions Before EU Courts' in Panara C and De Becker A (eds), *The Role of the Regions in EU Governance* (Springer 2011)

Tiebout C, 'A Pure Theory of Local Expenditures' (1956) 64 Journal of Political Economy 416

Tiebout C, Warren R, and Ostrom V, 'The Organization of Government in Metropolitan Areas: A Theoretical Inquiry' (1961) 55 The American Political Science Review 831

Torres P and Doubrava R, 'The Covenant of Mayors: Cities Leading the Fight against Climate Change' in Van Staden M and Musco F (eds), *Local Governments and Climate Change* (Springer 2010) 91

Trepte P, *Public Procurement in the EU: A Practitionner's Guide* (Oxford University Press 2007) 28

Tryfondiou A, 'Reverse Discrimination in Purely Internal Situations: An Incongruity in a Citizen's Europe' (2008) 35 Legal Issues of Economic Integration 43

Tuytschaever F, *Differentiation in European Union Law* (Hart 1999)

van der Leeuw K, Gupta J, and de Moel H, 'Climate Change: a "Glocal" Problem Requiring "Glocal" Action' (2007) 4 Environmental Sciences 139

Van Nuffel P, 'What's in a Member State? Central and Decentralized Authorities before the Community Courts' (2001) 38 Common Market Law Review 871

Van Staden M and Musco F (eds), *Local Governments and Climate Change* (Springer 2010)

Van Zeben J, 'Local Governments as Subjects and Objects of EU Law' in Fahey E and Bardutzky S (eds), *Framing the Subjects and Objects of Contemporary EU Law* (Edward Elgar 2017)

Vandamme T, 'Case C-212/06, Government of the French Community and the Walloon Government v. Flemish Government, Judgment of the Court of Justice (Grand Chamber) of 1 April 2008, nyr' (2009) 46 Common Market Law Review 287

Vara Arribas G and Bourdin D, *Tripartite Arrangements: An Effective Tool for Multilevel Governance?* (EIPA Publications 2005)

Verhoeven M, 'The "Costanzo Obligation" and the Principle of National Institutional Autonomy: Supervision as a Bridge to Close the Gap?' (2010) 3 Review of European Administrative Law 23

Verschueren H, 'La régionalisation de la sécurité sociale en Belgique à la lumière de l'arrêt de la Cour de justice européenne portant sur l'assurance-soins flamande' (2008) 2 Revue belge de sécurité sociale 173

Verschueren H, 'The Impact of EU Law on the Devolution of Social Powers in the Member States' in Elke Cloots, Geert de Baere, and Stefan Sottiaux (eds), *Federalism in the European Union* (Hart Publishing 2012) 265

Von Borries R and Hauschild M, 'Implementing the Subsidiarity Principle' (1999) 5 Columbia Journal of European Law 374

Wakefield J, 'The Plight of Regions in a Multi-Layered Europe' (2005) 30 European Law Review 406

Walker N, 'Federalism in 3D, The Reimagination of Political Community in the European Union' Edinburgh School of Law Research Paper No 2016/13

Warleigh A, 'On the Path to Legitimacy? The EU Citizens Initiative Right from a Critical Deliberativist Perspective' in Ruzza C and Della Sala V (eds), *Governance and Civil Society in the European Union* (Manchester University Press 2007) 55

Weatherill S, 'On Competence Creep and Competence Control' (2004) 23 Yearbook of European Law 1

Weatherill S and Bernitz U (eds), *The Role of Regions and Sub-National Actors in Europe* (Hart 2005) 157

Weatherill S, 'The Challenge of the Regional Dimension in the European Union' in Stephen Weatherill and Ulf Bernitz (eds), *The Role of Regions and Sub-National Actors in Europe* (Hart Publishing 2005) 1

Weinrib L, 'The Postwar Paradigm and American Exceptionalism' in Sujit Choudhry (ed), *The Migration of Constitutional Ideas* (Cambridge University Press 2006) 84

Wincott D, 'The Governance White Paper, the Commission and the Search for Legitimacy' in Arnull A and Wincott D (eds), *Accountability and Legitimacy in the European Union* (Oxford University Press 2002) 379

Windolf P, 'Wer ist der Schiedsrichter in der Europäischen Union? Der Konflikt Zwischen Europäischen Gerichtshof und Bundesverfassungsgericht' (2000) 40 Kölner Zeitschrift für Soziologie und Sozialpsychologie 39

Ziller J (ed), *L'européanisation des droits constitutionnels à la lumière de la Constitution pour l'Europe* (L'Harmattan 2003)

Ziller J, 'National Constitutional Concepts in the New Constitution for Europe' (2005) 1 European Constitutional Law Review 247

## BLOG POSTS

Graziadei S, 'Belgian Constitutional Court Upholds the "Essential Elements" of Power Sharing Deal' (*I-CONnect Blog*, 28 January 2015): http://www.iconnect-blog.com/2015/01/belgian-constitutional-court-upholds-the-essential-elements-of-power-sharing-deal/

## DOCUMENTS OF THE EUROPEAN INSTITUTIONS

Opinion of the Committee of the Regions on the Revision of the Treaty on European Union and of the Treaty establishing the European Community (1996) OJ C100/1

Opinion of the Committee of the Regions on The 2000 Intergovernmental Conference (2000) OJ C156/6

European Commission FOREN Network, 'A Practical Guide to Regional Foresight' (2001)

European Commission, 'A White Paper', COM (2001) 428 Final

European Commission, 'A framework for target-based tripartite contracts and agreements between the Community, the States and regional and local authorities', COM (2002) 709 Final

Opinion of the Committee of the Regions on the Draft Report of the European Parliament on the Division of Powers between the European Union and the Member States (2002) OJ C192/31

Opinion of the Committee of the Regions on the Treaty Establishing a Constitution for Europe (2005) OJ C71/1

Communication from the Commission to the European Council—A citizens' agenda—Delivering results for Europe, COM (2006) 211 Final

Question for written answer by MEP Izaskun Bilbao Barandica (ALDE) on the statistics on the early warning process, no. E-5865/2010: http://www.europarl.europa.eu/sides/getDoc.do?pubRef=-//EP//TEXT+WQ+E-2010-5865+0+DOC+XML+V0//EN

Communication from the European Commission, Europe 2020, A Strategy for Smart, Sustainable and Inclusive Growth, COM (2010) 2020 Final 2010

Communication from the European Commission, Europe 2020, A Strategy for Smart, Sustainable and Inclusive Growth, COM (2010) Final

Communication from the Commission to the European Parliament, the Council, the Economics and Social Committee and the Committee of the Regions, Regional Policy Contributing to Smart Growth in Europe 2020, COM (2010) 553 final

European Commission, Assessment of the Impact of the Regions of Knowledge Programme (2011)

European Commission, Regional Aspects in the 7th Framework Programme. Expert Advisory Group on 'Regions of Knowledge'—2012/2013 (2011)

European Commission, Assessment of the Impact of the 'Regions of Knowledge Programme' (2011): http://ec.europa.eu/research/evaluations/pdf/archive/other_reports_studies_and_documents/assessment_of_the_impact_of_the_regions_of_knowledge_programme.pdf

European Commission, Regional Aspects in the 7th Framework Programme. Expert Advisory Group on 'Regions of Knowledge' (2011): https://ec.europa.eu/research/fp7/pdf/advisory-groups/eag_regions_2011.pdf 4

Question for written answer E-009555/2011 on the Committee of the Regions and early warning system: http://www.europarl.europa.eu/sides/getDoc.do?pubRef=-//EP//TEXT+WQ+E-2011- 009555+0+DOC+XML+V0//EN

The Council Communication from the Commission to the European Parliament, the European Economic and Social Committee and the Committee of the Regions, Regional Policy Contributing to Sustainable Growth in Europe 2020 SEC (2011) 92 Final 12

European Commission FOREN Network, 'A Practical Guide to Regional Foresight' (2011): http://foresight.jrc.ec.europa.eu/documents/eur20128en.pdf

EU Smart Specialisation Platform, Guide to Research and Innovation Strategies for Smart Specialisation (RIS 3) (2012)

Committee of the Regions, Resolution of the Committee of the Regions on the Charter for Multilevel Governance in Europe (2014): http://cor.europa.eu/en/activities/governance/Pages/charter-for-multiLevel-governance.aspx

European Commission, Mobilising Regions for Jobs and Growth. Regions of Knowledge and Research Potential (2014) 62: https://ec.europa.eu/research/regions/pdf/publications/rec-13-056_rok_03.pdf

European Commission, Smart Specialisation Strategies—Focusing on Regional Strengths in Innovation Activities (2014): http://ec.europa.eu/growth/tools-databases/newsroom/cf/itemdetail.cfm?item_id=7901&lang=en

Urban Agenda for the EU, 'Pact of Amsterdam' Agreed at the Informal Meeting of EU Ministers Responsible for Urban Matters on 30 May 2016 in Amsterdam, The Netherlands: http://ec.europa.eu/regional_policy/sources/policy/themes/urban-development/agenda/pact-of-amsterdam.pdf

# Index


**2016 Urban Agenda**
polycentricity 19, 20, 133–4

**Åland islands**
competence to determine applicability of EU Treaty 56
special status 38
treaty revision process 65
***Anton Las* case** 169–70
***Aragonesa* case** 167–9
**Assembly of European Regions (AER)**
interregional/local communication, promotion of 51
'Knowledge Center' 51
'Smart Specialisation' 51
**assimilation, Member States/subnational authorities**
*Anton Las* case 169–70
*Aragonesa* case 167–9
*Azores* case 180–2, 183–7, 188–9
*Flemish Care Insurance* case 163–7
insider narrative and 25, 27, 162
outsider narrative and 5, 14–15, 25, 26
smart specialization agenda 171–2
**associations of subnational authorities**
Assembly of European Regions (AER) 51
city representatives 51–2
Conference of European Regions with Legislative Powers (REGLEG) 50–1
Council of European Municipal and Regional Authorities (CEMR) 51–2
European Groupings of Territorial Cooperation (EGTC) 53
thematic collaborations 52–3
***Azores* case**
state aid law and 180–3
'sufficiently autonomous' test 180, 183–7
subnational authorities as insiders 188–9
**Azores island**
independent tax rates 181
special status of 38

**Barroso Initiative** 46, 104
**bi-centric interaction**
bi-centric/polycentric transition 30
EU/Member States and 1–2, 3–4, 10–13
ordinary legislative procedure 88–90
subnational authorities and 12
**bipolar porosity** 21–2
**'blindness' narrative**
outsider narrative distinguished 5–6
recognition of subnational authorities 62

**C 40,** 52
***Carbonati Apuani* case**
fiscal autonomy and 147–9
***Casagrande* case**
subnational education competences 136–9
**Child Friendly Cities Initiative** 51
**cities**
alternative political scales, as 42
regulatory competence and 39
**citizens**
EU substantive objectives 64
European Citizens' Initiative 44, 122, 134–6
European Parliament 89
'Urban Agenda' 133
**climate change**
Covenant of Mayors 52, 130
polycentricity and 19–20
subnationals thematic collaboration, example of 52
**closer cooperation enhancement**
Member State, special right 72–4
subnational authorities and 73–4
**Committee of the Regions**
areas on which consulted 48
criticism of 49–50
EU advisory body 48
praise for 49
purpose of 48–9
**Committee of the Regions' Charter on Multi-Level Governance** 122, 132, 133–4
**competences**
regulatory *see* **regulatory competence**
sub to supranational transfers 45–6
variation in scope 38, 39–40
**Conference of European Regions with Legislative Powers (REGLEG)**
associations of regions and localities 50–1
**conferral, principle of** 8, 63
**contemporary governance challenges**
interconnection 34–6
modifications in European legal order 33
polycentric nature of 2
tripartite contracts 35, 160–2

**contributors to substantive law development**
insider narrative, aspect of 110
*Omega* case 1, 23, 111–23
outsider narrative and 110
**Council of European Municipal and Regional Authorities (CEMR)** 51–2
**Council of Europe's European Charter of Local Self-Government** 57
**courts**
adherence to monolithic nature of statehood 91–2
direct responsibility and 77–8
Member States' right to standing in front of ECJ 67–72
**Covenant of Mayors**
administration of 130–1
climate change objectives 52, 130
constitution of 130
polycentric nature of 122, 130
porosity and 131
regulatory nature of 131–2
relationship with Commission 130–1, 192
Sustainable Action Plan 130
thematic collaboration and 52
**cross-border**
cooperation 141–2
local government networks 43–4

**devolution**
asymmetric devolution 38–9
symmetric devolution 38–9
***Digibet***
heterogeneity of betting regulation 125–9
public interest criterion 126
**direct democracy**
European Citizens' Initiative and 44
**direct responsibility, Member States**
breaches of EU law and 77, 81–2
breaches, sole responsibility for 74–5
courts and 77–8
domestic mechanisms for holding SNAs liable 81
*effet utile* of EU Law 75, 81
EU secondary legislation 75–8
national institutional autonomy 76
*pacta sunt servanda* maxim 75, 81
principle of cooperation 80
supranational judgments, failure to comply with 78–9
transposing directives 79–80
treaty provisions 75–6
**diversity**
asymmetric devolution 38–9
competences, variation in scope 38, 39–40
decentralized states 38
disparity of internal institutional arrangements 38
federalism 38, 39
formal labels 39
Member States, variation between and within 38
politico-economic gravity dissimilarities 40
regulatory impact 39–40
symmetric devolution 38–9
unitary states 38–9
wide panoply of decentralized arrangements 39

**Early Warning System** 46, 56, 104–8
**education**
*Casagrande* case 136–9
**endorsement**
European Citizens' Initiative 44
**EU law**
bi-centric interaction between Member States/EU 1–4, 10–13
'blindness' of 5
contemporary structure of 19
formal status 70
insider narrative *see* **insider narrative**
Member States' special status under 13–15
outsider narrative *see* **outsider narrative**
subnational authorities and 2–3, 4, 10
**EUROCITIES**
network of city representatives 51
**Europe 2020 strategy** 133
**European Citizens' Initiative** 122
direct democracy at supranational level 44
polycentricity and 134–6
**European Climate Alliance** 52
**European Commission**
SNAs, direct relationship with 47–8
SNAs as policy makers, support for 130–1
**European Grouping of Territorial Cooperation (EGTC)** 53, 144–6
**European integration**
adaptation of subnational authorities to 46–7
competence transfers from sub to supranational 45–6
contemporary governance challenges 32–6
nature of 28–32
neofunctionalism and 28
origins of 62
state sovereignty and 7
spillover 28
subnational authorities and 28–31, 45, 47–8
transition from bi-centricity to polycentricity 30

**European legal order**
bi-centric nature 20
cooperative federalism and 28
evolving structure of 27–8
European integration *see* **European integration**
polycentricity, emergence of 20–1
subnational authorities and 1
**'European paradiplomacy'** 53–4
**European Union**
associations of regions/localities 50–3
Committee of the Regions 48–50
competence transfers 45–8
constant evolution of subnational autonomies 56–60
diversity *see* **diversity**
domestic phenomena, challenges to 37
'European paradiplomacy' 53–4
fragmentation of 121, 124–5, 128
governance challenges 32–6
integration *see* **European integration**
involvement in international affairs *see* **international relations**
norm generating capacity 40–4
SNAs, complex relationship with 191–2
transnational networks 35–7
wide plethora of 37

**federalism**
Austrian version of 39
'centralising effect' 58
European legal order and 28
integration and 16, 28
polycentricity and 18
subnationals authority and 39
symmetric devolution and 38, 39
***Flemish Care Insurance* case** 163–7
**formal legal perspective**
EU/Members States generators of norms 61
outsider narrative *see* **outsider narrative**
States' direct responsibility for breaches 81
subnational authorities and 61, 109, 191
**fragmentation**
between/within Member States 121, 124–5, 128
public authority 17, 124–5
regulatory 124, 126, 128–9
serving integration 16, 58
**functional legal perspective**
alignment of Member States/subnational authorities 192
*Casagrande* case 136–9
insider narrative *see* **insider narrative**
organic nature of 195
subnational authorities and 191

**gambling**
*Digibet* case 125–9
**globalization**
subnational authorities, effect on evolution of 60
**'globalization from below'** 43
**glocalization** 60
**Greater London Authority**
competences and 38

***Horvath* case**
assimilation 124–5
courts and 123–4
facts of 122–3
**human dignity**
*Omega* case 1, 23, 111–23

**implied powers, doctrine of** 137–8
**indirect responsibility, Member States** 82–4
***in foro interno in foro externo* doctrine** 54
**insider narrative**
assimilation characteristic 25, 27, 182
*Azores* case 180–2, 183–7, 188–9
*Carbonati Apuani* case 147–9
Charter on Multi-Level Governance *see* **Committee of the Regions' Charter on Multi-Level Governance**
contributors *see* **contributors to substantive law development**
Covenant of Mayors 122, 130–1
*Digibet* 125–9
direct relations emerging 3
duty of loyalty towards EU 155–60
European Citizens' Initiative *see* **European Citizens' Initiative**
European legal order and 15–17
fluid systems of power sharing 17
functional legal perspective of 2, 3, 4, 15, 25–7, 109
*Horvath* case 122–5
internal market participants *see* **internal market participants**
*Omega* case 1, 23, 111–23
outsider narrative contrasted 21
Pact of Amsterdam *see* **Pact of Amsterdam**
polycentricity characteristic *see* **polycentricty**
porosity characteristic *see* **porosity**
public procurement law 173–9
state aid law 179–83
supranational objectives, allies in achieving *see* **SNAs allies in achieving supranational objectives**
tripartite contracts 160–2

**internal market participants**
public procurement law 173–9
state aid law 179–83
subnational authorities as 172–3
**international relations**
Åland island 56
Bavaria and 55
Belgian subnational authorities and 54–5, 56
devolved UK territories and 55
'European paradiplomacy' 53–4
*in foro interno in foro externo* doctrine 54
London/Paris mayoral meeting 55–6
ratification of Treaties 56
Westminster's exclusive competence over 55
**INTERREG initiative** 141
**intertwining**
European Grouping of Territorial Cooperation 146
polycentricity 20–1, 44, 117
porosity and 15, 21, 109, 136
public authorities generally 59–60
sovereignty and 36
supranational objectives, achieving 131
tripartite contracts 161

***Josemans* case**
supranational objectives and regulatory competence 150–3

**local/regional authorities** *see* **subnational authorities**

**masters of the Treaties**
confers special rights *see* **special rights, Member States**
direct responsibility *see* **direct responsibility, Member States**
'founding treaties' 64
indirect responsibility 82–4
outsider narrative characteristic 62–7
privileged status of Member States 7, 13–15, 25, 62–6
procedures for revision 64
'revision treaty' 64–6
sovereign equality 63–4
special obligations of Member States 2, 11, 27, 61, 74
subnational authorities, non-recognition of 64
**Member States**
bi-centric relation of EU and 1, 10–13
conferral, principle of 63
diversity within 39–40
domestic decentralization arrangements and 7
masters of the Treaties, as 7, 11, 13–15, 61, 62–6
monolithic nature of statehood 6–9, 61, 84
sovereign equality principle 6, 10, 13, 63
special obligations 74
special rights 67
special status 63
state sovereignty 7
**monolithic nature of statehood**
accounts of bicentric interactions 10
courts adherence to 91–2
disadvantages of 9
indirect responsibility under EU law 82–4
indivisible sovereignty 8
Member States 6–9, 61, 84
nature of 6–9
ordinary legislative procedure, bi-centric nature of 89–90
outsider narrative and 6–9, 61, 84–8, 92–5
purely internal situations, doctrine of 85–8
sovereign equality and 13–15
subnational authorities and 14
treaty confirmation of 89

**national security** 74
**neofunctionalism, theory of** 29, 194
**norm-generating capacity**
cross-border local government networks 43–4
'globalization from below' 43
increased urbanization, effect of 41–2
locality regulation 41, 42
subnational authorities and 40–1
'urban liberalism' 42

***Omega* case**
human dignity, protection of 23, 116–18
local measure, justification of the 120–1
national identities, protection of 114–16
public policy exemption 118–20
public policy/human dignity, protection of 110–11
SNAs as generators of norms 111
**Open Method of Co-Ordination (OMC)** 45
**ordinary legislative procedure**
bi-centric nature of 88–9
monolithic statehood, confirmation of 89–90
subnational authorities, as passive outsiders 89

supranational law-making, governs 89
treaty provisions 89
**ordinary revision procedure**
treaty revision and 64–5
**Öresund Committee** 52
**outsider narrative**
assimilation and 5, 14–15, 25, 26
bi-centric nature of EU Law 10–13
blindness narrative, distinction 5–6
characteristics of 92–4
direct responsibility *see* **direct responsibility, Member States**
division/separate spheres narrative 61
EU law as a bi-centric structure 4, 61
EU/Member States bi-centric interaction 9, 10–13
EU/Member States generators of norms 61
formalist understanding of EU law 61–2
indirect responsibility 82–4
main features of 5
masters of the Treaties 62–7
Member States' special status under EU law 13–15
public authority, division/separate spheres of 92–4
public international law and 87–8
monolithic statehood *see* **monolithic nature of statehood**
regulatory competence under 93–4
special obligation of Member States 74, 75, 81–2
special rights of Member States *see* **special rights, Member States**
SNAs on outside 61–2
SNAs' status under EU law 4–5, 7, 11
subsidiarity and 100–2
supranational legal order and 9, 10
Treaty references to subnational authorities 95–9

**Pact of Amsterdam** 14, 33, 34, 122
polycentricity and 133–4
Urban Agenda, establishment of 133–4
urban authorities and 48
**Peace of Westphalia 1648,** 11
**PHARE programme** 141
**polycentricity**
2016 Urban Agenda 19, 20, 133–4
as a description of EU Law 109
Charter on Multi-Level Governance 122, 132, 133–4
contemporary governance challenges and 2, 19–20
Covenant of Mayors 122, 130
definition of 17–18
*Digibet* 125–9
emergence of 20
EU innovation policy, feature of 141–2
European Citizens' Initiative 134–6
European legal order, concept of 15–17
federalism and 18
fragmentation of State authority and 58
functional concept, as 17, 19
history of the term 17–18
*Horvath* case 122–5
insider narrative, aspect of 17–21, 122
Pact of Amsterdam 133–4
**porosity**
bipolar 21–2
*Casagrande* case 136–9
courts and 22–3
cross-border cooperation 141–2
cross-fertilization process 21
European Grouping of Territorial Cooperation 144–6
innovation and 142
insider narrative, aspect of 21–5, 136
international context 24
permeability of scales of public authority 21–5
*Regione Sardegna* case 139–41
Regions of Knowledge Initiative 142–4
subnational/supranational norms and 22, 24, 111
**public authority**
bi-centric division of 88, 102
bipolar division of 5, 8
breach of obligations 84
cross-border networking 141
insider narrative and 15, 17, 109, 111
intertwining of levels of 20–1, 44, 59, 146
outsider narrative and 9, 92–5
polycentricity and 17–8, 48, 122–3
porosity 21, 136, 192
subnational authorities and 37, 40
subsidiarity and 100–1
**public international law**
outsider narrative and 4, 7, 87, 102
polycentricity and 19
urban norm-generation and 41
subnational authorities and 59
**public policy exemption** 118–20
**public procurement law**
*Coditel Brabant* case 177–9
regulation of 173–4
*Rüffert* case 174–7

**purely internal situations, doctrine of**
consequences of 86
examples of 86–7
operation of 85–6
university fees 85

***Regione Sardegna* case** 139–41
**Regions of Knowledge Initiative** 142–4
**regulatory authority**
bi-centric division of 61, 73, 92
entities having relevant 164
of the State 9
subnational exercise of 170
**regulatory competence**
cities and 39
courts and defence of 67, 91
local 41, 150–1
national parliaments and 46
outsider narrative and 92–4
principle of conferral 8
subnational authorities and 9, 36, 70, 126
subsidiarity and 100–1
Westphalian ideal 11
**'revision treaty'** 64
**Riga Declaration** 20

**Saar-Lor-Lux collaboration** 52–3
**Schuman Declaration 1950** 29
**simplified revision procedure**
treaty revision and 64
**smart specialization agenda** 51, 171–2
**SNAs' allies in achieving supranational objectives**
*Carbonati Apuani* case 147–9
*Josemans* case 150–3
subnational authorities and 146–7
*Walloon waste* case 153–4
**SNAs in Europe**
Council of Europe's European Charter of Local Self-Government 57–8
decentralization of competences to regions 57, 60
'federalisation' in Europe 57
fragmentation of State authority 58
globalization, effect of 59–60
glocalization, 60
intertwining 15, 20–1, 59, 117, 131, 146, 161
regulatory processes, localization of 57
urbanization, effect of 60
**SolidarCity Network** 53
**sovereign equality**
importance of 63–4
monolithic statehood and 13–15
preservation in primary law 63
principle 6, 10, 13, 63
subnational authorities and treaties 64
**special obligations, Member States** 74, 75, 81–2
**special rights, Member States**
actions challenging legality of acts *see* **standing under Art 263 TFEU**
closer cooperation involvement 72–4
direct responsibility *see* **direct responsibility, Member States**
indirect responsibility 82–4
masters of the Treaties conferring 67
**standing under Art 263 TFEU**
actions challenging legality of acts 67
formal status, importance of 70
Member States' privileged standing 67–70
municipalities, the Luxembourg example 68–9
semi-privileged applicants 67
two-month time limit 67
subnational authorities, ways of challenging EU law 69–72
**State aid law**
*Azores* case 180–2, 183–7, 188–9
heeding 179–80
judgments 179–83
**subnational authorities**
associations *see* **associations of subnational authorities**
complex relationship
definition, difficulties with 1, 40, 60
diversity *see* **diversity**
domestic phenomena, as 4–5, 13, 37
European integration *see* **European integration**
explicit Treaty references to 95–9
image of 3
implementers of supranational norms, as 77
insiders *see* **insider narrative**
institutional structures, non-representation in 11
international relations *see* **international relations**
legal status, devoid under EU law 3–4, 12
norm-generating capacity *see* **norm-generating capacity**
regulatory authority and 9
outsiders *see* **outsider narrative**
polycentricity *see* **polycentricity**
porosity *see* **porosity**
secondary legislation and 14, 75–7

substantive development, contribution to 110
Treaties references to 95–9
treaty change, contribution to 65

**subnational/supranational norms**
conflicts between 22–3

**subsidiarity**
outsider narrative and 100–2
treaty provisions 100–4

**'sufficiently autonomous' test** 183–7

**supranational law**
formal analysis of 24
functional analysis 17, 19, 24
Member States, equal treatment of 7
polycentric 3

**supranational objectives**
hinging on subnational authorities 3
subnational authorities' role in 31

**supranational norms**
national norms, interaction with 12
national norms, fusion with 22
subnational norms, interaction with 109, 139, 148, 163

**supranational legal order**
bi-centric nature of 4
maturity of 27
outsider narrative and 9, 10
polycentricity and 3
porosity and 22
subnational authorities' interaction with 25

**symmetric devolution**
Austrian variant of federalism 39
formal labels inconclusive regarding autonomy 39
German variant of federalism 38
same category/same competences 38
wide panoply of decentralized arrangements 39

**TACIS programme** 141

**treaty revision**
bi-centric nature of process 65–6
'founding treaties', amendments to 64
Member States' monopoly over 65–6, 67
Member States' consent mandatory 65
ordinary revision procedure 64–5
revision treaty 64
simplified revision procedure 64
subnational authorities and 65–6

**tripartite contracts**
governance challenges and 35
supranational objectives, allies in achieving 60–2

**Urban Agenda** *see* **2016 Urban Agenda**

**'urban liberalism'** 42

**Walloon Region** 54, 163

***Walloon Waste* case** 23, 146, 153–4, 193

The manufacturer's authorised representative in the EU for product safety is Oxford University Press España S.A. of el Parque Empresarial San Fernando de Henares, Avenida de Castilla, 2 – 28830 Madrid (www.oup.es/en or product.safety@oup.com). OUP España S.A. also acts as importer into Spain of products made by the manufacturer.

www.ingramcontent.com/pod-product-compliance
Lightning Source LLC
LaVergne TN
LVHW011758200926
848484LV00003B/737

* 9 7 8 0 1 9 8 8 1 0 8 9 6 *